PRESIDENT
☆ A N D ☆
CONGRESS

PRESIDENT

☆ AND ☆

CONGRESS

BY

WILFRED E. BINKLEY

Professor of History and Political Science
OHIO NORTHERN UNIVERSITY

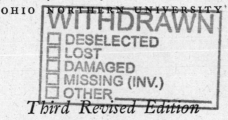
Third Revised Edition

VINTAGE BOOKS

A DIVISION OF RANDOM HOUSE
NEW YORK

VINTAGE BOOKS

are published by ALFRED A. KNOPF, INC.

and RANDOM HOUSE, INC.

Reprinted by arrangement with *Alfred A. Knopf, Inc.* First published in 1937 as *The Powers of the President* by Doubleday, Doran & Co. Rewritten, expanded, and reset edition published in 1947 by Alfred A. Knopf, Inc. Vintage edition extensively revised and augmented by the author.

TO

WENDELL,
LOWELL, LUDWELL,
ROBERT

Preface to the Vintage Edition

THE FIRST EDITION of this work was published with the title *Powers of the President* soon after the second inauguration of President Franklin D. Roosevelt and just before the tide began to turn in Congress against the New Deal. It has been found advisable in this Vintage edition to condense the treatment of Roosevelt's first term, add a chapter on World War II, and reinterpret somewhat the three full terms of the presidency of Franklin Roosevelt in the lengthening retrospect of the passing years. This edition provides the opportunity to evaluate President Truman's two terms as well as those of President Eisenhower.

WILFRED E. BINKLEY

Contents

Preface to the Second Edition

I AM convinced that we can never make any sense out of the perplexing problems of the presidency and its relation to the Congress unless we first ascertain precisely what our experience has been with these governmental institutions.

Surely now after more than a century and a half of experience with the functioning of the federal government the time has arrived for a comprehensive survey of the presidency and a frank appraisal of that great office in its relation to the Congress. This ought to dispel some popular delusions and put to rest a great deal of loose chatter as to what is and what is not constitutional, as well as what the fathers did or did not establish as to the presidency.

I had not suspected before I began the investigation of this subject the remarkable extent to which our major political parties have aligned themselves on opposite sides of the controversy regarding presidential leadership. No sooner had universal, white manhood suffrage been established and Jackson elected President than the masses turned to the President as a tribune of the people. The party that attracts the underprivileged has maintained this tradition now for more than a century.

Meanwhile Whig and Republican leaders have been only a little more critical of Democratic "tribunes" than of Presidents of their own party who essayed that role. Historically Republican party philosophy stresses the Congressional check of the Executive and views with jealous eye any pronounced shift of the center of gravity in the government to the President. Republican Congresses have been almost, if not altogether as severe in denouncing the "usurpations" of Abraham Lincoln and Theodore Roosevelt as they were in decrying Grover Cleveland, Woodrow Wilson, and Franklin Roosevelt, indeed any Chief Executive who essays vigorous leadership.

This book is a revision of my *Powers of the President* that extends to every chapter. Clarifying passages have been introduced at changes of administrations, at the beginning of major movements in American history, and indeed wherever they might help the reader to understand the setting of presidential or congressional developments in our political history. New interpretations of the theme of this work are included, and errors have been corrected. The years since the first edition have been covered, and a chapter on the presidency in the Second World War added.

I always considered the title of the first edition, *The Powers of the President,* a misnomer. Typographical considerations had led to its substitution for a longer but more accurate title of my own. It is gratifying to have this new and revised edition published under a more appropriate title.

WILFRED E. BINKLEY

PRESIDENT
☆ AND ☆
CONGRESS

The Problem in the Constitutional Convention

HOW SHALL THE EXECUTIVE BE RELATED TO THE LEGISLATURE?

★

THE RELATION of the President to Congress, though never static, has been conditioned by deep-seated and persistent forces throughout American political history. The Executive as an organ of American government got off to a bad start in the colonial period where it originated in the office of the colonial governor. All too often the King treated the appointment of this official as royal patronage to be dispensed to some court favorite. So lucrative indeed were the perquisites of the office that an appointment was considered a means of mending a broken fortune and to make matters worse, from the point of view of the colonists, the appointee frequently remained in England enjoying the emoluments of the office while a lieutenant-governor performed his functions in the colony. Here was a situation that intensified the habitual vigor of the colonial assembly's check upon what they considered potential executive despotism and they missed no opportunity to trim the governor's powers.

Even the governor's salary depended upon appropriation by the colonial legislature and he was consequently compelled to come to terms with the legislators at the same time that he struggled, as best he could, to execute his royal commission as governor. So he was reduced practically to the necessity of coming, hat in hand, to the door of the legislature begging for funds to carry out his duties and legislatures drove many a hard bargain with him. Indeed legislatures developed such habits as prescribing minutely detailed statutory provisions, by-passing the Governor by assigning the execution of laws to administrative commissions, and even circumventing the governor's appointing power by appropriating salaries, not to the offices, but to named persons. No wonder, it has been said, that the American Revolution was over twenty-five years before Lexington.

It is a curious fact that as early as 1742, half a dozen years before Montesquieu's *L'Esprit des lois* was published, the Massachusetts House of Representatives had explicitly expressed the doctrine of checks and balances in rejecting Governor Shirley's demand for a permanent salary on the ground that it "would lessen the just weight of the other two branches of the government, which ought ever to be maintained and preserved; especially since the governor has so great authority and check upon them." [1] A consequence of colonial experience was the conviction that political power, particularly executive power, is so dangerous that it must be checked with power. Early Americans would have reached this conclusion if they had never heard of

[1] W. S. Carpenter, "The Separation of Powers in the Eighteenth Century," *Am. Pol. Sci. Rev.*, XXII, p. 37.

Montesquieu but, if philosophy is to provide us good reasons for what we want to do anyhow, then *The Spirit of Laws* was made to order for the Founding Fathers. Suffice it to say that a deep-seated suspicion that implicit tyranny lurks in the executive office was planted early and persists to this very day in the American tradition, complicating the problem of integrating the determination of public policy with its execution.

How to adjust the relationship of the Executive to the legislature was an old American problem when the Fathers convened at Philadelphia in 1787. The framers of the Constitution did not have to cross the sea to find models for a plan of national government. These were close at hand in the governments of the thirteen states that had so recently made the transition from colonies. John Adams, who knew more about such matters than any of his contemporaries, even went so far as to say that it was from the constitutions of Massachusetts, New York, and Maryland that the Constitution of the United States was afterwards almost entirely drawn. Most of the others, of course, contributed something and none of them represented a sharp break with the government of the colony from which it had evolved.

Except in the charter colonies of Rhode Island and Connecticut, where the governor was the choice of the electorate, it was impossible for the office to be a popular one. The position of the royal governor was consequently particularly trying. An agent of the Crown, he was under almost constant pressure from the landed and commercial interests in England, mainly creditors, to prevent colonial action deemed disadvantageous to their interests. For one thing, the persistent scarcity of a circulating medium in the colonies and the consequent depressed price of produce made inflationists out of a majority of the colonists. Their demands for paper money were urged with the intense feeling which has characterized monetary controversies of debtors and creditors in every age. This pressure was resisted by the Crown authorities, and since the royal governor occupied the Crown's first line of defense, he bore the brunt of battle and incurred the odium of frustrating the desires of the colonists.[2] The fact that the governor was almost always from England, that he frequently did not even come to America, that he seldom had a sympathetic understanding of the problems of the colonists and was, moreover, often a court favorite, ill adapted for the duties of his office and mostly concerned with the feathering of his nest, all contributed to the bringing of the executive branch of the colonial government into pronounced disrepute almost from the very beginning.

The American legislature, on the other hand, from the earliest times, had been cast for a popular role. The assemblyman, chosen by popular election as a representative of his neighborhood, which was in most cases strictly agrarian, set forth to the provincial capital, commissioned, as he believed, to fight the people's battle against the governor. He was encouraged to go as far as possible in checking the Executive and thereby exalting the people's organ, the legislature. What if the governor did veto enactments? They were frequently put into effect pending the obtaining of the assent of the Crown authority in England, and if the governor was sustained, sometimes the legislation was re-enacted, perhaps in a slightly altered form, and put into effect pending another appeal to the Crown. Sometimes the requirement of the charters that *their acts* of the legislature be submitted to the assent of Crown was circumvented by the use of "votes or orders even to the repealing the effects of acts, suspending the establish-

[2] See E. B. Green, *The Provincial Governor,* Harvard Historical Studies, VIII, p. 163.

ment of pay, paying services, doing chancery and other judicatory business." [3] Thus the Crown might be ignored and the colonial executive disregarded.

The colonial legislature went to great lengths to curb the colonial executive by the creation of commissions for the performance of administrative functions instead of assigning them to the Governor and his subordinates. Through the jealous guardianship of the colonial purse it decisively reduced the governor's control of administration. Appropriations were often made in minute detail with the most meticulous provisions as to the purposes for which expenditures were to be made and executive discretion was reduced to a minimum. By 1757 it could be said of Massachusetts that "almost every act of executive and legislative power, whether it be political, judicial, or military, is ordered and directed by the votes and resolves of the General Court (the Legislature) in most cases originating in the House of Representatives." [4] When a governor of New York asked for fixed revenue for five years the legislature demanded the right to appoint every officer to be paid from the appropriation. Proroguing the legislature, the governor wrote home that the members had taken to themselves "the sole power of rewarding all services and in effect the nomination to all offices, by granting the salary annually, not to the office, but by name to the person in office." [5] Nor were these the only colonies where such paradoxes obtained.

Even before the American Revolution had reached the stage of an appeal to arms the legislature had at-

[3] Governor Pownall, "The Administration of the Colonies," p. 47, quoted in Allen Johnson, *Readings in American Constitutional History*, p. 29.

[4] "Board of Trade to Gov. Pownall," cited by E. B. Green, *op. cit.*, VIII, p. 194.

[5] Quoted in Beard and Beard, *Rise of American Civilization*, I, p. 117.

tained a position of practical sovereignty and had reduced the colonial governor to the necessity of begging at its door for needed appropriations. The last few years of the Colonial Era found the governors engaged in the hopeless task of attempting to maintain the authority of the Crown in the face of the rising tide of colonial discontent. When at last their offices had become utterly untenable and they were forced to flee we may say that the executive as a branch of government in America had reached its nadir. The popularly elected assemblies, however, remained in triumphant control of the governments of the thirteen emerging states. No wonder Locke's political philosophy, with its doctrine of legislative supremacy, was widely read and implicitly accepted by the Revolutionary patriots. Here were the doctrines by which they rationalized the accomplished facts of government in America.

So persistent are habits of mind that when the colonies, during the Revolution, made the transition to states, despite the powers with which the Governor was invested, that official became so subservient to the legislature that Madison, in the *Federalist* papers, declared the governors to be mere "ciphers" while the legislatures were "omnipotent." The framers of the federal Constitution in 1787, in creating the federal Executive, synthesized and fortified the provisions of several state constitutions for their executives with the consequence that the President of the United States, historically considered, is a sort of magnified state governor. This certainly did not extirpate the traditional legislative suspicion of the Executive. Just as the Speaker of the colonial assembly considered himself the people's champion in defying the governor, so the speaker of the state legislature and in turn the speaker of the national House of Representatives confronts the Executive as the assumed guardian of the people's interest.

Thus the evolution of the independent American state began at a time when the executive branch was suffering from the deepest degradation and the very word "governor" had become almost an expression of reproach. One Massachusetts town during the Revolution voted, "that it is Our Opinniun that we do not want any Goviner but the Guiviner of the universe and under him a States General to Consult with the wrest of the united stats for the good of the whole." [6] Several of the states even abandoned the term "governor" as the title of the chief executive and introduced instead that of "President." It might have been expected that the opprobrium attaching to the office would have been readily attributed to the fact that the officer had been a representative of the Crown and now that the executive had become an agent of the people he would be regarded differently. Mere words, however, gradually accumulate the power to evoke powerful emotional reactions and do not suddenly lose it. There was no reasoning about the matter. The governor was reduced to a titular head, a mere "cipher," in most states during the Revolutionary period. Accordingly by most state constitutions he was permitted no veto power and was chosen by the legislature, whose obedient servant he then necessarily became. It was no mere accident that in the government of the Union by the Continental Congress and under the Articles of Confederation there was no executive organ established distinct from the Congress. The colonial merchants who had sought freedom of trade, and had combined with the agrarian inflationists for the purpose of revolution, had achieved their heart's

[6] Quoted in W. M. West, *American History and Government*, p. 228n.

desire in one respect but, alas, they had lost it in another. Now the authority of the Crown was gone and there was no executive power anywhere to exercise the desired check on the issue of paper money, the enactment of bankruptcy laws, and the declaring of moratoria on the payment of debts. No power now could deny legislation facilitating the sale and settlement of Western land or control of the Indians there whose hostility had prevented settlement. Interstate and foreign commerce were even under the control of state legislatures, which resulted in commercial anarchy.

The treaty of peace negotiated at the end of the Revolutionary War had not yet been signed when it became apparent to many patriots that the long-sought-for consummation of independence now attained was in reality not proving to be an altogether happy one. There were marked disadvantages in omnipotent state legislatures. The central governments of the Continental Congress and the Congress of the Confederation had turned out to be scarcely governments at all. They were little more than makeshifts for obtaining collective action among the states, somewhat effective during the war but utterly inadequate in a period of peace. The Articles of Confederation, indeed, did little if any more than convert the *de facto* government of the Continental Congress into a *de jure* government. It is difficult to find in the Articles of Confederation a single power Congress had not already been exercising for years. These powers, however, did not consist of the making of laws in the sense that a law is a rule of conduct commanding what is right and forbidding what is wrong. Congress could enact no statute that any private person was thereby obligated to obey. For its first several years the resolutions of the Continental Congress were carried out by

executive committees of which a hundred were functioning at one time. Later four executive departments
served this purpose. Consequently no separate Executive was ever set up under the Articles. It fell to the
lot of the Philadelphia Constitutional Convention to
create a national executive *de novo*.

The cleavage of economic interests eventually became apparent between the proponents and opponents of the government of the Confederation. The
grain-growing agrarians and the frontiersmen were
usually relatively well satisfied with the Confederation and the "sovereign" state legislatures that gave
them what they wanted, such as legislation acceptable
to the debtor classes. Merchants, however, were becoming deeply distressed over the difficulty of collecting obligations due them, the chaos of conflicting
trade regulations among the states, and the serious
need of a commercial treaty with England. That
country was refusing to negotiate with the feeble
Confederation and threatened to open diplomatic relations with the separate thirteen states. Holders of
Continental securities were dissatisfied with the slowly
disintegrating and utterly insolvent government of
the Confederation, as were also the unpaid officers
and soldiers of the now disbanded Revolutionary
army. Speculators wanted an opportunity at Western
lands. Here was a powerful array of interests soon to
be welded into a compact group and destined in time
to make a determined drive to curb the omnipotent
state legislatures. There were among them some who
must have recalled almost fondly the time when
creditors were protected by Parliament and Crown
against the reprisals of the debtor class in control of
the provincial assemblies. British authority was, of
course, now gone forever, but might not a somewhat
similar central authority be established in America,

capable of protecting their interests against the agrarians? A central American government, sufficiently strong, might yet hold in check the state legislatures and make the country safe for business.

By and large it was these interests bent upon strengthening the central government that provided most of the delegates from the dozen states represented at Philadelphia. Exceptionally significant is the fact that thirty-five of the thirty-nine signers of the finished Constitution were to be found living adjacent to salt water. Lesser agrarians and frontiersmen were conspicuously absent from the delegations, which meant that the protests of the chief opponents of a strong Executive would scarcely be heard in the debates of the Convention. To these absent men the very term "Executive" conjured up a specter of tyranny incarnate in the person of King George. Only somewhat less odious was a central legislature endowed with broad specific powers in marked contrast with the provisions of the Articles of Confederation. So when the publication of the new Constitution eventually revealed that such powers were to be vested in the new federal legislature the cry arose, "We did not dethrone King George only to enthrone King Congress." Such were their phobias of central power wherever it might be lodged.

It would be difficult to discover a more striking example of the irony of history than is to be found in the chief structural problem of the Constitutional Convention. The delegates were groping in the dark to discover a solution of the old problem of the relation of the Executive to the legislature. Unfortunately they were not aware that a workable solution—one that has proved permanent—had emerged from the parliamentary conflicts of the very decade in which they sat at Philadelphia. Their deliberations show that they were somewhat influenced by the British constitution as they understood it, but the silence of their debates concerning the meaning of the younger Pitt's recent struggle with Parliament indicates that they could not have been aware, any more than the English themselves then were, of the most significant constitutional development of that generation. They missed one answer to their question that experience was just revealing.

The problem of a workable adjustment of the relation of Parliament to the Ministry had puzzled English statesmen particularly since the days of the Restoration and the Revolution of 1688. From the point of view of Parliament the questions were: How can the organ of government, now recognized as possessing the power over the nation's purse, control the agents who spend what Parliament supplies? How can the Legislature which Locke declared to be sovereign exert its power? The ministers were the king's by appointment and by ancient custom; but unless the power of Parliament were to remain little more than a shadow that body must be able to exercise some control over the Ministry. How could it be compelled to obey its master? There was also the problem of the ministers themselves. Unless they enjoyed the confidence of Parliament they could not hope to obtain the supply necessary to maintain the functions of the state.

By the seventeenth century impeachment by the British House of Commons and trial by the House of Lords had evolved into the standard means of enforcing responsibility of the King's ministers to Parliament. Since the King as Sovereign "could do no wrong" and was consequently immune to impeachment that procedure was directed against his ministers who were charged with treason. Notable seventeenth century examples of this use were the impeachment of the Duke of Buckingham, 1626 in the reign of James I, and the impeachment, conviction, and execution of the Earl of Stafford and of Archbishop Laud in the reign of Charles I.

The ministers of Charles II had sought to come to a working understanding with the parliamentary leaders through informal conferences, but Parliament bristled with suspicion of intrigue and treachery against them. Yet they were helpless to provide a remedy.[7] They were deeply concerned, some years later, when William III accidentally discovered that a workable government could be obtained by selecting all his ministers from the majority in Parliament. How could these ministers be held responsible to Parliament? Impeachment, the old device, seemed absurd under the circumstances. But the conferences of King William with a select group of parliamentary leaders smacked of intrigue and cabal.[8] Was Parliament to be subordinated once more to the king and the fruits of the "Glorious Revolution" to be lost?

Soon a supposed remedy was devised. In 1692 Parliament passed what is commonly known as the Place Bill. It provided for the exclusion from seats in the House of Commons of all persons holding offices or pensions from the Crown. This would prevent a group of the king's friends, that is the ministers, from sitting in their midst, and through royal prestige and patronage exerting pressure to impose the king's will upon Parliament. William refused his assent to the measure.[9] Again in the Act of Settlement (1700) it was provided that after the accession of the House of

7 G. B. Adams, *An Outline Sketch of English Constitutional History*, pp. 154, 155.

8 *Ibid.*, pp. 157-58.

9 Edward Jenks, *Parliamentary England*, p. 82.

Hanover any person who held an office or a place of profit under the king was to be excluded from the House of Commons. Once more the opportunity for the development of the ministerial system was saved, this time by the repeal of this provision in the Act of Settlement before it went into effect.[10] Almost a century later the Philadelphia Convention succeeded, after considerable debate, in putting just this kind of provision in the federal Constitution.[11] Thus did the delegates unwittingly preclude the solution left open to the English by royal veto and parliamentary repeal of provisions that would have prevented the development of a ministerial system.

William III fulfilled his days and was gathered to the fathers. Queen Anne reigned out her years and then came the four Georges. During the reign of the first two Georges Prime Minister Walpole was giving the evolving cabinet government something of its modern form and procedure at the same time that he was perfecting his technique for the control of elections through patronage and slush funds. The indifference of George I to affairs of state gave Walpole a free hand. When, however, in 1746 George II, alarmed at the declining royal influence, attempted but failed to establish a personal government, he revealed his frustration by exclaiming, "Ministers are kings in this country." [12] Here was a reluctant recognition of a now accomplished fact. The ministerial system was, perhaps, in its infancy, but it had arrived. Yet the Tories did not permit the new institution to go unchallenged. Their opposition to the develop-

10 F. W. Maitland, *The Constitutional History of England*, p. 292.

11 *Documents Illustrative of the Formation of the Union*, p. 261.

12 M. T. Blauvelt, *The Development of Cabinet Government in England*, p. 177.

ment of the ministerial system under Walpole and the Pelhams found expression in a pamphlet of 1761 which declared that "a cabal of ministers had been allowed to erect themselves into a fourth estate, to check, to control, to influence, nay to enslave others." [13]

George III came to the throne in 1760 determined to restore the Constitution of 1689. It is to be doubted whether he was influenced any more by his mother's injunction, "Be a King," than by the precepts of his illustrious tutor, Sir William Blackstone, who read to his young royal pupil as instruction the manuscript of his then unpublished *Commentaries on the Laws of England*. Here the prince learned an authoritative exposition of royal prerogative. He was taught that the king was not only the chief but, properly, the sole magistrate of the nation and that all others were acting by commission from him and in due subordination to him.[14] The prince was no less deeply impressed by Bolingbroke's ideal of the "Patriot King" who was to begin to rule as soon as he began to reign, who was "to espouse no party but to govern like the common father of his people." [15]

No sooner was George III crowned than practice followed precept. At once he took over the patronage previously dispensed by the Ministry, and, utilizing the corrupt methods matured by Walpole, he built up an ostensibly nonpartisan following of the "King's Friends" as they came to be called. This was to be the instrumentality through which the "Patriot King" would rule. To his surprise these tactics drove the Whigs, both English and American, into the opposi-

---

[13] Quoted, *ibid.*, p. 246.
[14] William Blackstone, *Commentaries on the Laws of England*, I, p. 190.
[15] Quoted, M. T. Blauvelt, *op. cit.*, p. 246.

tion and made them the popular party.[16] The objective of the king's attack was of course, the cabinet system with its growing ministerial responsibility to Parliament and its seeming usurpation of royal functions. In 1770 he found in Lord North a congenial minister, completely in accord with him on constitutional theory, and for twelve years this faithful royal servant continued as prime minister. This long and subservient Ministry came to an end only upon the arrival of the news of the surrender of Cornwallis at Yorktown. Yorktown thus became, in effect, a landmark in English constitutional development, marking the failure of the last attempt at personal government on the part of an English king. It is scarcely too much to say that George III lost his colonies and the control of the ministry simultaneously.[17]

After some experimenting with ministers the king called on the younger Pitt to form a Ministry in the face of a majority hostile to him. Almost singlehanded the youthful statesman contended against an overwhelming opposition. The issue was finance. Unless supply were voted, the army, the navy, and other essential public services could not be maintained. But Parliament was at last making a discovery of a weapon to control the Ministry, a discovery which it made in spite of the fact that Pitt ultimately had his way. "The passing of the appropriations and of the annual mutiny bill," wrote the late George Burton Adams, "was postponed and from that date (1784) it had been understood that *the Parliamentary weapon compelling the appointment of a minister of its choice is the refusal to do business with any other*." [18]

---

16 *Ibid.*, p. 252.

17 G. B. Adams, *op. cit.*, p. 162.

18 *Ibid.*, p. 164 (Italics mine, W. E. B.). See Edward Jenks, *op. cit.*, pp. 275-80.

The fact that Pitt neither resigned nor appealed immediately to the country need not concern us here. These practices under such circumstances were not yet thoroughly conventionalized and the opposition made the mistake of trying to prevent an appeal to the country, thereby calling down upon themselves public disapproval.[19] Finally when the opposition had dwindled to a majority of but one Pitt got his election and was overwhelmingly sustained by the electorate. Thus established was another fundamental precedent, that if the ministers of the Crown do not possess the confidence of Parliament they may appeal to the electorate.[20]

In a few months Pitt's experience had done more to clarify the relation of the Ministry to Parliament than a century of previous parliamentary history. Quite naturally the significance of these events was not perceived by those who participated in them. Not until the dawn of the new century did Englishmen begin, and then only imperfectly, to perceive the nature of the institution of cabinet government. Indeed descriptions of the system that convey anything like our modern understanding of it did not begin to appear until about half a century later.[21]

It is not to be wondered at that the framers of the Constitution of the United States had no clear understanding in 1787 of the stage of development then reached by the British constitution to which they so often turned for illustration. When such a keen and discerning delegate as Gouverneur Morris, protesting against the proposed election of the Executive by Congress declared, "Our President will be the British

[19] E. Jenks, *op. cit.*, pp. 278, 279; M. T. Blauvelt, *op. cit.*, p. 282.
[20] A. Lawrence Lowell, *The Government of England*, I, p. 33.
[21] G. B. Adams, *op. cit.*, p. 167. See J. W. Garner, "Executive Participation in Legislation as a Means of Increasing Legislative Efficiency," *Proc. Am. Pol. Sci. Assoc.*, X, p. 180.

Prime Minister, yet we are about to make him appointable by the legislature," [22] his statement provoked no challenging criticism. No one on either side of the Atlantic then saw that practice was settling down to a set of conventions that in effect amounted to the virtual choice of the Ministry by Parliament. The constitutional fathers were under the spell of Montesquieu and Blackstone, both of whom had written their classics long before Pitt's struggle with Parliament and still longer before the treatises that interpret cabinet government as now understood had been published.

The vogue of Montesquieu in America at this time is not difficult to understand, for his political philosophy provided the formula with which Americans could rationalize their political experience. The titular head of the colony, and later of the state, was the governor. In a majority of the colonies he had represented the king or the proprietor. The popularly elected assembly came naturally to be regarded as the people's essential bulwark against executive autocracy. When they read in Montesquieu that power is always prone to be abused and that the remedy is to check power with power they simply saw well stated what they had already learned from experience with government. The colonists would have learned the importance of legislative control of the purse without wide reading of English history and they used this weapon with telling effect on the colonial governors. The prejudice engendered against the colonial executive carried over into the Revolutionary state governments where, according to Madison, the governors became "mere ciphers." The state legislatures gained

---

22 *Documents Illustrative of the Formation of the Union of the American States*, 69th Cong., 1st Session, House Document 398, p. 446.

what the governors lost. So, in spite of explicit statements of separation of powers in the early state constitutions, by 1787 power had largely gravitated to a single department. On both sides of the Atlantic practice had run away with theory. When the Fathers gathered at Philadelphia widespread was the feeling that the remedy for the governmental maladies of the "critical period" was a return to the sound doctrines of the great philosopher, Montesquieu. Once more, they thought, power would have to be checked with power.

The Philadelphia Convention wrestled for weeks with the problems of creating the executive and adjusting its relation to the legislature, the body they regarded as peculiarly representative of the people. This was the very matter that had just been finally adjusted through decisive ministerial responsibility to Parliament on the other side of the Atlantic. Despite the manifest devotion of the framers to the supposed principles of the British constitution we shall find them, nevertheless, deliberately separating the legislature from the executive in the very decade when that constitution had definitely integrated the two departments.

It is a curious fact that the early deliberations of the Philadelphia Convention, starting with the Virginia plan, inclined in the direction of a parliamentary system. The seventh resolution of that plan proposed "that a national executive be instituted to be chosen by the National Legislature . . . and that besides a general authority to execute the national laws, it ought to enjoy the Executive rights vested in Congress by the Confederation." [23] When on June 1 the subject of the executive was taken up by the convention, Roger Sherman said that "he considered the execu-

<hr />

[23] *Documents Illustrative of the Formation of the American States*, p. 117.

tive magistry as nothing more than an institution for carrying the will of the legislature into effect, that the person or persons ought to be appointed by and accountable to the legislature only, which was the depository of the supreme will of society." He proceeded to urge that the legislature be left free to appoint an executive consisting of one or many, as experience might dictate. In the same debate he further expressed himself as in favor of making the executive absolutely dependent on the legislature. An executive independence of the supreme legislature was, in his opinion, the very essence of tyranny if there was any such thing.[24] More or less inclined to this view were also Pinckney, Rutledge, Mason, and Randolph. No less than five times did the convention vote in favor of election of the executive by the legislature before finally rejecting that method.[25]

The appearance of this early proposal to establish a quasi-parliamentary system in the Constitutional Convention is easily explained. We have only to recall that the existing national government of the Articles of Confederation, which the convention had been called merely to revise, represented a union of legislative and executive functions. Congressional committees were responsible for carrying out the resolutions of Congress and whenever it was not in session a committee consisting of one representative from each state sat continuously in order to see that its policies were executed. The multiple executive proposed by Sherman would have been but a smaller Committee of the States provided for by the Articles of Confederation and suggestive of the present Swiss executive.

The development of a parliamentary type was not, however, destined to be initiated by the framers of

24 *Ibid.*, p. 132.
25 Max Farrand, "Compromises of the Constitution," *American Historical Review*, IX, pp. 479 ff.

the Constitution. The matter was determined otherwise in the secrecy of the deliberations of the Committee of Eleven, where there was a return to "true principles." On this committee were some strong nationalists who thought of the executive as essentially a part of the whole of government and who conceived of the Chief Executive as representative of the people of the nation. The committee had substituted for election by the legislature the plan of a choice by presidential electors. When, on September 4, after a partial report of this committee had been made, Randolph and Pinckney inquired as to the reason for changing the methods of electing the Executive, Gouverneur Morris, answering for himself and the committee, gave among other reasons, "the danger of intrigue and faction if the appointment should be made by the Legislature" and "the indispensable necessity of making the Executive independent of the Legislature." [26] The Beards have pointed out that: "If either the Virginia or New Jersey plans had been adopted, parliamentary government would have been developed in America and modern publicists would have displayed their enthusiasm in demonstrating the merits of that particular system." [27]

Let it be kept in mind that the framers of the American Constitution were essentially Whigs and that party affiliation and dogma played their parts in shaping the fundamental instrument. When the great issues that led to the American Revolution were being discussed on this side of the Atlantic, excitement was running high in England over the Middlesex election of 1769. Mass meetings, reform associations, and committees of correspondence were results. American Whigs sympathized with these English activities, the

26 *Ibid.*, pp. 662, 663.
27 Charles A. and Mary R. Beard, *Rise of American Civilization*, I, p. 322.

provincial assembly of South Carolina even attempting to vote funds in their support. Arthur Lee, a Virginian then in London and active in these movements, wrote to Samuel Adams suggesting the organization of committees of correspondence in America to maintain contact with their fellow partisans in England.[28] Adams acted on the suggestion and the American Whigs were soon knit into an extragovernmental organization that promptly seized the reins of government when the Revolution shattered British authority. In the course of the war the American Tories were ruined and the Whigs came into possession of the political field, divided only by faction.

Disciples of Locke, these Whigs believed that the union of legislative and executive functions in the same hands was the essence of tyranny. Montesquieu had taught them that power had to be checked by power. The greatest American exponent of Whig philosophy, John Adams, was in England when Pitt's dramatic struggle with Parliament was giving definite form to the new system of ministerial responsibility based on a continuous acceptability of the Ministry to Parliament. Yet in all his voluminous writings no mention is made of this significant development. Such an admission would have proved fatal to his cherished theory of separated powers. The only instrument for maintaining ministerial responsibility which he deigned to notice was the ancient and obsolete device of impeachment.[29] Had Adams been a delegate to the Constitutional Convention instead of Minister to England he would doubtless have protested vehemently against the persistent tendency of the Convention to make the Executive the choice of the Legislature.

Yet the American Whigs, including, no doubt, even

---

[28] Henry Jones Ford, *The Rise and Growth of American Politics*, pp. 7, 8.
[29] C. M. Walsh, *The Political Science of John Adams*, pp. 97, 98.

John Adams, were not unaware that something had happened to alter the English constitution. Certainly it no longer conformed to Montesquieu's clear-cut dogma and Blackstone's eloquent exposition. But this, they reasoned, was because it had somehow been abused. What if the king did not rule? He ought to. That was his function. The Ministry had been guilty of a usurpation, a temporary one, certainly, it was supposed, but in any case the change was unconstitutional; that is to say, a violation of sound and established practice.[30]

These aberrations of the British constitution from established practice were to be corrected in the new instrument formulated in Philadelphia.[31] It was to be constructed on the mechanistic scheme that had captivated the imagination of the English Whigs.[32] As Madison frankly put it, the stability of the departments was to be maintained "by so contriving the interior structure of the government as that its several constituent parts may, by their mutual relations, be the means of keeping each other in their proper places." [33] They might have been fortified in their faith by Burke's contemporary expression of the idea of checks and balances as "that action and interaction which in the natural and in the political world, from the reciprocal struggles of discordant powers draw out the harmony of the universe." [34]

Nothing in the Constitution has done more to insure the separation of the Executive from Congress than the provision that no person holding any office under the United States shall be a member of either house during his continuance in office. This, of course,

---

[30] See H. J. Ford, *op. cit.*, p. 276.
[31] *Ibid.*, p. 51.
[32] See Woodrow Wilson, *Constitutional Government in the United States,* pp. 56, 57, 70, 203.
[33] *The Federalist*, No. 51.
[34] Quoted by H. J. Ford, *op. cit.*, p. 29.

prevents a member of Congress from being, at the same time, a member of the President's Cabinet, as well as his holding any other federal office. This provision was just the kind that, we have seen, failed to get fixed in the British constitution despite two attempts in the reign of William III. The provision in the federal Constitution had been debated in the Philadelphia Convention on June 22, but there is no hint in the debate that the members sensed the momentous effect of their decision on their doctrine of separated powers. They manifested concern only over the corruption that might prevail without such a provision. English-born Butler, of Georgia, cited the example of his native land: "This was the source of corruption that ruined the government." [35] Several delegates, notably Hamilton, wanted to retain this opportunity for officeholding by congressmen. That Machiavellian realist thus expressed his views: "It was known that one of the ablest politicians (Hume) had pronounced all that influence on the side of the Crown which went under the name of corruption, an essential part of the weight which maintained the equilibrium of the Constitution." [36] Whether Hamilton hoped to see a ministerial system established in America no one can certainly say, but his peculiar conduct during Washington's administration in trying to play the part of a parliamentary prime minister while filling the office of Secretary of the Treasury renders the supposition a very plausible one. A motion to omit from the Constitution under preparation the provision mentioned led to four votes for omission and four for retaining the restriction.[37] Thus narrowly did the Fathers avert the possibility of a radical change in their plan of government.

[35] *Documents of the Formation of the Union*, p. 261.
[36] *Ibid.*
[37] *Ibid.*

The Philadelphia Convention met at a time when reform of the legislature was a subject of discussion on both sides of the Atlantic. Burke had declared that the "distempers of monarchy were the great subjects of apprehension in the seventeenth century; in the eighteenth century the distempers of Parliament." [38] Even then, half a century before the Reform Bill of 1832, Pitt was declaring that unless Parliament reformed itself from within it would be reformed from without. The American state governments, though generally acceptable to the interior counties, had proved unsatisfactory to the commercial, financial, and planting interests of the tidewater. "The legislative department," complained Madison, "is everywhere expanding its sphere of activity, and drawing all power into its impetuous vortex." [39] The most specific provisions for separation of powers had proved powerless to stem the current. No one wrote a more vigorous protest against the tendency than Jefferson. "All the powers of government, legislative, executive, and judicial, result to the legislative body. The concentration of these in the same hands is precisely the definition of despotic governments. . . . 173 despots would surely be as oppressive as one." [40] Corwin sees nothing mysterious about this accumulation of powers in the legislatures. The recognition of separation of powers in the state constitutions "was verbal merely, for the reason that the material terms in which it was couched still remained undefined." [41]

What did the terms "legislative power," "executive power," "judicial power" mean? To modern Americans these expressions represent quite definite concepts, clarified, as they have been, by a century and a

[38] Quoted by M. T. Blauvelt, *op. cit.*, p. 244.

[39] *The Federalist*, No. 48.

[40] Thomas Jefferson, *Notes on the State of Virginia*, p. 211.

[41] "The Progress of Constitutional Theory, 1776-1787," *Am. Hist. Rev.*, XXX, 1925, p. 514.

half of experience and judicial definition. To the men who made our earliest constitutions the conceptual content of these terms was inchoate. Consequently, in spite of the precise statement of the principle of separated powers in the constitution of New Hampshire, its legislature "vacated judicial proceedings, suspended judicial actions, annulled or modified judgments, canceled executions, reopened controversies, authorized appeals, granted exemptions from the standing law, expounded the law for pending cases, and even determined the merits of disputes." [42] Virginia used her "right of original and complete legislation to abolish the privileges of primogeniture, cut off entail, forbid the slave trade and established the principle of freedom in religion as the inherent and inalienable possession of spiritual beings." [43] An elaborate bill of rights in the Virginia constitution did not restrain the legislature from suspending the sittings of courts, from attempting twice to place the state under a dictator, from enacting tender and other ex post facto laws. They attainted a man of treason and declared his life forfeited without trial.[44] In brief, legislative power in 1787 was whatever power the legislature chose to exercise. If the question is raised as to how a legislature could deal with such fundamental rights without constitutional amendment, it need only be recalled that there had been no direct popular ratification of the earliest state constitutions and that consequently they were solely the creations of state legislatures. The Fathers were learning that constitutions are not self-executing.

Here were experiences with government and especially the legislative branch that profoundly im-

---

[42] *Ibid.,* p. 514.

[43] George Bancroft, *History of the United States* (1892), **V,** p. 329.

[44] See *The Federalist* (Ford ed.), p. 55n.

pressed the delegates at Philadelphia. Where the makers of the state constitutions had feared and subdued the Executive, the dominant element in the Philadelphia Convention was deeply concerned lest the popular organ, the Congress, would play the tyrant. No wonder "the perils of democracy" was a favorite topic of discussion behind the closed doors of the Constitutional Convention that long hot summer of 1787. Among the delegates there developed a pronounced consensus that the national legislature would have to be decisively checked. Even the great liberal, James Wilson, declared that legislatures had come to believe that "the exercise of rights by either the executive or judiciary is a breach of their prerogatives and an outrage to their dignity." [45] Their experience with state legislatures quite naturally led the framers of the Constitution to believe that the House of Representatives would possess a tremendous inherent vitality as the immediate representative of the people. It would require no such special safeguards for its protection as the other co-ordinate branches of the government.[46]

The framers probably greatly overestimated the inherent strength of the lower house and left it too weak. Contemporary liberals thought so. Richard Henry Lee, opposing ratification of the Constitution by Virginia, protested that "the only check to be found in favor of the democratic principle in this system, is the House of Representatives which, I believe, may justly be called a mere shred or ray of Representation." Mason bitterly complained that the House of Representatives is "the shadow only, not the substance of representation." [47] Here are foreshadowings of that championing of the pre-eminent place of Congress in the Federal system by the early Virginia Republicans

---

[45] James Wilson, *The Works of James Wilson,* II, pp. 286, 393.
[46] *The Federalist,* No. 63.
[47] J. Elliott, *Debates,* I, p. 503.

and their drive against the "monocrats," as Jefferson denominated the Federalists who vigorously defended the Executive power as administered by Washington and Adams.

The vaunted "power of the purse" left in the Representatives' hands has proved in practice to be little more than the pretense of power. What is the advantage in the sole power to initiate revenue measures when the Senate, under its constitutional power to amend such measures, can alter and has altered every word of such a measure except the title, or when the conference committee, an organ unknown to the Constitution, can radically change a revenue measure, substituting rates outside the limits approved by either house before the measure went to conference.[48] Moreover revenue measures once enacted can be altered not by the House alone but only upon the concurrence of the Senate and the President. Let a permanent money provision once be made and the two agencies can defy the lower house to alter or amend it. Is it not possible that in their eagerness to establish a strong executive the framers left the lower house an "incurably deficient and inferior organ of government"?[49]

The sorry spectacle of the impotent state executives of 1787, the "mere ciphers," in contrast with the despotic state legislatures led the Fathers to invest the President with extraordinary authority. The Constitution, in contrast with the Articles of Confederation, provided for direct action of the central government on the individual which rendered imperative a distinct executive organ. We have seen that the Congress of the Confederation could pass a resolution declaring a policy but when it applied to private persons,

[48] James Ford Rhodes, *History of the United States from Hayes to McKinley,* pp. 176, 178.
[49] H. J. Ford, *op. cit.,* p. 55.

unless state officials chose to enforce it, it would become a dead letter. We have the testimony of a contemporary, John Quincy Adams, that "the Federal party was that which had struggled to give effect to the recommendations of Congress under the Confederation. . . . Their exertions were confined to action upon the several state legislatures. . . ." [50]

The framers were concerned over the current belief that a republic was inherently weak. Then a strong republican executive was widely assumed to be a contradiction in terms; only monarchies had strong executives. Hamilton, whose preference for monarchy was no secret, frankly asserted in the Constitutional Convention that obtaining a good republican executive was impossible. The framers would essay the innovation of creating a strong executive in a republic. Consequently there was as much effort in the convention to strengthen the executive as there had been to check the House of Representatives.[51]

The prototype of the office of President was found in the governor in two of the states, for in two of them that officer was not a "cipher." In Massachusetts and in New York the governors were popularly elected, thus providing them with popular mandates, which inevitably must have added prestige to the office. The framers were impressed by Governor Bowdoin's recent achievement in subduing the revolting followers of Daniel Shays in Massachusetts.[52] But to a greater degree the governorship of New York, where the office was not so hedged about,[53] as elsewhere, by

[50] Adrienne Koch and William Peden, *The Selected Writings of John and John Quincy Adams*, p. 325.

[51] See Charles C. Thach, Jr., *The Creation of the Presidency*, Johns Hopkins Studies in Historical and Political Science, Series XL, No. 4, p. 77. See Hamilton's speech in Farrand, *Records*, I, p. 289.

[52] See S. E. Morison, *The Oxford History of the United States*, I, p. 92.

[53] C. C. Thach, *op. cit.*, p. 27.

constitutional restrictions, captured their attention. The influence of the office in that state on their handiwork is seen in the extent to which the provisions for it in the New York constitution found their way into the federal Constitution.[54] There was some inclination to regard New York as having almost a model constitution.

The first clauses of the first and second articles of the Constitution seem to betray on the part of the framers a distrust of Congress and a solicitous concern for the Executive. Before the Constitution had been in force half a dozen years Hamilton was driving the Jeffersonian Republicans to fury by pointing out that while the Constitution granted legislative power in specific terms, the executive power in blanket form is vested in a President of the United States. Except for enumerated prohibitions the Executive, Hamilton argued, has plenary powers.[55] It seems to have been no accident, on the part of those who gave the Constitution its phrasing, that the President's oath was made to read that he "execute the office" of President, not merely enforce the law. Executive prerogative as well as whatever duties Congress might assign by statute had thus been apparently constitutionally authorized for the Chief Executive, argued Hamilton.

Few rejections of proposals by the Philadelphia Convention caused more bitter disappointment than that of an executive council.[56] In every state there was then a council of advice without which the chief magistrate could not act.[57] The ultimate abandoning of

54 See Alexander Johnson, "What the Federal Constitution Owes to the Several States," *New Princeton Review,* Sept., 1887.

55 Alexander Hamilton, *The Works of Alexander Hamilton* (Lodge ed.), IV, pp. 142-44.

56 See the objections of George Mason to the federal Constitution, P. L. Ford, *Pamphlets on the Constitution of the United States,* pp. 327 ff.

57 Elliot, *Debates,* V, p. 150.

this proposed agency immensely strengthened the President. The Executive is further fortified by the requirement of a two-thirds vote of the Senate for conviction on impeachment by the House. Consequently he cannot thus be punished for a veto. In fact the extraordinary majority required renders conviction practically impossible. Moreover, the President's power is enhanced by his freedom either to enforce or to neglect to enforce a particular law. His oath as already noted does not even specifically obligate him "to enforce the law." [58] The framers had taken pains to insure the independence of the executive branch. We shall see how the failure to define its necessary relations to Congress confronted the new government with a problem of transcendent importance from the day it began to function.

[58] One of the ablest exponents of the doctrine of state rights, Able P. Upshur, President Tyler's secretary of state, expressed the fears of his school on this point in his exceptionally keen criticism of Story's *Commentaries:* "The most defective part of the Federal Constitution, beyond all question is that which relates to the executive department. It is impossible to read that instrument without being forcibly struck with the loose and unguarded terms in which the powers and duties of the President are pointed out. So far as the Legislature is concerned, the limitations of the Constitution are perhaps as precise and strict as they could safely have been made; but in regard to the Executive, the Convention seems to have studiously selected such loose and general expressions as would enable the President, by implication and construction, either to neglect his duties or to enlarge his powers. We have heard it gravely asserted in Congress that whatever power is neither legislative nor judicial is, of course, executive, and as such belongs to the President under the Constitution. Be this as it may, it is a reproach to the Constitution that the executive is so ill-defined as to leave any plausible pretense, even to the insane zeal of party devotion, for attributing to the President of the United States the powers of a despot—powers which are wholly unknown to any limited monarchy in the world." *A Brief Enquiry into the True Nature and Character of Our Federal Government* (1840), pp. 116, 117.

★ ★ ★ II ★ ★ ★

The Solution of
the Federalist Party

★

IN ONE RESPECT there can be no doubt that every
President since Washington has had an advantage
over him. In respect to almost every important presidential function Washington's successors have been
able to ask "How has this matter been handled before?" Washington was acutely aware that he had no
precedents to guide him and that his presidency
would set the precedents. Thus he observed in a letter
to Madison: "As the first of everything, in *our* situation will serve to establish a precedent, it is devoutly
wished, on my part, that these precedents may be fixed
on true principles." [1] So the Electoral College was a
perfect organ of the public will in casting a unanimous vote for him. The legislatures of the eleven

[1] Quoted by James Hart, *The American Presidency in Action,
1789* (1948), p. 9.

states that had ratified the Constitution proceeded to elect the twenty-two senators who were to sit in the First Congress. In the absence of specific directions in the Constitution the members of the lower house were chosen in some states on a general ticket, in others by districts, and in still others by a combination of the two methods. With the inauguration of Washington, April 30, 1789, the legislative and executive branches were ready to institute the new government prescribed by the Constitution.

In a very proper sense the first Congress under the Constitution may be regarded as a constituent assembly. The product of the Philadelphia Convention was after all only a framework, parts of which were slender indeed, with here and there strange omissions in the structure. Consequently the deliberations of the First Congress over the starting of the new government are suggestive of the debates of the Constitutional Convention. Questions apparently settled there are raised again and debated once more, sometimes even by the same statesmen. This ought to remind us that approximately the same group that framed the Constitution at Philadelphia were on hand in New York to put the instrument into operation. Eighteen delegates of the Philadelphia Convention sat in the first session of Congress and every state represented there except New York had one or more delegates among either its senators or representatives.[2] "It is safe to say," wrote Charles A. Beard, "that four-fifths of the active, forceful leaders of the Convention helped to realize as a process of government the paper constitution they had drafted."[3] Specifically twenty-six of the thirty-nine signers of the Constitution came to occupy places in the new government.

[2] C. C. Thach, *op. cit.*, pp. 141, 142.
[3] *The Economic Origins of Jeffersonian Democracy*, p. 105.

We are concerned here with a major problem confronting this First Congress: How is the administrative apparatus to be geared to the governmental machine or, more concretely, what is to be the relation between the executive departments and the principal political organs, the President, the House of Representatives, and the Senate? The Constitution was vague on the matter. It assumed that there would be a "principal officer in each department" without even prescribing the establishment of any departments. The President, of course, would appoint these principal officers by and with the advice and consent of the Senate and might require their opinion in writing "upon any subject relating to the duties of their respective offices." [4] It is evident that the framers had in mind the departments established during the Revolutionary War. The debates of the Constitutional Convention throw almost no light on the matter, but contemporary correspondence reveals an assumption that these existing departments would be continued and that even the incumbents would be reappointed to the principal offices in their respective departments. This explains how General Knox came to be Washington's Secretary of War, as well as President Washington's efforts to ensure a continuation of the services of Robert Morris as Secretary of the Treasury and John Jay as Secretary of Foreign Affairs as soon as Congress had established these departments.[5]

These are important facts because they constitute an important part of the mental equipment of the members of the First Congress when they attacked the problem stated. The debates revealed that these departments in the government of the Confederation both in form and procedure were constantly suggest-

---

[4] Art. II, Sec. 2, Clause 1.
[5] See H. B. Learned, *The Creation of the Cabinet*, pp. 111-15.

ing precedents to aid them in their legislation. Moreover the precedents thrust upon them the question whether within the limits permitted by the Constitution any such relation of the departments to Congress should be provided for as would suggest a ministerial system. The practices under the old Congress looked decidedly in that direction. For example the Secretary of Foreign Affairs, John Jay, had been accustomed to appear freely on the floor of the Congress of the Confederation and he occasionally spoke in an advisory capacity. A keen and observing chargé d'affaires, representing the French government, was quick to note the effect of this practice and to report to Vergennes that "Mr. Jay, especially, has acquired a peculiar ascendancy over the members of Congress. All important business passes through his hand." [6] Later this same official wrote home to his chief, "Congress seems to be guided only by his directions. . . . Congress does not perceive that it ceases to be any more than an organ of its chief minister. . . . He inspires the majority of the resolutions of Congress." [7] In these declining days of the Congress of the Confederation John Jay became virtually the Chief Executive of the government. Other executive heads also were accustomed to appear before the Congress. Here was a practice that looked like a precedent for a procedure under the government about to be established in order to implement the Constitution.

Since the first department to be considered by Congress was that of the treasury it is necessary to survey briefly the ideas of the First Congress concerning the handling of public finance. Let it be remembered that both colonial experience and the prevailing state practices, as well as the system of the government of the

---

[6] Quoted by George Bancroft, *History of the Constitution of the United States* (1882), I, p. 473.

[7] Quoted *ibid.*, I, p. 479.

Confederation, had established the treasury almost absolutely under the control of the legislature, particularly of the popular branch.[8] Long accustomed to such an arrangement, it must have then seemed to most Americans of that period a part of the established order of nature. To the Founding Fathers the Treasury Department must have seemed to be a congressional rather than an executive organ. The Constitutional Convention had accordingly seriously considered providing for the election of the Secretary of the Treasury of Congress.[9] This arrangement was still being considered by the convention even as late as September 12 [10] and was voted down finally on September 14, [11] only a week before that body finished its work. The ill repute of legislatures in general, due to the excesses of state legislatures and the bad reputation of the Continental Congress and the Congress of the Confederation, had determined the framers finally to place the appointment of the Secretary of the Treasury in the hands of the President.

But when Congress took up the question of the establishment of the Treasury Department it did not at once conclude that the Constitution had closed the matter of its relation to Congress and the President. Old habits of thought persisted and strong efforts were made to subordinate the Secretary of the Treasury quite decisively to Congress. Gerry pleaded for a continuance of the old Treasury Commission of three under which Robert Morris had functioned, and he would have had these three appointed and supervised by Congress.[12] He thought the Secretary of the Treasury ought "to recommend general systems of finance

8 H. B. Learned, *op. cit.*, p. 101.

9 *Documents of the Formation of the Union*, p. 475.

10 *Ibid.*, p. 706.

11 *Ibid.*, p. 723.

12 *Annals of the Congress of the United States*, 1st Cong., I, p. 384.

without having anything to do with actual administration of them, because if he engages in the executive business, we shall be deprived of his talents in more important things." [13] Gerry evidently had in mind an official who, as a specialist in finance, would advise Congress in that field. Hamilton was soon to act in that very capacity, but without being divorced from administration.

Representative White thought that the question of the relation of the departments had been settled in the Constitutional Convention. "We are told we ought to keep the legislative and executive departments distinct; if we were forming a constitution the observation would be worthy of due consideration and we would agree to the principles: but the Constitution is formed and the powers blended; the wished-for separation is therefore impracticable." [14] Exception was taken to this interpretation and the debate proceeded.

The bill before Congress, which was the subject of debate, followed almost the exact words of the act creating the superintendent of finance under the Articles of Confederation.[15] It authorized the secretary to "digest and report plans for the improvement and management of revenue and the support of the public credit." [16] Representative Page objected that this would render the office too powerful. It might lead to the ministers of the government being admitted to the floor to explain and support their plans, "thus laying the foundation for an aristocracy or a detestable monarchy." [17] Certainly, thought he, revenue bills could not be said to originate in the House if they were reported by the minister of finance. This led Ames to inquire "what influence could a plan re-

13 *Ibid.*, p. 386 .
14 *Ibid.*, p. 383.
15 W. S. Carpenter, *Democracy and Representation*, p. 46.
16 *Annals*, 1st Cong., I, p. 592.
17 *Ibid.*, pp. 592-93.

ported openly and officially have on the mind of any member more than if the scheme and information were given privately at the Secretary's office." [18] And Boudinot pointed out further that "if he can secrete himself behind the curtain, he might create a noxious influence, and not be answerable for the information." [19] Boudinot's idea represented what was to become the Federalist party doctrine. The Federalists wanted the departments so organized that the secretary would function in the light and be unable to evade responsibility.

To compose the difference revealed by the debate there was proposed an amendment to strike out from the bill the word "report" and insert instead "prepare" which was carried.[20] It is just possible that this apparently insignificant change of a single word in the phrasing of the statute may have had a profound effect on our constitutional development. At any rate it is a link in a chain of events leading to a distinct and awkward separation of the legislative and executive branches in a manner certainly not required by the letter or apparent intention of the Constitution.

So circumscribed by congressional authority did the statute establishing the Treasury Department leave the secretary that half a century later, during the controversy over Jackson's veto of the rechartering of the Second Bank of the United States, Congress was debating the question of whether it was an "executive" department at all. Was it not really a congressional agency? This question did not arise with respect to the War and State departments since they were recognized as performing executive functions and were specifically designated as executive departments. That Congress hesitated to give the Treasury Department

18 *Ibid.*, p. 596.
19 *Ibid.*, p. 600.
20 *Ibid.*, p. 604, 608.

specific executive classification is not to be wondered at when we recall that their colonial, state, and Confederation experience had led them to the conviction that the control of the purse is a function of the "sovereign legislature." Years later Presidents Madison and Monroe were embarrassed by the statutory requirement that the Secretary of the Treasury report directly to Congress.[21] This chief officer is to this day subject at any moment to the direction of Congress "generally to perform all such services relatively to the finances as he shall be directed to perform."[22] It was the unique and somewhat ambiguous standing given this department from the beginning that led to the furious controversy between Andrew Jackson and the Senate over the removal of government deposits from the Bank of the United States.

From the day of his appointment as Secretary of the Treasury, Alexander Hamilton began to impress upon that office the stamp of his imperious personality. His conception of the functions of the finance minister may be gathered from an examination of the thirty-sixth number of *The Federalist:* "Nations in general, even under governments of the more popular kind, usually commit the administration of their finances to single men or to boards composed of a few individuals, who digest and prepare, in the first instance, the plans of taxation which are afterwards passed into laws by the authority of the sovereign legislature." This was not a generally accepted dogma in 1789 and with a less aggressive secretary in the Treasury Department we might not have started with that practice. We certainly would not have had Hamilton's name attached to the financial policy of the First Congress.

This brilliant and aggressive young statesman had

---

21 H. B. Learned, *op. cit.,* p. 102.
22 *Statutes at Large,* I, pp. 28, 49, 63, 68.

been confessedly disappointed in the product of the Philadelphia Convention, but he missed no opportunity now to fashion the new government in accordance with his political theory so far as possible within the terms of the fundamental instrument. We shall soon find him manifesting a capacity for deriving unexpected meanings from the Constitution through the magic of "documentary exegesis." The Treasury Act, in the adoption of which he is reputed to have played an important part,[23] appeared to afford ample latitude for the employment of his undoubted talents as an administrator and political leader.

Could Hamilton play the commanding part in shaping a financial program that the younger Pitt was then performing in England and present his plans face to face with the congressmen as Robert Morris, the finance minister, had done in appearing before the Congress of the Confederation? The need of leadership in Congress was already becoming apparent and the Virginia agrarians seemed to be unwittingly leaving wide open the gate of opportunity for the young and ambitious Federalist leader. The congressional delegation from that state had brought from the Virginia House of Delegates a very exalted opinion of the adequacy of the Committee of the Whole and a pronounced antipathy to the use of select and standing committees. Their stubbornness in the matter provoked Fisher Ames to write, "Virginia is stiff and touchy against any change of the Committee of the Whole. . . . They are for watching and checking power; they see evils in embryo; are terrified with possibilities and are eager to establish rights and to explain principles to such a degree that you would think them enthusiasts and triflers."[24] Congress had

---

23 J. Q. Adams, *Memoirs of John Quincy Adams,* IV, p. 217.
24 Fisher Ames, *Works of Fisher Ames,* I, p. 64.

been in its first session only a few months when a ways and means committee was "discharged from further proceedings on business referred to them and the business was referred to the Secretary of the Treasury to report thereon." [25] Hamilton, as well as other department heads, was soon drafting bills for Congress. Apparently invited to do so, the Secretary of the Treasury readily proceeded to organize his department as an organ of Congress in the preparation of financial measures. Hamilton's theory as he had described it in *The Federalist* was becoming practice. In brief, the initiation and preparation of legislation for the consideration of the House during the Federalist administrations were becoming the business of "ministers" as it is in the British parliamentary system to this day, and not of the specialized committees to be firmly established later by the Jeffersonians.

Instead of taking immediate alarm at Hamilton's increasing part in shaping legislation Congress was soon facilitating further development in that direction by referring financial matters of every description, including even petitions, to the Secretary of the Treasury. He was rapidly acquiring a command of legislation in his field that was erelong to raise the specter of ministerial government in the minds of timorous Republicans. Could he have but held his impetuous nature in check his dream of legislative leadership might have been completely and permanently established and our federal system, at this point, might have been stabilized in a different form by a set of conventions that only narrowly missed being established. Curiously enough the very housing of the new federal government seemed to invite the most intimate relations between Congress and the executive

25 *Annals,* 1st Cong., I, pp. 1, 929.

department. New York City, not without hope of capturing permanently the seat of the federal government, had constructed Federal Hall for housing officers of the entire government. Thus the Senate, the House, and the executive department began functioning in the closest proximity, all of which suggested the integration rather than the separation of powers.

During its first session Congress had instructed Hamilton to prepare for their consideration a financial program. When that body convened for its second session the secretary informed the House that he was ready to report. The question now was the manner in which he was to report. The statute creating his office directed him "to make report and give information to either branch of the legislature in person or in writing respecting all matters referred to him." [26] Here the House was confronted with an alternative. Hamilton undoubtedly preferred to report in person. There seemed to be good American precedent for this. He must have been familiar with the appearance of the secretaries before the Congress of the Confederation. Was he not in a sense the successor of Robert Morris? Moreover, it would have been in accordance with British ministerial practice, which made a profound impression on Hamilton's mind, and he was perfectly at home in the give and take of debate. Boudinot "hoped that the Secretary of the Treasury might be permitted to make his report in person in order to answer such inquiries as the members might be disposed to make." [27] But after a brief and one-sided debate on the question it was decided that the report should be presented in writing.[28] It is possible that Representative Madison, then regarded as

[26] *Statutes at Large,* I, pp. 65-67.
[27] *Annals,* 1st Cong., I, p. 1043.
[28] *Ibid.,* pp. 1044-45.

an administration man, did not care to risk his leadership of the House through the appearance before it of the magnetic and masterful treasury head whose prestige was enhanced by the implicit confidence President Washington had in him. At any rate Hamilton was compelled to convert his brief for a speech into a written report.

The alternative so lightly disposed of by Congress was unquestionably of momentous consequence in our constitutional development. If we brush aside externals we reach the fundamental question here involved: Shall the leadership of Congress be provided internally or shall that body frankly accept leadership from without? The agrarians, including Jefferson, who was soon to be their chieftain, were evidently not even aware of the existence of this problem. They believed that public policies were to be evolved from the free and unrestricted discussions of the Committee of the Whole. Jefferson as Secretary of State clung tenaciously to the idea that, as an executive official, he must keep clear of Congress. The Federalist leaders, Washington, Hamilton, Marshall, and Ames, both in word and deed, were giving expression to a more realistic and businesslike view of the necessities of the case. They would have preferred the frank and free appearance of the secretaries before Congress in order to keep responsibility in the full light of publicity and discourage intrigue and backstair methods. When later the agrarians, in control of the House, ended the system of reference to the executive heads and substituted standing committees the Federalists turned to the congressional caucus where, free from House rules and an annoying opposition, Hamilton could exercise an easy mastery of the party and consequently of Congress. Shut out of the House, the Executive through Hamilton nonetheless manifested a masterful leadership, the outcome of which was the enactment of Hamilton's financial program.[29]

That Hamilton from the very first, despite his exclusion from the House, assumed the functions of a Crown minister was the opinion of his opponents, notably Senator Maclay, who stated that the rest of the department heads followed him in this view of his office.[30] "Anything which comes from a Secretary is adopted almost without any examination." [31] "It is totally vain to oppose the Bank Bill." [32] "Nothing was done without him [Hamilton]." [33] "Congress may go home. Mr. Hamilton is all-powerful and fails in nothing he attempts." [34] Hamilton was even looking after the selection of committees (in the Senate apparently) in order to prevent his measures falling into unfriendly hands[35] and he attended committee meetings to give advice.[36] His control of legislation was arousing some resentment in the lower house early in the first session. Representative Jackson remarked that "according to the ideas of some gentlemen, the House had no right to add to the appropriations proposed by the Secretary" and that "according to this doctrine the whole business of legislation may as well be submitted to him, so in fact the House would not be the Representative of their constituents but of the Secretary." [37] Hamilton may have been astonished that Jackson's objection was even raised, for again it was a long-established British practice that the Congress-

29 See R. V. Harlow, *The History of Legislative Methods in the Period before 1825*, pp. 140, 145.

30 *Journal of William Maclay*, p. 272.

31 *Ibid.*, p. 246.

32 *Ibid.*, p. 364.

33 *Ibid.*, p. 385.

34 *Ibid.*, p. 387.

35 *Ibid.*, p. 331.

36 *Ibid.*, p. 385.

37 *Annals*, 1st Cong., II, p. 1449.

man condemned. For nearly a century a standing order of the House of Commons had forbidden the consideration of any question of supply except on the recommendation of the Crown.[38] But this was contrary to American theory and practice as developed in colonial and state handling of finance by the legislature and was destined to be but a temporary usage in Congress.

Hamilton did not stop with the mere assumption that he was a crown minister. He presumed that he was the chief one, the prime minister. Something more than his aggressive disposition is needed to account for this. No doubt he was influenced by the example of Pitt who was the prime minister at the same time that he was first lord of the treasury and chancellor of the exchequer.[39] He went so far as to ask his friends to speak of him as the first lord of the treasury. Hamilton's biographer, the late Henry Cabot Lodge, who treated his subject sympathetically, admitted that "he could not rid himself of the idea that he was really the prime minister, a notion encouraged by the way Congress had thrown all sorts of questions into his hands for decision." [40] Further still, the implicit trust of President Washington in Hamilton encouraged him in another assumption suggested by English parliamentary practice. Like a prime minister he would be the channel of communication between the legislature and the Executive. Washington was to enjoy something of the detachment from Congress that befitted a monarch in a constitutional system.

---

[38] "This House will receive no petition for any sum relating to the public service or proceeding upon any motion for a grant or charge upon the public revenue, whether payable out of the consolidated fund or out of money to be provided by parliament, unless recommended from the Crown." *Standing Order of the House of Commons*, No. 66.

[39] M. T. Blauvelt, *op. cit.*, p. 281.

[40] H. C. Lodge, *Alexander Hamilton*, p. 156.

It is a strange fact that the heads of the other departments and the Attorney General who had not yet been given the status of a department head, acquiesced somewhat in Hamilton's assumption of a premiership. The evidence of this is incontrovertible. On January 11, 1791, we find him replying to Jefferson's request for an opinion concerning our treaty with France and writing, "I have perused with attention your intended report to the President, and will, as I am sure is your wish, give my opinion with frankness."[41] Later Jefferson was asking him what the Senate would do in regard to certain proposals for a treaty with Algiers.[42] Hamilton and not the Secretary of War wrote to the House "that it is the opinion of the secretary for the Department of War that it is expedient and necessary that the United States should retain and occupy West Point."[43] Hamilton wanted to make all purchases for the War Department. When Knox demurred, Hamilton persuaded Congress to give him such authority.[44] Hamilton prepared the list of questions that constituted the agenda at the Cabinet meeting to consider the conduct of Genêt, the irrepressible young minister from the new Republic of France whose recall had to be requested by the President. Washington had recopied the questions in his own handwriting but Jefferson knew the usurper of his prerogative in the field of foreign affairs.[45] It was Hamilton and not Jefferson who issued the instructions to Jay when he went to London to negotiate the treaty that bears his name. Moreover, Hamilton took liberties revising and altering important state papers prepared by other

[41] A. Hamilton, *Works* (Lodge ed.), IV, p. 52.

[42] A. Hamilton, *Works* (1851), p. 215, quoted by H. J. Ford, *The Rise and Growth of American Politics,* p. 82n.

[43] *Ibid.*, p. 82n.

[44] Noah Brooks, *Henry Knox*, p. 213.

[45] Thomas Jefferson, *Anas*, I, p. 268. Cited, Claude Bowers, *Jefferson and Hamilton*, p. 215.

executive heads. He wrote the Attorney General advising changes in a paper drafted by that officer, objecting that "there appears too much tartness in various parts." [46] He is said even to have written many of the papers Randolph felt constrained, as Attorney General, to sign.[47] When he dealt with Congress, Hamilton's well-known close association with President Washington and the latter's confidence in him made him appear to be speaking for the President and the other secretaries hesitated to interfere or even demur.[48]

The movement for a strong executive which we saw crystallize in the Constitutional Convention and which was dominant throughout the first term of Washington's administration had practically run its course by the end of that term. Washington would start his second term with a hostile Republican majority in the lower house. Even before the new Congress was seated the emboldened Republicans in the House started the campaign against Hamilton that was in time to drive him back to private life. They attacked his "premiership" and his "unconstitutional" promotion of money bills.[49] They attacked him by offering a series of resolutions charging him with violation of law, neglect of duty, transgression of proper limits of his authority, and indecorum in his attitude toward the House, and refused to permit him to appear in person to defend himself.[50] Although the resolutions failed to carry, the new Congress was to render Hamilton's position as secretary scarcely tenable.

The Republicans in the Third Congress proceeded in the demolition of the Federalist system of executive leadership, through a system of sabotage. They har-

[46] Hamilton, *Works* (1851), IV, p. 544.
[47] H. S. Randall, *The Life of Thomas Jefferson,* II, p. 244n.
[48] *Ibid.,* I, pp. 635-36.
[49] *Annals,* 1st Cong., II, pp. 349-54.
[50] *Ibid.,* pp. 907-63.

assed the departments with demands for information.[51] They stopped using the departments as agencies for formulating measures for their consideration and fell back on the cumbersome Committee of the Whole as in the first session of Congress before the departments had been organized. The House began to flounder and lapse into confusion and incompetence, which provoked the disgusted Ames to write, "Congress is too inefficient to afford stuff for a letter." [52]

In the Fourth Congress Albert Gallatin sought to rescue the House from its confusion by getting a Ways and Means committee appointed, to the disgust of the Federalists and the alarm of some of the Republicans.[53] Nevertheless the House hesitated, drifted, and refused to assume responsibility.[54] Congress was suffering from just such a set of legislative circumstances as must have led John Stuart Mill to declare that while a legislature is the best way to get good laws it is the poorest kind of a body to make them.[55] The Republicans had rejected the competent agencies employed by the Federalists because they were executive. Internal organs then had to be devised and gradually a system of specialized standing committees began to develop and became a part of the Republican body of doctrine, constituting a kind of corollary of the grand theory of the "sovereignty" of the legislature.

Strange to say, the standing committee in America owes its origin to the rise of that type of committee in the British Parliament as early as 1571.[56] Eventually it disappeared there, owing, we may suppose, to the

[51] George Gibbs, *Memoirs of the Administrations of Washington and John Adams* (1846), I, pp. 127, 129.

[52] Fisher Ames, *Works*, I, p. 169.

[53] Henry Adams, *The Life of Albert Gallatin*, p. 157.

[54] George Gibbs, *op. cit.*, I, p. 443.

[55] *Autobiography* (New York, 1873), pp. 264, 265.

[56] J. F. Jameson, "Origin of the Standing Committee System," *Pol. Sci. Quarterly*, 1894, pp. 246, 247.

development of the cabinet system which rendered it scarcely necessary. Before the committees had disappeared in England, however, they had been carried to America by the English colonists, where they developed in the assemblies of the Middle and Southern colonies. The Revolutionary state governments witnessed a further development of this device and the multiplication of the committees. The Republicans now turned to these agencies, not as a matter of deliberate choice, but as a means of release from the debacle in Congress after it had refused to utilize the department secretaries any longer in shaping legislative proposals for consideration.[57]

The bitter disappointment of the Federalists at this supposed perversion of sound practice is reflected in their letters. Fisher Ames, from his seat as a member of the Fourth Congress, wrote to Hamilton, now practicing law in private life, "The efficiency of the government is reduced to its minimum, the proneness of the popular body to usurpation is already advancing to its maximum. Committees are already the ministers; and while the House indulges a jealousy of encroachments in its functions, which are properly deliberative, it does not perceive they are impaired and nullified by the monopoly as well as the perversion of information by the committees." [58]

Several episodes of Washington's administration served to contribute to the clarification of the relationship of Congress to the Executive. The first congressional investigation of an executive activity through a special committee was for the purpose of ascertaining the cause of the disastrous defeat of St. Clair's army by the Indians in 1791.[59] A perusal of the debate reveals that Congress based its right to investigate on

57 See Harlow, *op. cit.,* Chaps. I & IV.
58 Hamilton, *Works* (1851), IV, p. 201.
59 *Annals,* 2nd Cong., pp. 490-94.

its control of the expenditure of public money. The House was not successful in its purpose when it summoned the Secretaries of War and of the Treasury to appear before it, but these officials appeared before the congressional committee.[60] The committee grew so bold as to ask the President for the papers pertaining to the St. Clair campaign. The position taken by the Executive was the result of several Cabinet meetings leading to the unanimous conclusion that: "first, the House was an inquest and therefore might institute inquiries; second, that they might call for papers generally; third, that the executive ought to communicate such papers as the public good would permit and ought to refuse those the disclosure of which would injure the public . . . ; fourth, that neither the committee nor the House had a right to call on the head of a department who or whose papers were under the President alone, but that the committee should instruct their chairman to move the House to address the President." [61]

When Washington in 1793 issued his proclamation of neutrality in the war that had broken out between France and England, he provoked a furious outburst concerning his constitutional powers. Not only were his political opponents, the Republicans, generally pro-French in sympathy but they had come to be the chief exponents of legislative "sovereignty." That any branch of the government other than Congress should seek to determine the public policy was held to be in violation of sound constitutional interpretation. The proclamation, it was argued, was a clear case of executive usurpation. Did not Congress have the constitutional power to declare war and, by inference then, to determine peace? In Jefferson's opinion, expressed in a letter to Madison, Washington's Proclamation that

60 *Ibid.*, pp. 2, 679, 722.
61 Thomas Jefferson, *Writings* (1892), I, pp. 189-90.

the nation was at peace was equivalent to declaring it would not go to war which took on the character of executive encroachment on the legislature. Moreover had not the President wantonly set at naught our treaty of alliance with France and broken our plighted faith? The situation provided Hamilton with an opportunity to seize his pen and write one of the most daring interpretations of the executive power of the President that has ever come from the pen of a responsible commentator. After enumerating the specified constitutional powers of the President and contending that it would be unreasonable to suppose that his powers were confined to these alone he continued: "The different mode of expression employed in the Constitution in regard to the two powers, the legislative and the executive, serves to confirm this inference. In the article which gives the legislative powers of the government the expressions are 'all legislative power herein granted shall be vested in a Congress of the United States.' In that which grants the executive power the expressions are 'the executive power shall be vested in a President of the United States.'

"The enumeration ought therefore to be considered as intended to specify merely the principal articles implied in the definition of executive power, leaving the rest to flow from the general grant of power, interpreted in conformity with the other parts of the Constitution and with the principles of free government. The general doctrine of our Constitution then is that the executive power of the nation is vested in the President subject only to the exceptions and qualifications which are expressed in the instrument." [62] Whether or not Hamilton's arguments were a factor in determining the outcome, the doctrine or rule of interpretation applied has stood with respect to the President's power over unenumerated matters of for-

[62] A. Hamilton, *Works* (Lodge ed.), IV, pp. 142-44.

eign policy, but in regard to all other powers the President is still compelled generally to look to the specific grants of the Constitution or to the statutes. The Republicans did not let Hamilton's exposition go unanswered but Madison, at Jefferson's suggestion and under the pen name "Helvidius," maintained that Hamilton derived his concepts of executive power from the prerogatives of English royalty and that "no citizen could any longer guess at the character of the government under which he lives." [63]

So many controversies with England growing out of the Revolutionary War still remained unsettled that in 1794 President Washington sent Chief Justice Jay to London to negotiate a treaty. It was because the Federalists in the mid-term congressional elections of 1794 had lost control of the House of Representatives but retained a majority in the Senate that they turned to the treaty power for relief of commerce. The anti-administration forces, bitterly disappointed at Washington's proclamation of neutrality instead of a declaration of war against England in order to aid France, wanted no such treaty. When, in due time, Jay returned with a treaty containing extraordinary benefits for Federalist interests and not one item favorable to anyone south of the Potomac, the rage against it was, as Washington said, "like that against a mad dog." One of the immediate effects of the controversy over Jay's Treaty was that it induced the first party caucuses of the decade thus carrying the growth of party organization a step further. Quite naturally the agrarians prepared to employ to the limit their strength in the lower house against implementing the despised treaty. In the House debate on a resolution calling on President Washington for Jay's instructions and all the correspondence and documents relating to the treaty that it would not be improper to disclose, no less a statesman than Albert Gallatin rose to argue that a treaty is not a law without the approval of the House of Representatives. "To construe the Constitution consistently," he said, "we must attend to all sections of it. To interpret particular clauses of it by themselves, invites absurdities. By one section, it is declared that a treaty is the supreme law of the land, that it operates as a law; yet it is to be made by the President and Senate only. Here will be an apparent contradiction; for the constitution declares that the legislative power shall be vested in three branches (President, Senate, and House). By this construction there would appear to be two distinct legislatures. . . . If still it is insisted that treaties are the supreme law of the land, the constitution and laws are also; and it may be asked which shall have the preference? Shall a treaty repeal a law or a law a treaty? Neither of these can be done. A law cannot repeal a treaty because a treaty is made with the concurrence of another party—a foreign nation—that had no participation in framing the law. . . . It is a sound maxim in government that it requires the same power to repeal a law that enacted it." [64] Gallatin felt that to surrender this power would be tantamount to saying that the House abandons its share in legislation and consents that the power shall be centered in the other branches. Jefferson was so impressed by Gallatin's interpretation that he thought it worthy of a place in the *Federalist*.

Hamilton, in response to Washington's request for advice, suggested that the information was wanted for the purpose of impeachment. Employing Hamilton's phrasing, the President refused the request in the resolution because the concurrence of the two houses was not required to give validity to a treaty and "because of the necessity of maintaining the boundaries

[64] *Annals*, 4th Cong., 1st Session, pp. 471-74.

fixed by the Constitution." [65] He stated that a proposition that no treaty should be binding on the United States unless ratified by law was specifically rejected by the Philadelphia Convention. The House then disclaiming any share in the treaty-making power, insisted on its right to use its judgment in deciding whether or not to appropriate money when such is required to carry out a treaty.

It is impossible in our day to understand the heat generated by the prolonged controversy over Jay's treaty. The fate of the government seemed to be hanging in the balance. The Senate ceased its sittings. King bluntly declared that unless the House appropriated the required funds the Senate would regard all legislation at an end and the union dissolved.[66] Finally the House, exercising its recognized constitutional freedom of judgment, appropriated the needed funds and another constitutional crisis had passed.

President Washington resolutely rejected all proposals that he serve a third term. Each presidential elector, in accordance with the provisions of the Constitution, was still simply casting ballots for two persons without designating which was intended for President and which for Vice President. Inchoate though parties still were, the presidential election of 1796 turned out to be practically a referendum on Jay's Treaty; but Adams polled only three more electoral votes than Jefferson, which made the latter Vice President. Adams's close election by the margin of only three electoral votes, in contrast with Washington's two elections by unanimous votes, impaired from the very beginning of the administration his prestige as President.

[65] J. D. Richardson, *Messages and Papers of the Presidents*, I, pp. 194-96.
[66] Claude Bowers, *Jefferson and Hamilton*, pp. 298, 299.

Since the Federalists had recaptured the lower house in 1796, why did they not promptly re-establish the organic connection with the executive department? For one reason their majority was slight and rather nominal in the lower house, and, because of the uncertain political complexion of some Federalist members, the Republicans sometimes had their way.[67] Presiding over the Senate was Thomas Jefferson, the astute leader of the Republican opposition both in and out of Congress, a constant check on Federalist exercise of power. In the House of Representatives still remained Albert Gallatin, the exceptionally competent leader of the lower house Republicans. There was no likelihood of the House of Representatives turning confidently to the Secretary of the Treasury, Wolcott, as they had once depended on Hamilton. Wolcott felt himself fettered and complained that "the management of the Treasury becomes more and more difficult. The legislature will not pass laws in gross. Their appropriations are minute. Gallatin, to whom they yield, is evidently intending to break down this department, by charging it with an impractical detail." [68] For three years the Federalists retained or endured the Committee of Ways and Means and then in 1800 re-established their old system by instructing the Secretary of the Treasury, at the opening of each session, to lay his financial proposals before them.[69]

It is not to be assumed that the Federalist governmental system now began to function again as in the first administration of President Washington. The system at this time lacked a definite head like Hamilton within the executive branch. President Adams was hampered by the uncertain place of the department heads in the system. Usage had not yet given these

[67] Jefferson, *Works*, VII, p. 1451.
[68] Hamilton, *Works* (1851), VI, p. 279.
[69] *Annals*, 6th Cong., 1st Session, p. 709.

officials their present-day status. It would scarcely be an exaggeration to say that during most of President Adams's four years a multiple executive of the department heads conducted the government except in the field of foreign affairs, in which President Adams was unquestionably the chief.

Several reasons had led Adams to retain Washington's Cabinet. For one thing the positions were unattractive and Presidents had great difficulty in finding willing incumbents. Only a few years later President Jefferson offered the position of Secretary of the Navy to five different persons in succession before getting the office filled. Shutting the officers out of Congress while still leaving them subject to congressional criticism and investigation had left the offices hardly worth holding. The department heads had not yet come to be considered the personal representatives of the President and his executive subordinates. Adams's retention of the old Cabinet lends plausibility to the idea that they were rather looked upon as a part of a permanent bureaucracy. The Constitution seemed to imply that they were to be considered as experts in their respective fields, sufficiently detached from the President that he might "require their opinion in writing." Since they were regarded as expert administrators, serving during good behavior and removable by impeachment, loyalty to the President was not yet looked upon as necessary. As late as 1829 we find William Wirt, Attorney General during the presidency of J. Q. Adams, writing to James Monroe to inquire whether he ought to resign upon the inauguration of Andrew Jackson." [70]

In consequence of these facts an anomalous situation developed in the administration of President John Adams. Today the President would be considered the head of the party. But the Federalists de-

[70] J. P. Kennedy, *Memoirs of William Wirt*, II, p. 256.

nied the very legitimacy of political parties and never admitted that they themselves constituted one. In their own minds "Federalists" and "patriots" were synonymous. They never openly effected a nation-wide organization and bitterly denounced the opposition for having one. The local Republican organizations were "self-constituted democratic societies" according to President Washington. It was the Jefferson Republicans to whom Washington was paying his respects in the Farewell Address when he stated that "all combinations and associations under whatever plausible character, with the real design to direct, control or awe the regular deliberations of the constituted authorities, are destructive of this fundamental principle, and of fatal tendency." [71] Thus a hard-and-fast ideology prevented the Federalists from institutionalizing party leadership in the presidency.[72]

Such was President John Adams's diffidence at the time of his inauguration that in a letter to his wife he wrote, "If the Federalists go to playing pranks I will resign and let Jefferson beat them. . . ." [73]

In the late 1790's the leader of the Federalists, if they had any, was an aggressive and talented private citizen, Alexander Hamilton, whom Adams rightly regarded as his political enemy. The department heads were Hamilton men. When Adams, in accordance with the constitutional provision, sought their advice, they turned to Hamilton and relayed his recommendations to Adams, who unwittingly put the phrases of his enemy in some of his presidential messages. When at last Adams became convinced that he was the victim of treachery he reconstructed his Cabinet when his campaign for re-election was already in progress.

---

[71] J. D. Richardson, *Messages of the Presidents*, I, p. 217.

[72] See W. E. Binkley, *American Political Parties: Their Natural History*, pp. 50, 51.

[73] Adrienne Koch and William Peden, *The Select Writings of John and John Quincy Adams*, p.144.

This weakened Adams with the Federalists since their leaders discountenanced the President's disagreements with his Cabinet, which seemed more representative of the party than Adams did. Hamilton secretly circulated among the Federalists damaging letters opposing the re-election of Adams in the very midst of the campaign of 1800. So with the Federalists, discredited by their extraordinarily unpopular Alien and Sedition Acts and the drastic enforcement of the Sedition Act by Federalist judges, and divided on the re-election of Adams, the opposition could scarcely lose. By this time party lines were so tightly drawn that the blind voting of the Presidential Electors for "two persons" produced the tie between Thomas Jefferson and Aaron Burr. The House of Representatives broke the impasse by registering the undoubted will of the American people in choosing Jefferson.

The first decade of the republic may be looked upon as a period of the trial-and-error method in seeking a working adjustment of the relationship between the executive and the legislature, the net result of which was not decisive. The Federalists had started off the new government with a definite and workable plan, the advantage of which was the placing of the initiative in the shaping of legislation in the hands of the department heads. This, however, aroused the fears of the agrarian element because they regarded it as placing the center of governmental gravity in the Executive, which they considered the historic dwelling place of tyranny. When they captured control of Congress they made short work of the Federalist plan, but their shifting of the preponderance of power to the House resulted in an inefficiency of its functioning only moderately relieved by establishing standing committees. Thus matters stood when the Federalists started their trek into oblivion.

III

The Solution of the Jeffersonian Republicans

★

WHEN the new century opened with the triumph of a coalition of planters, grain-growers, and frontiersmen in the election of Jefferson, the great question was whether these Republicans possessed the competence to solve the question left unanswered by the Constitution: How can the President and Congress function together to accomplish the great ends of government? It remained to be seen how Jefferson would gear the Executive into the congressional organization to the end that the Republican program might be carried out. In the light of party principles, legislative theory, and practice the solution seemed impossible, short of a miracle. Jefferson's faith in the doctrine of separated powers was apparently as firm as almost a score of years earlier, when he had expounded it in his *Notes on Virginia.*[1] Since then, however, he had abandoned his extremely critical attitude toward the legislature and he had come, along with Republicans generally, to regard the Congress as the bulwark of the agrarians against executive usurpation. Republican doctrine made Congress the fundamental organ, the mainspring of government and peculiarly the agent of the people. This dogma could not be ignored now without inviting the charge of inconsistency and inviting party revolt. Congress under the Republicans could certainly not consistently turn to the heads of the executive departments for leadership, direction, or even aid in legislation. Had not the party rescued the constitutional powers of the lower house a few years earlier by divorcing Hamilton from legislation, and, in effect, driven him back to private life?

If Jefferson looked back to survey the achievements of the Republicans in Congress, the prospects for the future were anything but reassuring. During the four years of Washington's second term the party had been in the majority in the lower house and had had an opportunity to assume responsibility and demonstrate their capacity as legislators. They could not complain that they were hampered in their plans by either the Senate or the Executive. Yet that period is singularly barren of legislative achievement, contrasting strikingly with the preceding four years of constructive lawmaking. During the years that the Republicans had been in a majority they had distinguished themselves mainly as critics of Federalist policies. Could a party that had attained proficiency merely in obstruction be transformed into one of construction?

The greatest of all Jefferson's difficulties was that in 1801 he was at the head of an agrarian party of strict individualists. They were lacking in that solidarity of

[1] Jefferson, *Works*, VII, p. 108.

interests and capacity for compromising their internal differences that had characterized the Federalists and enabled Hamilton to direct a well-disciplined following. Jefferson's recognition of this Republican defect is revealed in his admission to De Witt Clinton that "our leading friends are not yet sufficiently aware of the necessity of accommodation and mutual sacrifice of opinion for conducting a numerous assembly where the opposition, too, is drilled to act in phalanx on every question." [2] Moreover the Republicans as an agrarian group were woefully lacking in business acumen and practical experience which go far toward accounting for the Federalists' proficiency in governmental matters: Jefferson lamented this lack in Republican congressmen. "We want men of business among them. . . . I am convinced it is in the power of any man who understands business and who will undertake to keep a file of the business before Congress and press it . . . to shorten the sessions a month one year with another . . ." [3] At one time early in the first session of Congress under Jefferson the Washington *Federalist* expressed doubt whether the House could proceed without adding more Federalists to the committees, and somewhat later that same journal predicted that, in the absence of certain leaders, "the President's sect in the House of Representatives will be obliged to relinquish the goodly work of reform for want of sufficient acquaintance with business to mature their plans and carry them into execution." [4]

How could a political philosopher, who was a proponent of separate powers and legislative supremacy co-ordinate his executive branch with a House of Rep-

2 *Writings,* VIII, pp. 282, 283.
3 *Ibid.,* p. 187.
4 Washington *Federalist,* Feb. 17 and Mar. 27, 1802. Quoted in Harlow, *Legislative Methods,* pp. 170, 171.

resentatives, a majority of whom consisted of undisciplined individualists? Strange to say, a hint of the answer to this question was given two months before Jefferson's inauguration in a letter of John Marshall to Hamilton, refusing to use his influence as a member of the House to support the election of Jefferson in the House of Representatives. This letter contains a shrewd and prophetic observation. "Mr. Jefferson appears to me to be a man," wrote Marshall, "who will embody himself with the House of Representatives. By weakening the office of President, he will increase his personal power. He will diminish his responsibility, sap the fundamental principles of government, and become the leader of that party which is about to constitute the majority of the legislature." [5] Marshall foresaw that there would be no opportunity in the new government for a frank and responsible contact with Congress on the part of the Executive. Intrigue, as the Federalists saw it, was to be the means of integrating the political branches of the government. And that is exactly how it turned out.

It ought to be said that the key to Thomas Jefferson's success in the face of the apparently insuperable obstructions enumerated above is that he was not disturbed by charges of inconsistency and he never let his philosophy prevent the exercise of his practical good sense. "What is practical must often control what is pure theory," wrote Jefferson in 1802.[6] He was in earnest in his determination to change the trend the Federalists had given governmental procedure and policy. This great end, he thought, would justify whatever employment of the means at hand was necessary. It

[5] Hamilton, *Works*, VI, pp. 501-03, quoted by A. J. Beveridge, *Life of John Marshall*, II, p. 537.

[6] Quoted by C. A. Beard, *Economic Origins of Jeffersonian Democracy*, p. 437.

was his good fortune that, for the first time since the appearance of distinct and fairly coherent parties, the President of the United States was the actual and unchallenged leader of the party in power.

There was a bit of guile, as time was to reveal, in these words of modest self-denial with which the President closed his first message to Congress. "Nothing shall be wanting on my part to inform, as far as in my power, the legislative judgment, nor to carry that judgment into faithful execution." [7] This was a public gesture quite becoming in a Republican President. But when the House of Representatives had elected its Speaker and the committee chairmen had been appointed it was apparent to the discerning that lieutenants of the President occupied every key position. Nominally the President had not appointed them, but his wishes, confidentially expressed, had determined them just as surely as if he had formally and publicly nominated them. Here was the fulfillment of Marshall's prediction that Jefferson would "embody himself in the House of Representatives." In time it came to be an accepted practice, but this was the first time a President had had just such an opportunity and it was then a startling innovation. Into the competent hands of William Branch Giles fell the reins of congressional leadership. A fellow Virginian with the President, he commanded the unbounded confidence of his chief. Never before had a floor leader been the personal representative of the President.

Soon it was being said, "In the House of Representatives Mr. Giles leads the ministerial phalanx, and is the only member whose capacity is adequate to the conducting of party measures." [8] He was being called

[7] Richardson, *op. cit.*, I, pp. 331-32.
[8] Washington *Federalist*, Feb. 17, 1802, quoted in Harlow, *op. cit.*, p. 167.

the "premier or prime minister of the day" [9] in the congressional debates. The terms, "first lord of the treasury" and "chancellor of the exchequer," [10] were in use to indicate Giles's leadership in the House. These expressions were not applied, as in Washington's day, to executive heads but to the chairman of the Committee on Ways and Means, which was again a shift to be expected in a Republican regime. When a competent leader retired from Congress or one was deposed as Randolph was, Jefferson busied himself writing to able men outside of Congress beseeching them to offer themselves as candidates.[11] The deposing of Randolph from the chairmanship of the Committee of Ways and Means was due to his refusal to move the appropriation the President desired for the purchase of Florida.[12] "The measure has been very reluctantly adopted by the President's friends, on his private wishes, signified to them in strong contradiction to the tenor of his public messages," wrote John Quincy Adams. "His whole system of administration," continued Adams, "seems founded on the principle of carrying through the legislature measures by personal or official influence." [13] In words reminiscent of Marshall's prediction Senator Pickering wrote that Jefferson tried "to screen himself from all responsibility by calling upon Congress for advice and direction. . . . Yet with affected modesty and deference he secretly dictates every measure which is seriously proposed." [14] It is no mean tribute to the political genius of Thomas Jefferson to say that this well-organized sys-

---

9 *Annals*, 7th Cong., 1st Session, p. 666.
10 Randolph to Gallatin in Henry Adams, *Gallatin*, p. 324.
11 See letter to W. C. Nicholas, Thomas Jefferson, *Writings*, XI, p. 162.
12 Gallatin to his wife. Henry Adams, *Gallatin*, p. 363.
13 *Memoirs*, I, p. 403.
14 Quoted in Harlow, *op. cit.*, p. 175.

tem worked with almost infallible precision, despite the fact that the machinery and its operation were concealed from the public. Through a hint dropped here, a diplomatic letter sent there, and a suggestion made to another the President had his way. To the Federalists Jefferson's system constituted a sheer travesty of sound government.

Nothing exasperated the Federalists more than the Republican practice of adopting, when they attained power, some of the very devices they had so loudly condemned when employed by the Federalists. They had once regarded it as particularly vicious and unconstitutional to refer matters of the House to Hamilton as Secretary of the Treasury. The Republicans had deliberately created a Ways and Means Committee to end that practice. But now that a Republican, Albert Gallatin, was Secretary of the Treasury there seemed to be no impropriety in reviving the practice once so roundly denounced, and they directed him to make reports and proposals to the House.[15] Gallatin now attended committee meetings and he prepared at least one report for the Committee on Foreign Affairs[16] which was presented to the House. He seems to have been almost as active as Hamilton had been in steering measures through Congress. He shared with the President the management of the party in that body.

The Republicans appropriated another device of the Federalists, the caucus, which they had vehemently condemned when it had been used effectively against them. In this extra-constitutional agency President, Cabinet, and congressmen of both houses could meet and circumvent the sacred dogma of separation of powers without doing violence to the tenderest

15 *Annals,* 7th Cong., 2nd Session, pp. 567-68, 664.
16 Printed in Gallatin, *Writings,* I, pp. 435-46.

Republican conscience. This organization seems to have been mentioned for the first time in a congressional debate in 1802, the member who spoke the word being called to order for it,[17] as was also Josiah Quincy half a dozen years later for the same offense.[18] In spite of the fact that the Federalists had been the first to use the caucus, they now condemned it when employed by the Republicans. Coming to a definite understanding in the caucus, the party membership would come on the floor prepared to present a united front. Jefferson himself is alleged to have presided over some sessions of the caucus. On the floor of the House his personal representative was at hand to hold doubtful members in line.[19]

By 1808 the caucus had become powerful enough to pass from being an instrument for executive control of Congress and start on its career of the control of the Executive. Jefferson like Washington had firmly refused a third term. Madison, his Secretary of State and long his protégé, as Jefferson's favorite, was the heir apparent. Thus he became the almost unanimous choice of the Republican caucus as the presidential candidate and the Electoral College did little more than execute the logic of the situation.[20]

Soon after his inauguration, however, it became evident enough that the "Father of the Constitution" had been miscast in the role of President of the United States. Madison's personality forbade his playing the part of the leader that Jefferson had been. A little clique in the Senate would not even permit him to determine his own Cabinet. The relations with England and France were critical and Madison

17 *Annals,* 7th Cong., 1st Session, p. 480.
18 *Ibid.,* 10th Cong., 2nd Session, p. 1143.
19 Washington *Federalist,* Feb. 21, 1802, cited by Harlow, *op. cit.,* p. 188.
20 J. Q. Adams, *op. cit.,* I, p. 507.

wanted to make Gallatin Secretary of State. The senatorial clique prevented this and compelled him instead to appoint the incompetent Robert Smith.[21] Gallatin remained in his old position of Secretary of the Treasury but now that Jefferson was no longer President the government was leaderless and Gallatin's influence in the lower house was reduced. He drafted what was known as Macon Bill Number One but his enemies in the Senate defeated it.[22] He very much desired that the Bank of the United States be rechartered but the House defeated that. There is no evidence that Madison exerted any influence whatever toward the rechartering of this first Bank at the time of the charter's expiration.[23]

In the absence of a leader in the presidency such as Jefferson had been Congress lapsed into the old confusion that had characterized it in Washington's second term when the Republicans were in control of the House. One cannot imagine Madison writing as Jefferson did more than once to induce some leader to enter Congress. A single episode reveals the confusion in the first Congress during Madison's administration. The lower house was endeavoring to reduce the military and naval establishment. A resolution to that effect was carried by a vote of 60 to 31. Resolutions to carry out the details were offered, "but no sooner did the House go into committee [of the Whole] than the members astonished themselves by striking out each section in succession. Gunboats, frigates, navy yards, and marines each managed to obtain a majority against reduction." [24] The results of the first session of the Eleventh Congress were succinctly

21 Henry Adams, *History of the United States*, V, pp. 5-12.
22 Adams, *Gallatin*, pp. 413, 415.
23 *Ibid.*, p. 427.
24 Henry Adams, *History of the United States*, V, p. 204.

summarized by John Randolph in a letter to Nicholson: "We adjourned last night a little after twelve, having terminated a session of more than five months by authorizing a loan of five millions and all is told. The incapacity of the Government has long ceased to be a laughing matter. The Cabinet is all to pieces and the two Houses have tumbled about their own ears." [25]

Madison's lack of leadership was matched by his lack of decision. So cautious were his communications to Congress that some of them were almost unintelligible. His message of January 3, 1810,[26] provoked Crawford of Georgia to declare, "This message in point of obscurity comes nearer my idea of a Delphic oracle than any state paper which has come under my inspection. It is so cautiously expressed that every man puts what construction on it he pleases." [27]

The repeated defeats of Madison on measures he desired passed amounted to votes of lack of confidence. Under a parliamentary system the government would have fallen and a new one been established or an election held to test the sentiment of the country. John Randolph, again writing to Nicholson, expressed his contempt by declaring, "The truth seems to be that he (Madison) is President *de jure* only. Who exercises the office *de facto* I do not know but it seems agreed that there is something behind the throne greater than the throne itself." Concerning Gallatin, "If his principal will not support him by his influence against the cabal in the ministry itself as well as out of it he ought to resign." [28] Gallatin did

---

25 Quoted, *ibid.*, p. 209.
26 Richardson, *op. cit.*, I, p. 478.
27 *Annals*, 11th Cong., 1st Session, p. 544.
28 Adams, *Gallatin*, pp. 430-31.

indeed ultimately offer his resignation on the ground
that the Cabinet was divided.[29]

With the assembling of the Twelfth Congress after
a "tidal wave" in the elections of 1810, practically a
new generation entered the arena of national politics
and took charge of the federal government. Seventy
of its one hundred, thirty members were young men
who could scarcely, if at all, remember the Revolutionary War.[30] A considerable proportion came from
the new Western states. They were an impatient
group, exasperated with the temporizing foreign policies of Jefferson and Madison. The outstanding Western member, Henry Clay, was elected Speaker of the
House the first day of his service in it. He had served
his apprenticeship in that office, with its peculiarly
American development, in the legislature of Ken-
tucky and he knew from experience the possibilities
of leadership inherent in the position. In colonial
times the Speaker of the popularly elected assembly
had provided the one official rallying point of the
people against royal encroachment as personified in
the governor. This trend continued after the Revolution in the state assemblies. The earliest speakers of
the national House of Representatives, however, assumed rather the function of an impartial moderator.
The floor leader was the outstanding partisan leader
of the majority, as we have seen manifested in Jefferson's constant concern to secure a competent congressman for that position.

Clay brought to the Speaker's office not only the
prestige that had accumulated through its historical
development but also the commanding personality of
a born leader of men. Under the circumstances Madi-

[29] Gallatin to Madison, Mar. 1811, Gallatin, *Writings,* I, pp.
495-96.
[30] Henry Adams, *History of the United States,* VI, p. 122.

son could scarcely have recovered executive initiative even if he had been disposed to do so. Gallatin did make a vain attempt to resume his former relations with Congress as Secretary of the Treasury.[31] Mastery of the government passed rapidly into the hands of the House of Representatives and the Executive could only follow. Clay, exercising his power of appointment, promptly organized his committees for war.[32] His own lieutenants, Calhoun, Grundy and Porter, all "War Hawks," were placed on the Committee of Foreign Affairs. These energetic young men proceeded to take the control of foreign policy out of the hands of the President, the clear intent of the Constitution to the contrary notwithstanding.[33] The pioneer Westerners whom these young "War Hawks" represented were seething with indignation against Madison, who seemed to be submitting tamely to British tampering with the Indians and outrages against American seamen. Moreover, these pioneers had been suffering from depressed agricultural prices which they attributed to the failure of the administration to extract trade concessions from the traditional enemy. Before long the "War Hawks" were demanding war. Clay took the initiative in this matter. Madison was kept in uncertainty as to renomination for a second term and action of the caucus on that matter was delayed until the pressure upon Madison made a war policy certain. Finally on June 1 Madison recommended war. Congress had enforced its will on the Executive.[34]

The congressional caucus, which had been employed by Jefferson as an integrating agency co-ordi-

[31] *Ibid.*, pp. 127, 128.
[32] *Annals*, 12 Cong., 1st Session, p. 343.
[33] *Ibid.*, p. 373.
[34] See D. R. Anderson, "The Insurgents of 1811," *American Historical Association Reports* (1911) I, p. 174.

nating the Executive and the legislature, was no longer serving the Executive for that purpose but was used by congressional leaders now for securing party solidarity in putting their program through Congress. The executive branch was being tied to the legislature through the developing system of congressional committees. In time there came to be a committee in the lower house corresponding to each executive department, such as war, navy, foreign affairs, post office, and ways and means.[35] Sometimes the legislative, sometimes the executive side exerted the greater influence, depending on which included the stronger personalities.

Certainly during Madison's administration, especially on domestic problems, Congress looked to the department heads rather than to the Chief Executive. For example, the first Bank of the United States had been chartered in 1791 upon the recommendation of Secretary of the Treasury Hamilton. In 1811 Secretary of the Treasury Gallatin recommended rechartering and, though the recommendation was rejected, a precedent had been established. When in 1816 the movement to charter a Bank of the United States started again, the House raised objection to the measure being considered unless "the proposition came in at the proper constitutional door." We have the opinion of Representative Thomas P. Grosvenor that "if such a necessity existed he wished the government to come forward and declare it, and not shrink from the responsibility of recommending the measure." Representative Gaston thought the recommendation ought to come from the Executive.[36] Evidently this did not mean the President since the Secretary of the Treasury then recommended the incorporation of a bank in his next report to Congress and the bank bill was framed along the lines recommended by the Secretary.[37] One cannot conceive of Madison's vigorously promoting the chartering of the bank and there is no more evidence of his promoting actively the movement in Congress in 1816 than there is that he had made the slightest gesture toward aiding his anxious Secretary of the Treasury, Albert Gallatin, in his earnest but futile efforts to persuade Congress to recharter the first bank in 1811.[38] He did nothing with the tariff beyond the formal recommendations of two messages, and the legislation on internal improvements provoked only the employment of his negative in a veto message. "Madison could hardly have played a less important part," concluded Professor Harlow, "during those eight uncomfortable years if he had remained in Virginia." [39] This could be an almost pardonable exaggeration.

In 1816 James Monroe was elected to the presidency with no more than a token opposition by the now rapidly vanishing Federalists. While Monroe had a happier career as President than his immediate predecessor he did no more than Madison to check the momentum of congressional aggrandizement. The outstanding conflict in Congress during Monroe's eight years was the prolonged struggle over the admission of Missouri to statehood, which was terminated by the famous compromise. There is no doubt of the President's deep concern over the nation-rocking controversy and the fierce sectional feeling it provoked. Unlike Jefferson, but like Madison in such circumstances, he kept aloof from congressmen,

37 *Ibid.*, 13th Cong., 3rd Session, pp. 403, 604; 14th Cong., 1st Session, pp. 494-514, 1229-33.

38 Adams, *Gallatin*, p. 427.

39 *Op. cit.*, p. 196. See also Adams, *Gallatin*, pp. 388-91.

merely holding in reserve his veto power if the measure as finally enacted should appear to be unconstitutional. His letters revealed an attitude of detachment, a hands-off policy, with respect to the activity of Congress.[40] It was shortly after this and at the time of Monroe's second inauguration that Clay gave his opinion that "he considered the situation of our public affairs now as very critical and dangerous to the administration. Mr. Monroe had just been re-elected with apparent unanimity, but he had not the slightest influence on Congress. His career was considered as closed. There was nothing further to be expected by him or from him. Looking at Congress, they were a collection of *materials,* and how much good and how much evil might be done with them, accordingly, as they should be well or ill directed. But henceforth there was and would not be a man in the United States possessing less *personal* influence over them than the President." [41]

While Clay's opinion is that of an unfriendly critic it would be difficult to discover evidence to invalidate his poor opinion of Monroe's influence with congressmen. A quite similar view was expressed by Representative William Plumer, Jr., of New Hampshire, who thought that "the very President who is just re-elected with but one dissenting voice throughout the Union, is not only the least deserving of all our Presidents but has actually at this moment fewer real friends and admirers, and less influence than any of his predecessors had. . . . We have lately given a pretty strong proof of the little influence possessed by the Administrations over the House of Representatives by the passage of the Army Bill. The Secretary of War and all his friends, in and out of doors, op-

[40] Monroe, *Writings,* VI, pp. 115, 116, 159, 161.
[41] J. Q. Adams, *op. cit.,* V, p. 324.

posed by every expedient in their power—the President was known to be against it—and probably other members of the Cabinet—but it was carried notwithstanding many defects in the details of the bill by an overwhelming majority.[42] A similar proof was given last year in the refusal of the House to proceed with the Yellow Stone Expedition, after the President had informed us that it was a subject of very great importance in which he took a particular interest and was willing to incur great responsibilities to secure its success." [43]

Had Monroe possessed but a trace of Jefferson's leadership in Congress he might have concerned himself over who was chosen Speaker of the House. The opportunity to take a part in this matter came to the President but he refused to have anything to do with it.[44] To such an extent had the public interest now become centered in the activities of Congress, particularly the lower house, that the election of the President had ceased, for the time being, to be connected intimately with public policies. The time would come when a presidential election could not follow by a few months such a furious conflict as the Missouri question without its being a vital issue in the election of the President. It is indicative of the status of the presidency then that Monroe's conception of his presidential obligations induced him to abstain from any intervention in the struggle in Congress over the Missouri bill until it came to him for his signature. Like-

[42] The vote was 109 to 48, *Annals,* 16th Cong., 2nd Session, pp. 936-37.

[43] William Plumer, Jr., *The Missouri Compromise and Presidential Politics, 1820-25, Letters of William Plumer, Jr.* (E. S. Brown, editor). Missouri Historical Society. It was Plumer who cast the one electoral vote against Monroe in 1820, thereby preventing his unanimous re-election.

[44] J. Q. Adams, *op. cit.,* V, pp. 428, 431, 434.

wise significant is the fact that the devastating financial panic of 1819 had not the slightest effect on Monroe's re-election in 1820. The most one-sided election in the history of the United States excepting that of Washington was the all but unanimous re-election of James Monroe in the midst of a terrifying business depression. Twenty years later Van Buren found a depression a decisive factor in preventing re-election and no President since has been able to overcome the handicap of such a calamity during his term and win a re-election.

A striking example of Monroe's disposition to defer to Congress appears, of all places, in the field of foreign relations. The Spanish provinces of South America had apparently decisively established their independence. In due time the government of the United States was confronted with the question of the recognition of the new governments. This had been assumed to be exclusively an executive function as prescribed by the Constitution's provision that the President "shall receive ambassadors and other public ministers." Monroe, however, sent a message to Congress in which, among other things, he said, "When we regard, then, the great length of time, which this war has been prosecuted, the complete success which has attended it in favor of the Provinces, the present condition of the parties and the utter inability of Spain to produce any change in it, we are compelled to conclude, that its fate is settled, and that the Provinces which have declared their independence and are in enjoyment of it ought to be recognized." In the closing paragraph the President refers twice to the measure (recognition of independence) he is "proposing" evidently to Congress and closes the message with the sentence: "Should Congress concur in the view herein presented, they will doubtless see the propriety of making the necessary appropriations for carrying it into effect." [45] Apparently the President was implying that he would exercise his constitutional power of recognition if Congress would agree to provide for the diplomatic and consular representatives required for the governments to be recognized.[46]

By 1825 the presidency must almost inevitably have been at a disadvantage in its relations with Congress because of the part the latter had for a quarter of a century been playing in the election of the President. Jefferson had been elected for his first term by the House of Representatives and was renominated by the caucus which also, four years later, dutifully nominated Jefferson's personal choice, Madison, as his successor. Henceforth, however, the Republican caucus ceased to be an instrument whereby the Executives controlled Congress. By 1812 it was the means by which the new masters of the House of Representatives laid down, by implication at least, the conditions on which Madison would be renominated by the Republican caucus, and in 1825 the House itself elected John Quincy Adams President. Monroe was twice nominated by the Republican caucus. Thus in the first quarter of the century Congress, by direct election or through the caucus, had chosen every President. So merely nominal was the opposition of the Federalist party that the Electoral College had done little more than ratify whatever choice the Republican caucus made. The constitutional framers had considered the election of the Executive by the legislature and had rejected it in order to protect the independence of the Executive but a chain of cir-

---

45 Richardson, *op. cit.*, II, pp. 117, 118.
46 On the history of the Jeffersonian Republican party see W. E. Binkley, *op. cit.*, Chapter IV.

cumstances had come to pass that practically reversed their decision. Such a long trend in the actual process of choosing the President must inevitably have left its mark upon the office. Jefferson, through the force of his personality, delayed the effect, but Madison and Monroe offered no such resistance to congressional subordination of the presidency.

An important factor in this decline of the presidential office was the practical extinction of our two-party system by the 1820's.[47] Nothing gives more vitality to our party system today than the quadrennial struggle to win the stakes of power and prestige vested in the great office. By 1816, however, the Federalists had given up all hope and had indeed become so insignificant that it became customary to disparage political parties. "Now is the time to exterminate the monster called party spirit," wrote Andrew Jackson to President-elect Monroe in 1816. "The chief magistrate of a great and powerful nation should never engage in party feelings," continued this future prince of partisans, and father of Jacksonian Democracy. By 1820 the presidential electors in Massachusetts who, of course, all voted for Republican Monroe, consisted of seven old-line Republicans and eight former Federalists, among whom were ex-President John Adams and Daniel Webster. Four years later, however, there were four presidential candidates—Crawford, Clay, Adams, and Jackson, all Republicans. Under the circumstances the votes of the Electoral College were too scattered to give any one a majority, whereupon the House of Representatives elected Adams.

Indeed, it is scarcely too much to say that by 1825, unless the trend were checked, the presidency bade fair to represent, in time, not much more than a

---

[47] Charles S. Sydnor, "The One-Party Period of American History," *Am. Hist. Rev.*, LI (April, 1946), pp. 439 ff.

chairmanship of a group of permanent secretaries of the executive departments to which Congress at times paid more attention than to the President. Since Jefferson, no President had appointed a completely new Cabinet and this permanency of tenure had its inevitable effect on the incumbent's idea of the position. We have already noted the case of William Wirt. Monroe had appointed him Attorney General and John Quincy Adams had retained him in that position. In 1829 he wrote to Monroe to inquire whether he ought to offer his resignation upon the inauguration of Andrew Jackson as President.[48] The later conception of the department heads as the trusted personal representatives and advisers of the President, and hence obligated to loyalty to him, is not at all apparent.

The most convincing evidence that the executive heads were then thought of as just administrative officials rather than the President's trusted official family is found in the fact that President John Quincy Adams wanted to retain in the Cabinet Crawford, who was associated with Calhoun in consolidating the South against the administration. Adams desired to appoint Jackson Secretary of War despite the fact that he was smarting over the loss of the presidency through the alleged "corrupt bargain" between Adams and Clay. The President refused to break with Postmaster General McLean, though cognizant of his current activities promoting Jackson as a candidate for President. President John Quincy Adams's utter indifference to cultivating potential presidential prestige and the consequent power to rule through his influence on the public and his subordinates measures the vast difference between the presidency then and now. "Strategically," writes Richard Neustadt, "the

48 J. P. Kennedy, *op. cit.*, p. 256.

question is not how he masters Congress in a peculiar instance but what he does to boost his chance for mastery in any instance looking toward tomorrow from today." [49] Not only did the personnel of the Cabinet not necessarily change with the election of a new President, but for a quarter of a century through the process described above Congress had merely promoted the Secretary of State to the Presidency, that is to say, among other things, to the chairmanship of the group or heads of executive departments. Thus, Jefferson's Secretary of State, Madison, followed him as President; Madison's Secretary of State, Monroe, became the next President; and in turn Monroe's Secretary of State, John Quincy Adams, was elected by Congress as his successor.

So thoroughly established had this practice become, so generally accepted was the precedent, that when John Quincy Adams appointed Clay Secretary of State in 1825 it was said, as a matter of course, that Clay was "in the succession" to the presidency. And when the established usage was discredited and broken up by the election of Jackson a political sensation was created. A visiting foreigner with a keen and penetrating insight into political realities in America might have contributed an interesting chapter on our unwritten constitution in 1825. He might have observed that under the circumstances of congressional influence on presidential elections these events did not constitute popular referenda on presidential policies. But in any case the end of an era was near at hand and the coming revolution was to change definitely the relative importance of the political branches of the government and leave no question as to the location of the center of gravity in the government.

[49] *Presidential Power: the Politics of Leadership*, p. 2.

The administration of John Quincy Adams marked the end of an era. Madison and Monroe had not been temperamentally equipped to play the part of decisive leaders in their relations with Congress. Adams was a more vigorous executive but he was baffled by circumstances that made a happy leadership impossible and his utter indifference to personal prestige as a means of executing the office of President. The era of one-party government was drawing to a close. The mid-term elections of 1826 gave a heavy majority against an administration for the first time in American history.[50] The opposition consisted of the personal followers of Andrew Jackson, embittered by the defeat of their candidate in the recent election of Adams by the House of Representatives when Jackson had already received a plurality of the popular vote cast for the four candidates. They looked upon Adams as the beneficiary of a "corrupt bargain" by which Clay was alleged to have delivered his following to Adams in the latter's election in the House of Representatives and, moreover, as a party to the crime as they assumed to be implied by his rewarding Clay with an appointment to the position of Secretary of State.[51] Both houses were antiadministration and in a spirit of vengeance the opposition faction broke with a well-established precedent and organized the committees of the House on a four-to-three ratio against the administration. This meant the end, for the time being, of the quite practical co-operation between the congressional committees and the executive departments dealing with the same governmental services. The administration could not get its measures effectively presented to Congress.[52] Disregarding the Pres-

50 *Dictionary of American Biography,* I, p. 87.
51 Thomas H. Benton, *Thirty Years View,* I, p. 55.
52 *Ibid.,* p. 92.

ident's messages and program, Congress spent its energy in a grand inquest into the conduct of the Executive. Only the absence of great issues prevented serious conflict between Congress and the President.

The social unrest induced by the severe and prolonged depression of the 1820's was destined to stimulate a major political revolution. There then took possession of the American masses a conviction that the old governing class, the rural and urban gentry, had betrayed its trust by neglecting the welfare of the people. Only the discovery of a leader who could symbolize justice for the common man was needed to channelize this conviction into political action. For this purpose the anti-Adams politicians drafted Andrew Jackson, the hero of New Orleans, and the translation of the theory of popular sovereignty into an established fact was at hand. In 1828 the re-election of Adams was prevented by the concentration of the opposition on the election of Jackson in his stead.

IV

The Jacksonian Revolution

★

JACKSON became the first President since Washington to be chosen in a manner involving Congress neither for nominating the candidate by the congressional caucus nor outright election by the House of Representatives as in the cases of Jefferson in 1801 and John Quincy Adams in 1825. Jackson's election was also practically coincident with the cessation of the choice of presidential electors by state legislatures and with the prevalence of popular election of them.[1] Consequently he may be said to have been the first popularly elected President of the United States and his career in the executive office is strongly colored by his firm conviction that he bore a mandate fresh from the hands of the "sovereign" people. This will be revealed in the famous papers he produced as a result of the controversies his unprecedented conduct in office provoked. Moreover President Jackson en-

[1] Alexander Johnson, *History of American Politics*, p. 102n.

joyed the support of a friendly majority in the lower house and the committees were once again organized for effective co-operation with the administration.[2]

The place of the President in the American constitutional system may be said to have been the outstanding constitutional question raised by Jackson's eight years in the presidential office. The Jeffersonian method of achieving mastery through secret influence with Congress had proved transient. Since the presidency of Jefferson the American political background had been transformed through the growth of the trans-Allegheny population and the diffusion throughout the older states of the doctrine of popular sovereignty with its practical manifestation in universal, white manhood suffrage. Here was a factor of enormous potency just as certain to leave its impress upon the character of the presidential office as had the congressional caucus. Nothing had more to do with the rescuing of the presidency from the hegemony of the congressional caucus and making it peculiarly the people's office, a rallying point of the agrarian and laboring masses. "As a matter of plain fact," wrote McLaughlin, "we only exaggerate and over emphasize when we say that Jackson was in stark reality the first President of the American people." [3]

This transformation of the presidency from a congressional to a popular agency was not to take place without a gigantic struggle, which came to a head in Jackson's veto of the bill to recharter the second Bank of the United States four years before the expiration of its charter. The first Bank of the United States had been chartered in 1791 by act of Congress upon the urgent advice of Secretary of the Treasury

[2] T. H. Benton, *op. cit.*, p. 121.

[3] A. C. McLaughlin, *Constitutional History of United States*, p. 423.

Hamilton against the opposition of the agrarians. Though a private corporation the federal government owned one-fifth of the capital stock and the Bank was used as a fiscal agency for federal funds, at the same time that it furnished the nation with a sound currency and exerted a salutary check on the inflationary tendency of state banks by presenting their paper currency to them for redemption and compelling them to maintain an adequate specie reserve for that purpose.

Because of its deflationary tendency the B. U. S. was extraordinarily unpopular in the newer sections at the same time that it stirred up deep-seated animosity as a monopoly, in fact, a super-monopoly since its branches were located in certain cities thoughout the United States. In 1811 this opposition had prevented the rechartering of the Bank. Financial disaster consequently followed during the War of 1812, culminating in widespread suspension of specie payment and the practical bankruptcy of the United States Treasury. Influenced by this disastrous experience, Congress chartered a second bank in 1816. In the 1820's this bank also became extraordinarily unpopular in the rural West through its wholesale foreclosures of mortgaged farm land as a consequence of the severe depression of the early 1820's. Strangely unaware of this animosity, Senator Henry Clay sought to make political capital and perhaps advance his presidential candidacy by confronting Jackson with a measure rechartering the bank in 1832, four years before the expiration of the charter. If Jackson should decide to veto the bill, Clay believed it would ruin him politically, strengthen the National Republicans, as the anti-Jackson party was now called, and perhaps make Clay the next President.

Jackson decided against the Bank Bill and his veto

message is a landmark in the evolution of the presidency. For the first time in American history a veto message was used as an instrument of party warfare. Through it the Democratic party, as the Jacksonians were now denominated, dealt a telling blow to their opponents, the National Republicans. Though addressed to Congress, the veto message was an appeal to the nation. Not a single opportunity to discredit the old ruling class was missed. It utilized the bitterness of the state banks against the monster bank, the poor man's envy of the rich, and the nativist prejudice against the foreigners who owned considerable stock in the Bank. So adroitly was it phrased that the common man saw in it the apt expression of his own sentiments. It became a Democratic campaign document and even the National Republicans with the fatuity of reactionaries printed and distributed widely the veto message in the confidence that it would end the political career of President Jackson. Instead it contributed powerfully to his overwhelming re-election.

Half a dozen years before the veto message Marshall, giving the opinion of the Supreme Court, in *McCulloch vs. Maryland,* had declared that Congress had the power to establish the Bank of the United States. With such a precedent the National Republicans were dumfounded by Jackson's arguments in the veto message that the Bank was unconstitutional. At this point he had made the suggestion that if he had been asked, he would have been ready to lay before Congress a bank bill that could not have been criticized on the ground either of constitutionality or expediency.[4] Somehow the apparent audacity of the President's suggestion fairly took the breath of the Senate majority including, as it did, such eminent

4 Richardson, *op. cit.,* II, p. 589.

National Republicans as Webster and Clay. The latter sarcastically declared that if the President were to furnish the draft for laws the country should be governed by "ukases and decrees" and not be subject to the useless expense of Congress.[5]

The President seems to have been protesting against the failure of the congressional committees to consult in advance the views of the administration through the Treasury Department. It was thus a request that established procedure be followed, the procedure practiced in all previous legislation with respect to the bank. Hamilton had laid before Congress the proposal for the first bank, and we have seen Gallatin in that office in 1811 beseeching Congress to recharter the bank. It was shown above that Congress even insisted upon the proposal of the second bank coming from the Executive.[6] President Jackson's suggestion becomes a reasonable one in the light of all the previous legislation on this subject. Why, then, the violent wrath of the senators?

The debate in the Senate on the veto of the Bank Bill marks the first appearance of that House in a prominent role, particularly in the capacity of an organ to check the Executive. The great debates on the organization of the government and on Hamilton's financial program took place in the lower house. The lower house held the center of the stage during the great controversies preceding, throughout, and following the War of 1812 and was still prominent in the debate on the Missouri Compromise. Gradually, however, the leaders who had maintained the pre-eminence of the House of Representatives were being graduated into the Senate, which, by the time

[5] Von Holst, *Constitutional History of the United States,* II, p. 45.
[6] *Supra,* p. 72.

of Jackson's presidency, was rapidly becoming the
chief forum for the discussion of national issues. President Jackson and his partisans held the House in
their firm control but the Senate was untrammeled
and in a position to challenge the President's policies and pretensions as to executive prerogative.

This veto of the Bank Bill which stirred the Senate
so profoundly contained the famous passage setting
forth Jackson's opinion that the three great departments possessed co-ordinate power to determine questions of constitutionality. It had been contended by
the proponents of the bank that since the Supreme
Court, in the opinion given in the case of *McCulloch
vs. Maryland,* had decided that Congress could constitutionally charter a bank then the opponents
ought no longer to raise the question of constitutionality on any bank bill. Webster, had said, "One
bank is as constitutional as another *bank.*" [7] That question, it was claimed, should be regarded as settled and
no longer debatable. In endeavoring to dispose of
this point, the President had declared, "If the opinion of the Supreme Court covered the whole ground
of this act, it [still] ought not to control the co-
ordinate authorities of the Government. The Congress, the Executive and the Court must each for itself be guided by its own opinion of the Constitution.
Each public officer swears that he will support it as
he understands it, and not as it is understood by
others. It is as much the duty of the House of Representatives, of the Senate, and of the President to decide upon the constitutionality of any bill or resolution which may be presented to them for passage or
approval as it is for the supreme judges when it may
be brought before them for judicial decision. The
opinion of the judges has no more authority over

[7] Daniel Webster, *Writings and Speeches,* VI, p. 174.

Congress than the opinion of Congress over the judges, and on that point the President is independent of both. The authority of the Supreme Court must not, therefore, be permitted to control Congress or the Executive when acting in their legislative capacities, but to have only such influence as the force of their reasoning may deserve." [8]

Such constitutional doctrine drew from the National Republican lawyers of the Senate opposition a prompt and emphatic denial. Webster, alarmed at the threatened specter of tyranny stalking through the land, struck back with the consummate skill of the great advocate. "According to the doctrines put forth by the President," he declared on the floor of the Senate, "although Congress may have passed a law, and although the Supreme Court may have pronounced it constitutional, yet it is nevertheless no law at all, if he, in his good pleasure sees fit to deny its effects; in other words to repeal and annul it. . . . Statutes are but recommendations, judgments are no more than opinion. Both are equally destitute of binding force. Such a universal power of judging over the laws and over the decisions of the judiciary, is nothing else but pure despotism. If conceded to him, it makes him at once what Louis the Fourteenth proclaimed himself to be when he said, 'I am the State.' " [9]

Webster, in the heat of the debate, exaggerated the danger of despotism and it is almost certain that he misrepresented and may have even misunderstood the meaning of the passage quoted above from the President's message. Jackson lacked capacity for clear and accurate expression of his ideas and on this occasion evidently failed signally to say just what he

8 Richardson, *op. cit.*, III, p. 582.
9 Webster, *op. cit.*, VI, pp. 167-68.

intended. Close attention to the phrasing in the passage quoted from the veto message reveals that he must have meant to say that the mere fact of Marshall's having given the opinion that the establishment of *a* bank was within the constitutional competence of Congress did not place Congress and the President under the necessity of considering any and every proposed bill for a bank constitutional. That is to say, the opinion of Marshall placed them under no obligation to recharter the bank and in no manner hindered them from terminating its existence. Congress was still free to exercise its policy-determining function in this field.

Although Jackson here appeared to be defending Congress and the Executive against the assumption of dominating authority by the courts, he was really striking at the attitude of the Senate, which seemed to be seeking to force acceptance of the bill by invoking the compelling power of the Court's opinion. The Supreme Court under Marshall's influence seemed to assume to be the interpreter of the powers of every department of the government instead of confining itself, as it did later, to questions of private right.[10] This was before the days when the Court had learned the way of caution and security by renouncing jurisdiction over political controversies. It then seemed in the habit of taking cognizance of questions primarily of political science and public law and even of public policy. The National Republicans could not see that after the long eclipse of presidential power President Jackson was only vigorously asserting the independence of the Executive and placing the co-ordinate branches of the government in a position apparently more nearly like that intended by the framers of the Constitution. The late

10 See J. W. Burgess, *The Middle Period*, p. 209.

Professor Burgess thought that Jackson in his veto message was rescuing the check and balance system from the domination of a single department, that is, the judiciary.[11] The people, in sustaining Jackson, may be said to have made his principles of interpretation a permanent part of Constitutional doctrine.

Jackson's personal friend, Senator White, of Tennessee, replied to Webster's argument. He declared that according to Webster's reasoning the Constitution had provided for the Supreme Court to settle constitutional questions after which every other great department of the government must acquiesce. He held instead that the true view is that: "Whenever a suit is decided by the Supreme Court, as that is the court of last resort, its decision is *final and conclusive between the parties.* But as an authority it does not bind either the Congress or the President of the United States." Such a decision, claimed the senator, left the other departments free in the performance of official acts to their own conscientious judgment as to the constitutionality of their conduct. When departments interpret differently, the people is the tribunal to decide the issue, since each department is but the agent of the people.[12] Lincoln, in 1857, used precisely White's line of reasoning in attacking the Dred Scott Decision. Moreover, in this connection Lincoln quoted approvingly Jackson's famous passage to the effect that each department decides the constitutionality of questions.[13]

Martin Van Buren was the intimate friend of President Jackson and had developed a sympathetic understanding of his brusque old chief. He has given an

11 *Ibid.*, pp. 206-09.
12 Quoted in Martin Van Buren, *Political Parties in the United States* (1867), p. 330.
13 A. J. Beveridge, *Lincoln*, IV, p. 150.

illuminating interpretation of the controversy under consideration. He admitted that the President was not on his guard as to his language when he wrote, "Each public officer who takes an oath to support the Constitution swears that he will support it as he understands it and not as it is understood by others." But Van Buren pointed out that the only reasonable interpretation of the President's meaning was that he had in mind those officers "who singly as was his own case, or in conjunction with others as was the case with some, constituted the three great departments of the government whilst acting in their respective official capacities. . . . The plain and well-understood substance of what he said was that in giving or withholding assent to the bill for the recharter of the bank it was his right and duty to decide the question of constitutionality for himself, uninfluenced by any opinion or judgment which the Supreme Court had pronounced upon that point further than his judgment was satisfied by the reason which it had given for its decision." In short, we might say, President Jackson considered that he had the right in the exercise of his discretionary power to reach the conclusion: "This particular bill which Congress has submitted to me is, in my opinion, not constitutional and I shall accordingly veto it." [14]

Mr. Van Buren maintained that if Mr. Webster was correct in his claim that the final decision of all constitutional questions belongs to the Supreme Court, then "the incumbents of the legislative and executive departments in respect to questions of constitutional power are *ministerial officers only.*" [15] Jackson's words consequently appear to be just the kind of a protest to be expected from the leader of a party claiming to

14 *Ibid.*, pp. 316, 317.
15 *Ibid.*, p. 316.

represent the doctrines of Thomas Jefferson. That statesman had expressed himself on this very point a dozen years before the bank veto in words of which Jackson's sound almost like an echo. "My construction of the Constitution," Jefferson explained, "is that each department is truly independent of the others and has an equal right to decide for itself what is the meaning of the Constitution in cases submitted to its action; and especially where it is to act ultimately and without appeal." [16]

President Jackson regarded his re-election in 1832, following the thorough public discussion of his bank veto, as a vindication of his veto and he slowly and deliberately matured the determination to withdraw the public funds from the bank three years before the expiration of the charter.[17] Since Congress had already refused to pass a measure authorizing him specifically to do this,[18] he decided to act through the Secretary of the Treasury under the authority conferred upon that official by the statute chartering the bank. Attorney General Roger B. Taney had advised the President that sufficient authority for such action existed.[19] The particular passage of the charter invoked for the purpose provided that: "the deposits of the money of the United States in places in which the said bank and branches thereof may be established shall be made in said bank or branches thereof *unless the Secretary of the Treasury shall at any time otherwise order and direct,* in which case the Secretary of the Treasury shall immediately lay before Congress, if in session, and, if not, immediately after

[16] Letter to Judge Spencer Roane, Thomas Jefferson, *Writings* (Ford ed.), XII, pp. 135-40.

[17] John Spencer Bassett, *Correspondence of Andrew Jackson*, V, pp. 32, 33.

[18] Schouler, *History of the United States,* IV, p. 137.

[19] J. S. Bassett, *op. cit.,* V, pp. 35, 69.

the commencement of the next session, the reason for such order or direction." [20] Taney claimed that according to the terms of the statute Congress could not remove the deposits but the Secretary of the Treasury could do so.[21]

Before the President could get a Secretary of the Treasury willing to execute his decision on the removal of the government deposits from the bank he had to transfer the incumbent of that office to another department and appoint W. J. Duane who, however, resolutely refused to accept the President's persistent and patient advice on this matter.[22] Dismissing Duane, Jackson then transferred his Attorney General, Taney, to the treasury. Because of the peculiarly close relationship that had always obtained between Congress and the Treasury Department the President's dismissal of Duane in order to force the removal of government deposits appeared to the Whigs[23] a particularly audacious and violent act of executive "usurpation." The astonishment and indignation the Senate had manifested over the bank veto seemed mild indeed when compared with the later wrath and fury of the Whigs at the Executive usurpation of what had long been considered as undoubted congressional prerogative. Jackson was assuming power over the acts of the Secretary of the Treasury which neither the Constitution nor Congress had granted. Not only had Congress assigned the duties in question specifically to the Secretary of the Treasury with the direction that he report his activities in this line directly to Congress,

[20] *Statutes at Large,* III, p. 274; italics mine.

[21] J. W. Burgess, *op. cit.,* p. 279.

[22] J. S. Bassett, *op. cit.,* V, pp. 111, 113, 129, 142, 204, 206.

[23] Jackson's re-election so discredited the National Republicans that their name had to be discarded. The opposition to Jackson with a somewhat different group-composition then adopted the party name of Whigs.

but the Supreme Court in one of its famous decisions had held that Congress could thus assign duties to officers who would then be solely responsible to them for their execution. Thus the existence of the power Jackson was indirectly exercising had apparently been expressly denied by the Supreme Court.[24]

The question at issue now became: Can the President of the United States, through his constitutionally implied power of dismissal, dictate to the Secretary of the Treasury how he shall exercise the discretionary power vested by Congress exclusively in the latter? The dismissal of Duane because he would not obey Jackson and remove the deposits was apparently based on the assumption that this officer was without question subject to the orders of the President.[25] With Jackson's view Congress, and particularly the Senate, could be depended on to take issue. Accordingly no sooner had Congress assembled in December, 1883, than Henry Clay opened the contest. His first move was a resolution introduced and promptly approved by the Senate, inquiring of the President whether a certain paper reported to have been read at a Cabinet meeting and later published was genuine.[26]

This was the famous paper in which the President had revealed to his Cabinet his determination to have the government deposits removed to state banks. He reviewed, in this long statement, the deliberate course of reasoning by which he had arrived at his decision. The law gave the Secretary of the Treasury *unqualified* power over deposits. The requirement that he report any removal to Congress was in order to enable that body to judge whether further legislation was

24 *McCulloch vs. Maryland, 4 Wheaton*, 316, L ed.
25 Jackson to Van Buren, J. S. Bassett, *op. cit.*, V, p. 205.
26 *Congressional Globe*, I, pp. 20, 21.

needed. As early as 1817 Secretary of the Treasury Crawford had "without contradiction" asserted the right to remove deposits from the Bank of the United States to state banks. The removal of funds, argued the President, should be started at once and be gradual before the charter expired. "The President would have felt relieved from a heavy and painful responsibility if Congress had reserved this power and not devolved it exclusively on an executive department." After detailing the propaganda and other activities of the Bank against public interests the President said that he "could not in justice to the responsibility which he owes to the country, refrain from pressing upon the Secretary of the Treasury his views of the considerations which impel immediate action. Upon him has been devolved by the Constitution and the suffrages of the American people the duty of superintending the operation of the Executive Departments of the Government and seeing that the Laws are faithfully executed." [27]

Such an inquiry as Clay's resolution made on the part of either house of Congress in our day respecting a Cabinet meeting would be simply incomprehensible and the resolution becomes intelligible only when considered against a background of almost a quarter of a century of subordination of the Executive to Congress. What Clay wanted to get at was, who was responsible for the removal of deposits—the Secretary of the Treasury or the President?

When Clay introduced his resolution he took occasion to condemn the governmental revolution in progress in the intemperate language that has been heard in every struggle of Congress with the Executive. "We are in the midst of a revolution," said he, "rapidly tending toward a total change of the pure republican character of our government, and to the

[27] Richardson, *op. cit.,* III, pp. 5-19.

concentration of all power in the hands of one man. The powers of Congress are paralyzed, except when exerted in conformity with his will, by frequent and extraordinary exercise of the executive veto, not anticipated by the founders of our Constitution and not practiced by any predecessors of the present Chief Magistrate." [28]

Clay's resolution proved to be a strategic blunder, in fact, a boomerang. Few shrewder American politicians ever lived than Andrew Jackson and he knew how to employ the legal talents and political sagacity of his lieutenants in turning the attacks of his enemies back upon themselves. The Senate resolution proved to be an excellent opportunity to confound the opposition to the President while giving the Whigs an elementary lesson in constitutional law as interpreted by the new political school. In a burning message the President informed the upper house that: "The Executive is a co-ordinate and independent branch of the Government equally with the Senate, and I have yet to learn under what constitutional authority that branch of the legislature has a right to require of me an account of any communication, either verbal or in writing, made to the Departments acting as a Cabinet council. As well might I be required to detail to the Senate the free and private conversations I have held with those officers on any subject relating to their duties and my own. . . . Knowing the constitutional rights of the Senate, I shall be the last man under any circumstances to interfere with them. Knowing those of the Executive, I shall at all times endeavor to maintain them agreeably to the provisions of the Constitution and the oath I have taken to support and defend it." [29]

Three months later Clay carried the war against

28 *Congressional Debates*, X, Part I, p. 60.
29 Richardson, *op. cit.*, III, 136.

the President a step further by putting through the Senate the famous resolution of censure: "Resolved that the President, in the late executive proceedings in relation to the public revenue, has assumed upon himself authority and power not conferred by the Constitution and laws and in derogation of both." [30] The President countered the new challenge with a protest to the Senate worthy of the occasion and with a skill that put the Senate Whigs at a disadvantage before the country. He declared that a charge as serious as that made in the resolution of censure called for impeachment, in which case the Senate could act only as judges. "The President of the United States has been by a majority of his constitutional triers, accused and found guilty of an impeachable offense, but in no part of this proceeding have the directions of the Constitution been observed." Of course the President was ignoring the very patent fact that the Senate had resorted to censure instead of waiting for impeachment because Jackson's partisans controlled the lower house and there was consequently not the slightest possibility of getting that procedure in motion.

The President closed his protest with words that exasperated the Whig senators at the same time that they inspired his followers with renewed enthusiasm for their chief. "I do hereby solemnly protest against the aforementioned proceedings of the Senate as unauthorized by the Constitution, contrary to its spirit and to several of its express provisions, subversive of that distribution of the powers of the government which it has ordained and established, destructive of the checks and safeguards by which those powers were intended, on the one hand to be controlled and on the other to be protected, and calculated by their

[30] *Senate Journal,* 23rd Cong., 1st Session, p. 197.

immediate and collateral effects, by their character
and tendency to concentrate in the hands of a body
not directly amenable to the people a degree of influence and power dangerous to the liberties and
fatal to the Constitution of their choice." [31] Thus while
Clay and his colleagues were trembling at executive
usurpation and threatened despotism the President,
with a better understanding of the mood of the American people, struck a more popular chord by raising
the specter of a senatorial oligarchy.

Before passing to the debate provoked by the President's protest it might be well to note that it was
during these conflicts between Congress and the President that the heterogeneous aggregation of anti-
Jackson men came to assume the party name of
"Whig." Historically the term carried the connota-
tion of opposition to executive prerogative, particularly on the part of the king, and on the other hand
an attachment to parliamentary or, in this case, congressional superiority to the Executive. No doubt the
Whigs meant by their name to imply that their opponents were Tories, the "King's Friends," as the
party of King George III had been named, friends
of "King Andrew the First." These Whigs claimed
to be the only genuine disciples of Thomas Jefferson,
true exponents of constitutional government with its
separated powers and checks and balances. With a
sort of strange political blindness the great Whig
chieftains had convinced themselves that they were
the champions of a popular movement. They were in
reality fighting the rear-guard actions of the retreat
of the old Republicanism that had begun its career
resisting the Hamiltonian system with its executive
initiative in legislation, the Republicanism that had
culminated in the supremacy of Congress during the

31 Richardson, *op. cit.*, III, p. 92.

administrations of the Virginia dynasty. In a sense these American Whigs, like the English Whigs, constituted an aristocracy and, like aristocracies throughout history, when they could not govern directly, they sought to control the Executive through the legislature.[32]

The debate over Jackson's formal protest against the resolution of censure was long and bitter. The ablest critic of the conduct and particularly of the protest of the President was Senator Daniel Webster. He warned his fellow senators that "the contest for ages has been to rescue liberty from the grasp of executive power. . . . Throughout all this history of the contest for liberty, executive power has been regarded as a lion which must be caged. . . . The President carries on the government; all the rest are but sub-contractors. Sir, whatever *name* we give him we have but one executive officer. A Briareus sits in the center of our system, and with his hundred hands, touches everything, moves everything, controls everything. I ask, Sir, is this republicanism? Is this legal responsibility?"[33]

Coming more definitely to the specific matter of the President's "usurpation" of Congress's power over the purse, the orator continued, "After half a century's administration of this government, Sir; after we have endeavored by statute upon statute, and by provision following provision, to define and limit personal authority; to assign particular duties to particular public servants; to define those duties; to create penalties for their violation; to adjust accurately the responsibility of each agent with its own powers and its own duties; to establish the prevalence

---

[32] See Raymond G. Gettell, *History of American Political Thought*, p. 247; also J. W. Burgess, *op. cit.*, p. 282.
[33] Webster, *op. cit.*, VII, pp. 133, 134, 137.

of equal rule; to make the law, as far as possible, everything, and the individual will, as far as possible, nothing; after all, this astounding assertion rings in our ears, that, throughout the whole range of official agency in its smallest ramifications as well as in its larger masses, there is but *one responsibility, one discretion, one will.*" [34]

Youthful Samuel J. Tilden as a private citizen entered the lists in defense of the President's dismissal of Duane and presented what may be regarded as the accepted contemporary Democratic justification, in a legal sense, of that act. His researches convinced him that the Treasury Department had always been considered an executive department and "the right of supervision and direction is of necessity included in and coextensive with that of removal." Passing from historical investigation to logic, he reasoned that "to give one department the right of requiring a conformity to its will without the power of enforcing it and to the other the power of enforcing that conformity without the right of requiring it" seemed absurd. "Under this arrangement of powers and rights, if the Secretary of the Treasury should squander the public money by millions, the President could not remove him, because that officer is not accountable to him. Congress to whom he is accountable could not because it does not possess the power at all." [35]

The humiliation of the Whigs was not yet complete. To Senator Thomas H. Benton, the leader of the Jackson senators, the Senate's vote of censure of the President was a perversion of popular government to be tolerated no longer than compulsion enforced

[34] *Ibid.*, p. 139.
[35] John Bigelow, *Public Writings and Speeches of Samuel J. Tilden* (1885), pp. 31. 32.

it. He pledged himself never to rest until the resolution was expunged.[36] Under the persistent pressure of the President and his partisans one state legislature after another forced the resignation of senators who had voted for the resolution of censure, and as new senators were chosen the Jackson men gradually gained control of the Senate which was widely interpreted as signifying that the public had sustained the President.[37] In December, 1837, Senator Benton's opportunity came. The phrasing of his expunging resolution is deserving of close attention, marking as it does the complete victory of the Executive and the final blow to the Republican system of congressional supremacy. Referring, of course, to the vote of censure, the resolution provided: "That the said resolve be expunged from the journal: and for that purpose, that the Secretary of the Senate, at such time, as the Senate may appoint, shall bring the manuscript journal of the session of 1833-34 into the Senate, and, in the presence of the Senate draw black lines round said resolves, and write across the face thereof in strong letters the following words: Expunged by order of the Senate, this ——— day of ———— in the year of our Lord, 1837." [38]

The debate on this resolution aroused the senatorial gladiators to a final fray. The solemnly presented arguments of the Whigs betray their astonishing lack of touch with the main currents of popular opinion. Every one of these conflicts with Jackson reveals their inability to comprehend the character of the democratic revolution in progress. The great Whig statesmen were lawyers, experts in refinements of

[36] T. H. Benton, *op. cit.*, I, p. 428; Henry A. Wise, *Seven Decades of the Union*, p. 137.

[37] For an account of the pressure of the administration on state legislatures, see H. A. Wise, *op. cit.*, p. 137.

[38] *Senate Journal*, Dec. 20, 1837.

juristic analysis. Is it too much to suggest that Jackson and his lieutenants with their keen awareness of political realities were better political scientists than Clay and Webster? A profound change had taken place in the very nature of the American body politic in this era so aptly designated, "The rise of the common man." This common man was beginning to look to the one official of the federal government who was not only chosen by his vote but could speak the voice of the people of the whole nation. Clay and Webster had certainly not sensed this change. They could not conceive of the President as a popular representative. To these disciples of John Locke that particular function was, by tradition, by philosophy, by the nature of things, they thought, monopolized by the legislature. When Webster contended that the Senate was standing as the guardian of the people against the tyranny of President Jackson[39] his blindness to reality and his insensibility to the prevailing popular conception of things placed him in a position of almost pathetic absurdity.

Clay could not see that in exercising the veto power President Jackson was endearing himself to the people by expressing quite precisely their sentiments. In vain did this frontier Whig statesman, with his florid rhetoric, paint harrowing pictures of the despot. "In one hand he holds the purse," he cried, "and in the other brandishes the sword of the country. . . . He has swept over the government, during the last eight years, like a tropical tornado. Every department exhibits traces of the storm. . . . When disabled from age any longer to hold the scepter of power, he designates his successor and transmits it to his favorite. What more does he want?" shouted the indignant orator, referring to the resolution to expunge the

[39] D. Webster, *op. cit.*, VII, p. 147.

vote of censure. "Must we blot, deface, and mutilate the records of the country to punish the presumptuousness of expressing any opinion contrary to his?" [40]

Clay's speech against expunging was one of the greatest of his life. It made a profound impression on the Senate and is said almost to have defeated the resolution. It was, however, all in vain, and in the bitterness of his defeat the vanquished senator declared, "The Senate is no longer a place for a decent man. . . . I shall escape from it with the same pleasure that one would fly from a charnel house." [41] Clay's disappointment was far more than a personal reverse. He had looked with incredulous eyes upon what seemed to him to be the ultimate collapse of republican government, which to him meant that political system he had personally played so large a part, as Speaker of the House, in building—a proud and efficient legislature, the essential organ of the public will and the motive power of the Executive. Before the advent of Jackson it had seemed to possess the enduring stability of a mature and permanent system. Now this governmental structure was topsy-turvy, wrecked beyond repair. The people's legislature lay prostrate, the conqueror's heel upon its neck, unable even to protest against the abuse of executive power. As if that were not enough, Clay had just been forced to witness the proud Senate compelled to mutilate its own records at the behest of the Executive and through a campaign on the floor of the Senate literally directed from headquarters in the White House.[42]

[40] Henry Clay, *Life and Speeches* (1843), II, p. 277.
[41] Letter of Clay to Francis Brooke, *Works of Henry Clay*, V, pp. 10, 17.
[42] Henry A. Wise, *op. cit.*, p. 137.

V

The Jacksonian View
of the Presidency
Prevails

---

*

WHEN Andrew Jackson's last term had ended and he had retired to private life the outstanding questions were: Has a permanent change been effected in the presidential office? Is the strong executive type to be considered as the accepted form of our constitutional system? Must Congress now orient itself to an external leadership claiming to speak with the authentic voice of the American people? It was no accident that the Democratic party was focused in the presidency rather than in Congress. Jacksonian Democracy originated as the personal following of one who symbolized the idea of justice for the masses. He was represented as a champion of the underdog and the

Democratic party long relied for its voting strength upon the counties with poorer soils and the crowded wards of the great cities largely populated with recent immigrant stock. Quite naturally then these segments of American society sought security by electing a national champion to the presidency which they conceive to be peculiarly their office.

To the well-to-do, however, Jackson was a demagogue, an inciter of social discontent, and the prosperous became the backbone of the opposition to Jackson. The dominant elements of the Whig party consisted of the great financial, commercial, and emerging industrial interests of the East, the more prosperous agrarians of the North and the great slaveholding planters of the South. These latter were obsessed with a phobia of a strong central government and when Jackson in 1832 let out his blast against the nullificationists these states rightsers allied themselves with the Whigs. Here then was a combination that never elected a president on a program but only through the stratagem of confusing issues by nominating the military heroes William Henry Harrison and Zachary Taylor.

To the three questions at the head of this chapter the Whig party gave an emphatic negative. That heterogeneous aggregation never came nearer to perfect party solidarity than when it shouted its challenge to the assertion and exercise of strong executive power and assumed a militant guardianship of the powers of Congress. Here was the one principle on which they could present a united front to the common enemy of "republican" government. In this matter of congressional supremacy the Whigs came closest to making their permanent contribution to American political ideas. The later Republican party, as their spiritual heir, never abandoned the old Whig reliance upon Congress nor quite dispelled a deep-seated distrust of the strong Executive, even though a Republican. The record of history is incontrovertible that Republican Congresses were as unhappy with Abraham Lincoln as with Theodore Roosevelt.

In 1836 Jackson's faithful followers ratified their chieftain's choice of a successor by electing Martin Van Buren President. This "Little Magician," as he was called, had been Jackson's shrewdest and most confidential political adviser and as President he followed in the master's footsteps. President Van Buren resolutely resisted the most powerful pressures to rescind Jackson's Specie Circular, an executive order which required the payment for public lands in hard money and even outdid Jackson in the policy of internal improvements by ordering the government's tools and other equipment for that purpose sold at public auction. The Whigs chose to consider the Van Buren administration as the "third term of Andrew Jackson." Near its close Clay expressed the Whig view when he declared that "during the last twelve years the machine, driven by a reckless charioteer with frightful impetuosity has been greatly jarred and jolted and it needs careful examination and a thorough repair." [1]

Henry Clay hoped to be the mechanic called to repair the disordered mechanism. What would have become of the doctrine of congressional supremacy had the electorate elevated to the Presidency a man with such a dominating personality as Clay? Given the opportunity, would he have taken himself in hand, restrained his impetuous nature and played a less masterful role than Jackson? History denied us the opportunity to know, for the Whigs nominated instead William Henry Harrison, a superannuated mili-

[1] *Cong. Globe,* 27th Cong., 2nd Session, p. 164.

tary hero, and after an issueless but hilarious campaign won a signal victory.

Issueless though the campaign may have been, constitutional theory was not neglected. The Whig candidates and campaigners had stressed their central doctrine of resistance to executive autocracy and proclaimed the coming restoration of Jeffersonian republicanism. Typical of their propaganda is an extract from the Richmond *Whig* of January 13, 1840: "If ever there was a genuine Republican party in the country it is that party which General Harrison now worthily leads and leads to victory. What are its objects and ends? To restore the Constitution, the charter of public liberty, to authority, to reduce the more the monarch's power of the President of the United States. . . ." [2] Harrison declared in his famous address to the immense audience at Dayton, Ohio: "the Augean stables of Van Burenism can be cleaned only by a Jeffersonian broom";[3] and Daniel Webster, with a convenient forgetfulness of his early partisanship as a Federalist and his conviction in 1801 that Jefferson's election was "an earthquake of popular commotion," now avowed himself to be "a Jeffersonian Democrat" [4]

As soon as the Whigs had elected a President, the practical manifestation of the doctrine of legislative guardianship over the Executive was in evidence. Senator Daniel Webster patronizingly offered the President-elect a ready-made inaugural address.[5] Concerning the demands for patronage Harrison felt impelled to declare that the Clay and Webster Whigs "were bent upon seizing the reins of government" [6]

[2] Quoted by Lyon G. Tyler, *Letters and Times of the Tylers,* I, p. 612.

[3] *Niles Weekly Register,* LIX, p. 71.

[4] *Cong. Globe,* 1840, Extra, p. 324.

[5] Morison, *op. cit.,* II, p. 33.

[6] L. G. Tyler, *op. cit.,* II, p. 64.

and he is reported to have been driven to the point of saying frankly, "Mr. Clay, you forget that I am President." [7] Ultimately he informed Clay that he would no longer deal with him except by letter.[8]

The Whig leaders had been thrown into consternation by the news that Harrison had, single-handed, prepared an inaugural address. Only with difficulty was he persuaded to permit Webster to aid in revising it.[9] Clay also is said to have had a hand in reshaping this long address,[10] and much of it consists of the ideas Clay had been expounding for years against the Jacksonian system. The address accordingly went straight to the heart of the cardinal Whig governmental theories. With recent history in mind the President declared: "the great danger to our institutions . . . appears to me to be . . . the accumulation in one of the departments of that which was assigned to the others." After mentioning the concern when the Constitution was first published lest the position assigned to the single executive "at no very remote period would terminate in monarchy," he modestly admitted, "it would not become me to say that the fears of these patriots have been realized." He had no doubts, however, that "the tendency for some years past had been in that direction."

In this inaugural address are passages which raise the suspicion that designing Whig leaders may have practically persuaded the aged President-elect to prepare a mortgage of his office to Congress. "I cannot conceive," said he, "that by fair construction any or either of its [the Constitution's] provisions would be

7 James Lyon, report of conversation with Harrison, letter to *New York Times*, Aug. 31, 1880.

8 Nathan Sargent, *Public Men and Events from the Commencement of Monroe's Administration*, II, p. 116.

9 Benjamin Perley Poore, Reminiscences, I, p. 250.

10 Schurz, Carl, *Life of Henry Clay*, II, p. 194.

found to constitute the President a part of the legislative power. . . . And it is preposterous to suppose that a thought could be entertained for a moment that the President, placed at the capital, in the center of the country could better understand the wants and wishes of the people than their own immediate representatives who spend a part of every year among them . . . and [are] bound to them by the triple tie of interest, duty, and affection."

Adverting to the conflict of the Whigs with Jackson over the treasury, he declared that the "delicate duty of devising schemes of revenue should be left where the Constitution has left it—with the immediate representatives of the people." They should prescribe the mode of keeping the public treasure "and the further removed it may be from the Executive the more wholesome the arrangement and in accordance with republican principle. . . ." And then, referring to Jackson's removal of Secretary of the Treasury Duane in order to ensure the removal of the deposits from the Bank of the United States, Harrison continued, "It was certainly a great error in the Framers of the Constitution not to have made the officer at the head of the Treasury Department entirely independent of the Executive. He should, at least, have been removable upon the demand of the popular branch of the Legislature. I have determined never to remove a Secretary of the Treasury without communicating all the circumstances to both Houses of Congress.[11] These, we may reasonably assume, were the sentiments of the President when a month later, as he lay dying, he said, perhaps imagining he was speaking to Vice President Tyler, "Sir, I wish you to understand the true principles of the Government. I wish them carried out; I ask nothing more." [12]

11 Richardson, *op. cit.*, IV, pp. 7, 8, 9, 10, 13, 14.
12 L. G. Tyler, *op. cit.*, II, p. 1.

Although deeply grieved, the Whig leaders were not alarmed over the death of Harrison. Did not Tyler owe his election to the Whig party? Had he not condemned the removal of the deposits and voted for the resolution censuring Jackson for his ordering removal of the deposits? Had he not resigned his seat in the Senate rather than be coerced into submission to the arbitrary Chief Executive? Such was the vice president, upon whom, in accordance with the Constitution, would devolve the duties of the presidential office. Of course it must have been somewhat disconcerting to have the new incumbent promptly assume the title of the office as well as all the prerogatives of an elected President instead of strictly observing the constitutional implication to "act as President." It must have seemed particularly presumptuous to see him give a presidential inaugural address to the people after the manner of an elected President.

But there was great comfort for the Whigs in that Tyler had retained Harrison's Cabinet and that his inaugural address contained the conventional Whig doctrines concerning the nature of the government. Among other things he said, "In view of the fact, well attested by history, that the tendency of all human institutions is to concentrate power in the hands of a single man and that their ultimate downfall has proceeded from this cause, I deem it of the most essential importance that a complete separation should take place between the sword and the purse. No matter where or how the public money shall be deposited, so long as the President can exert the power of appointing and removing at his pleasure the agents selected for their custody the commander-in-chief of the army and navy is in fact the treasurer." [13]

Clay himself had never stated the doctrine more clearly and the Whig leaders were accordingly jubi-

[13] Richardson, *op. cit.,* IV, pp. 37-38.

lant over the conciliatory tone of the message. Congress would apparently have a free hand in handling finance. Thomas H. Benton opened up on Tyler for apparently deserting his long consistent record of opposition to a bank of the United States. Clay, thinking the way clear, prepared to assume leadership in the government as the most prominent Whig member of Congress. It is indeed indicative of the Whig doctrine of legislative supremacy that he introduced in the Senate at this time a set of resolutions which he expected to be accepted as the party program. He prepared to push vigorously this program in the face of the protest of some of Tyler's intimate friends who thought the President was being ignored.[14] Again exemplifying Whig dogma was Clay's rejection of the offer of the Cabinet post of Secretary of State in order that he might exercise leadership in the Tyler administration as a Senator.[15] Following the precedent of Hamilton in the 1790's, Clay evidently expected to harness the dominant social forces of the nation in the 1840's and hitch them to the national government.

John Tyler, as a spokesman of the tidewater tobacco planters, represented pre-eminently the resentment of the great agrarians of the South against Jackson's vigorous executive policies and especially his denunciation of the South Carolina nullificationists. Tyler's nomination for the vice-presidency on the Whig ticket had been made to capture these dissenting Democrats who were allies rather than members of the Whig party. Here were patent facts Clay and his fellow partisans chose deliberately to ignore after Tyler reached the presidency.

No matter how much he had protested against Jackson "usurpations," Whig leaders were soon to

14 Schouler, *op. cit.,* IV, p. 378.
15 See *Dictionary of American Biography,* IV, p. 178.

discover that they had in John Tyler no complaisant President of the pre-Jacksonian type. Cabinet as well as Congress was to have that fact impressed upon it. Robert Tyler, the son of the President, relates that when the President confronted the Cabinet at the first meeting following Harrison's death the Secretary of State, Webster, said, "Mr. President, I suppose you intend to carry out the ideas and customs of your predecessor, and that this administration, inaugurated by President Harrison, will continue in the same line of policy." Seeing that Tyler assented, Mr. Webster continued, "Mr. President, it was the custom of our cabinet meetings of President Harrison that he should preside over them. All measures relating to the administration were to be brought before the Cabinet and their settlement was to be decided by the majority of votes, each member of the Cabinet and the President having but one vote." Thus the Whigs had applied their dogma by reducing their first President to a status of *primus inter pares* in his own Cabinet. To Webster's astonishing suggestion Tyler replied to the effect that he could never consent to being dictated to. "I am the President," said he, "and I shall be held responsible for my administration." [16] It was evident that, no matter how much Tyler disliked Jackson, he was resolved to continue the Jacksonian type of President.

Pursuant to the call for a special session issued by President Harrison shortly before his death, Congress convened and on June 1, 1841, received Tyler's first message. After dwelling on the need of a new fiscal agency to be substituted for the independent treasury instituted under Van Buren, the new President with becoming modesty declared that the nature of the

16 John Tyler, Jr., quoted by John Fisk in J. G. Wilson, *The Presidents of the United States,* II, p. 73n.

substitute belonged to the legislative province. While he did not think it possible that Congress would devise a measure he would be called upon to veto, he was "expressly reserving to himself, however, the ultimate power of rejecting any measure which might in his view of it conflict with the Constitution, or otherwise jeopardize the prosperity of the country, a power he could not part with even if he would." [17]

President Tyler had already, before the convening of Congress, sketched in principle the broad outlines of a new fiscal agency which a majority of his Cabinet had approved. The head of the Cabinet, Webster, was enthusiastic over it. In a speech delivered in Faneuil Hall, September 30, 1842, he declared, "I am ready to stake my reputation . . . that if the Whig Congress take the measure and give it a fair trial for three years it will be admitted by the whole American people to have proved the most beneficial institution ever established, the Constitution only excepted." [18] This is significant since Webster had been a champion of the Bank in the conflict with Jackson. The President desired that Congress follow the time-honored procedure of calling on the Secretary of the Treasury for advice in shaping the legislation.[19] Henry A. Wise in the House and Henry Clay in the Senate made the necessary motions and the Secretary of the Treasury Ewing, in harmony with Cabinet and President, framed the bill. When this measure, however, reached Clay's committee in the Senate, a new bill was framed resembling the old bank bill which Jackson had killed by his veto. The institution was to have the power to establish branches in states without their consent, which was particularly obnoxious

17 Richardson, *op. cit.*, IV, p. 46.
18 *Niles Register*, LXIII, p. 93.
19 N. Sargent, *op. cit.*, II, p. 124.

to the state's-rights President, and when, after passing the two houses, it was presented to him, Tyler vetoed it.[20] Clay wanted Congress to adjourn and let the people visit their wrath upon the President.[21] He seemed to have learned nothing from his failure to discredit Jackson by challenging him to veto the Bank Charter in 1832.

The friends of the Bank, however, insisted on another attempt. At a Cabinet meeting the President authorized Ewing and Webster to confer with caucus representatives in framing a second bill without, however, committing the President. He cautioned them to guard against an appearance of executive dictation to Congress on account of Whig sensitiveness on that score. They might express their opinion that the President, in the light of his known views, would probably approve such and such a bill but before it was presented to Congress, he would like to see whatever was framed.[22] The President, through Representative Wise, warned the House that the bill must avoid his specific constitutional objections.[23]

He would approve a fiscal institution to perform necessary governmental functions but he stood firm against the chartering of another bank that could establish branches in any state against that state's consent. This would be "unconstitutional." All efforts were, however, in vain. The President's wishes were disregarded when the administration project reached Congress and the second measure was met by another veto.[24]

The ensuing outburst of fury against the President

20 Richardson, *op. cit.*, IV, p. 63.

21 Wise, *op. cit.*, p. 185.

22 Statement of John Bell, quoted in L. G. Tyler, *op. cit.*, II, p. 86.

23 H. A. Wise, *op. cit.*, p. 189.

24 Richardson, *op. cit.*, IV, pp. 68 ff.

at this second veto has probably been equalled only by the merciless attack on Andrew Johnson and his supporters by the Radical Unionists after the Civil War. The savage enginery of social terror was let loose by the Whigs on John Tyler. Effigies of him were burned by thousands and his private secretary received hundreds of letters threatening assassination.[25] A decade of Whig warfare with the Executive had driven the party to hysteria with this final frustration of its plans. Whether it lost or won presidential elections, the results were the same. Congress could not regain its old mastery of the government. From the frantic rage of the rank and file the party leaders in Congress turned to more deliberate measures for forcing Tyler out of the presidency.

Immediately after the second veto all the members of Tyler's Cabinet except Webster suddenly resigned. Had they postponed this action a few days the Senate would not have been in session, due to the adjournment, and the President would not have been under the compulsion of immediate senatorial consideration of his nominations to Cabinet positions. The unseemly haste of the conjoint resignations was due, apparently, to a conspiracy to prevent the President from reconstructing his Cabinet deliberately through recess appointments. Webster, who was not with the Clay faction, and was not eager to enhance the prestige of another presidential aspirant, refused to resign with the rest of the Cabinet.[26] The President said, "It was declared to him that if he [Webster] would resign, I would necessarily have to vacate the government by Saturday night." [27]

In every one of these movements of the Whigs

25 L. G. Tyler, *op. cit.*, II, p. 92.
26 J. Q. Adams, *op. cit.*, XI, p. 14.
27 L. G. Tyler, *op. cit.*, II, p. 94.

there is apparent the persistence of their belief that the Executive ought to be subordinate to and act in harmony with Congress. The presidential succession law then in force[28] would have devolved the office on the president pro tem of the Senate and the statute provided for a new election to be held on the first Wednesday of the ensuing December if there remained time for a two-months' notification; if there was not time then the election would be held one year later unless the term had expired in the meantime. It was four months until such election date and Clay thought Tyler ought to resign and permit the election.[29] Clay and his partisans would have been happy to see W. L. Southard, president pro tem of the Senate, in the meantime exercise the office of President, for he would have offered no veto to the congressional program. A quarter of a century later there was a remarkable similarity in the situation when the Radical Unionists hoped to remove Andrew Johnson from the presidency following impeachment and conviction and elevate the president pro tem of the Senate, Benjamin F. Wade, to the chief magistracy.

Somehow Clay could not rid himself of the Whig notion that the precedents of a parliamentary system ought to apply here. As early as Tyler's first Bank veto he thought the President ought to have resigned. He wanted to know why he could not resign then, since he had resigned as Senator when he could not obey the instructions of the Virginia legislature on the expunging resolution. Why should he not likewise resign when he could not approve the action of Congress? This was a natural question for a Whig to raise. It brought the characteristic Democratic answer of Senator Rives that the Executive was an inde-

28 *Statutes at Large*, I, pp. 240, 241.
29 T. H. Benson, *op cit.*, II, p. 321.

pendent branch of the government as well as was Congress, and the President was not called upon to resign just because he differed with them in opinion.[30]

Another manifestation of the peculiar Whig doctrine of parliamentary responsibility for the Executive through the party in Congress appeared in the address to the people of the United States prepared by the Whig caucus following the second Bank veto. In part it said: "We grieve to say to you that by the exercise of that power in the Constitution which has ever been regarded with suspicion, and often with odium, by the people—a power which we had hoped was never to be exhibited on this subject by a Whig President—we have been defeated in two attempts to create a fiscal agent. . . . The first consequence is that those who brought the President into power can no longer, in any manner or degree, justly be held responsible or blamed for the administration of the executive branch of the government." [31] Caleb Cushing provided the Democratic answer to this in a letter to his constituents: "A caucus dictatorship has been set up in Congress, which, not satisfied with ruling that body to the extinguishment of individual freedom of opinion, seeks to control the President in his proper sphere of duty, denouncing him before you for refusing to surrender his independence and his conscience to its decree, and purposes, through subversion of the fundamental provisions and principles of the Constitution, to usurp the command of the government. It is a question therefore, in fact, not of legislative measures but of revolution." [32]

President Tyler's veto of a tariff measure a year later induced the first move in our history toward the

---

[30] *Cong. Globe,* 27th Cong., 1st Session, app., pp. 366-68.
[31] T. H. Benton, *op. cit.,* II, pp. 357, 359.
[32] *Ibid.,* II, p. 359.

impeachment of a President of the United States. Representative John Minor Botts introduced the impeachment resolution charging the President "with the high crime and misdemeanor of withholding his assent to laws indispensable to the just operation of the government, which involved no constitutional difficulty on his part, of depriving the government of all legal sources of revenue, and of assuming to himself the whole power of taxation, and of collecting duties of the people without the authority or sanction of law." [33]

On the motion of John Quincy Adams a select committee of thirteen was appointed which drew up a report formulated by Adams and arraigning Tyler for strangling legislation through the misuse of the veto power.[34] In reply the President sent to the House a vigorous protest [35] which that body, following the precedent set by the Senate in the case of Jackson's protest, treated as a breach of privilege and refused to receive on the ground that the House has the constitutional right of impeachment.[36]

To the present generation the Whig movement to impeach a President for the exercise of the veto power must seem absurd. So popular has the exercise of this power become that its employment rarely fails to elicit popular applause. This generation has to be reminded that a century ago it had not yet become generally accepted that the President possessed the right to pass independent judgment as to the wisdom of a piece of legislation. He might resort to the veto to protect his office against encroachments or he might refuse his signature to a measure he

33 *Cong. Globe,* Jan. 10, 1843.
34 J. Q. Adams, *op. cit.,* XI, p. 238.
35 Richardson, *op. cit.,* IV, p. 190.
36 J. Q. Adams, *op. cit.,* XI, pp. 245-46.

considered unconstitutional but many believed that only Congress should determine the legislative policies of the government.

The simple fact is that the veto power of the President was irreconcilable with the Whig theory of executive subordination to Congress. This along with the current exigencies of politics, impelled Clay to propose an amendment to the Constitution whereby Congress could overcome a veto by a mere majority. In a strong speech he pointed out that in legislative strength the President was equal to almost two-thirds of Congress, and "in practice this power drew after it that of initiating laws, and would ultimately amount to conferring the entire legislative power of the Government upon the Executive. The President must ultimately become the ruler of the Nation." Clay's argument against the aggrandizement of the Executive was squarely met by one of the exponents of the Jacksonian system. Said Senator W. C. Preston of South Carolina, "In truth there was but one department of the Government that was truly democratic and that was the Executive. . . . He [the President] was the only officer that came on the broad basis of the whole Union, and was therefore the proper exponent of the popular will. . . . The Executive was elected by the people of the United States." [37] Judge Levi Woodbury, who had been a Cabinet member under Jackson and Van Buren, epitomized the Democratic doctrine in a speech delivered in Faneuil Hall when he said, "It [the veto power] is the people's tribunative voice speaking again through their Executive." [38] Nothing came of the movement to impeach and Tyler gave no thought to resigning, and the movement for a constitutional amendment of the

[37] *Cong. Globe*, 27th Cong., 2nd Session, p. 167.
[38] Levi Woodbury, *Writings*, I, p. 571.

veto met only public indifference. The stubborn courage with which President Tyler had countered the Whig efforts to curb him had prevented a backset in the evolution of the presidential office and prepared the way for the completion of the movement toward executive leadership started by Andrew Jackson.

Party organization had now matured into a system that has not changed fundamentally to this day. It was possible then in 1844 for the party system itself to produce a relatively unknown candidate. In that year the Democratic convention nominated the first "dark horse" in American party history. It is significant that when the telegraph bore from Baltimore to Washington the first message ever conveyed by wire —the news that Polk had been nominated—Democrats went about the Capital City shouting "Hurrah for Polk" and only pausing now and then to inquire, "Who the hell's Polk?"

It was perhaps due to the bias given to the interpretation of American history by Whig and by abolitionist historians that the successor to John Tyler was long misunderstood as much as Tyler himself.[39] James K. Polk gave in his inaugural address perhaps the earliest official acknowledgment in a state paper of the importance of party government. "Although in our country," he said, "the Chief Magistrate must almost of necessity be chosen by a party and stand pledged to its principles and measures, yet, in his official action, he should not be the President of a party only but of the whole people of the United States." [40] If Tyler saved the presidency from suffering a backset, Polk carried it deliberately forward to a

[39] See J. F. Rhodes, "The Presidential Office," *Scribner's Magazine*, Feb., 1903.
[40] Richardson, *op. cit.,* IV, p. 382.

more firmly established place in our constitutional system. He possessed a resolute determination reflected in a letter written ten weeks before his inauguration. After expressing a desire for a harmonious set of Cabinet counselors he wrote that "in any event I intend to be *myself* President of the United States." [41] Gideon Wells, whose private opinion of the new President was a poor one, was compelled to admit that "several of them [Cabinet members] have been at particular pains to tell me that the President has his own way . . . does as he has a mind to." [42] History has confirmed the testimony of the Cabinet members. Soon after Polk's inauguration Judge Catron wrote to Jackson, "Our friend is very prudent and *eminently* firm, regardless of consequences. He came here to be . . . The President . . . which at this date is as undisputed as that you was THE GENL at N. Orleans." [43] Even Jackson was soon to discover that, despite his own prestige, Polk could not be dominated by him.

Perhaps the most remarkable testimony as to Polk's capacity as an executive fell half a century later from the lips of the last surviving member of his Cabinet, the eminent historian, George Bancroft. In 1887 Mr. Bancroft said that on the day of his inauguration Mr. Polk had told him that he had four definite objectives: the reduction of the tariff, the re-establishment of the independent treasury, the settlement of the Oregon boundary, and the acquisition of California.[44] It is a matter of history that in all four of

[41] Polk to Cave Johnson, quoted by E. I. McCormac, *James K. Polk, a Political Biography*, p. 287.

[42] Welles to Van Buren, Apr. 29, 1845, quoted by McCormac, *op. cit.*, p. 324.

[43] Jackson Papers, quoted, E. I. McCormac, *op. cit.*, pp. 321, 322.

[44] George Bancroft, "James K. Polk," Appleton's *Cyclopedia of American Biography*, V, p. 55.

these he took the initiative before Congress assembled in its first session and carried out the first three of them in co-operation with Congress before the end of the session. The fourth was accomplished before the end of his term. Here is perhaps the finest example of the functioning of the Jacksonian type of Chief Executive. "His administration," wrote Bancroft, "viewed from the standpoint of results, was perhaps the greatest in our national history, certainly one of the greatest. He succeeded because he insisted on being its center and in overruling and guiding all his secretaries to act so as to produce unity and harmony." [45] As the historian James Schouler aptly put it, "What Polk went for he fetched."

Polk's fourth objective, the acquisition of California, was attained as a result of the Mexican War. Ever since the annexation of Texas in 1845 provocation by the Mexican government had been accumulating. Perhaps no powerful nation was ever more patient with a weaker one than was the United States with Mexico. It was characteristic of Polk to act with decisiveness in moving American troops on what he believed to be American soil, whereupon the clash with Mexican forces occurred and war began. The President's initiative left Congress no choice but to accept a *fait accompli* by declaring that a state of war existed.

Let no one assume that Polk's achievements were due to a complaisant Congress. A militant Whig minority was present in both houses during the first half of his administration and during the latter half the lower house had a belligerent Whig majority. In no case could a Whig House remain silent in the presence of such a remarkable demonstration of the strong executive as Polk presented but the issues of

45 Letter to J. G. Wilson, Mar. 8, 1888, quoted in J. G. Wilson, *The Presidents*, II, p. 230.

the Mexican War and the related slavery controversy induced that party to conduct a persistent guerrilla warfare against the President. This impelled Polk to incorporate in his last annual message to Congress a vigorous assertion of his executive functions. His Cabinet doubted the propriety of such matter in a message delivered under the constitutional injunction to inform Congress concerning the state of the Union. It might better be presented with some veto message.[46] The President decided, nevertheless, to deliver the Whigs another lecture on the nature of our constitutional system.

"Any attempt," declared the President, "to coerce the President to yield his sanction to measures which he cannot approve would be a violation of the spirit of the Constitution palpable and flagrant and if successful would break down the independence of the Executive department and make the President clothed by the Constitution with the power to defend their rights the mere instrument of a majority of Congress." After this thrust at Whig theory, he continued, "The people by the Constitution have commanded the President as much as they have commanded the legislative branch of the Government to execute their will. . . . If it be said that the Representatives in the popular branch of Congress are chosen directly by the people, it is answered, the people elect the President. . . . The President represents in the Executive department the whole people of the United States as each representative of the legislative department represents portions of them." [47]

Polk had been elected in 1844 with the slogans "The re-annexation of Texas and the re-occupation of Oregon" as far as "Fifty Four Forty or Fight." The

[46] J. K. Polk, *Diary*, IV, pp. 219, 220.
[47] Richardson, *op. cit.*, IV, pp. 663-65.

design of Democratic leaders was to satisfy the intense imperialistic urge of both southern and northern Democrats. When, however, by the treaty with England Polk settled for only half the Oregon claim Northern Democrats were indignant, particularly since the southern wing of the party got not only Texas but also the vast cessions of the Southwest through the Mexican War. Thus the Democratic party was so split and disorganized in 1848 that the Whigs nominated and elected General Zachary Taylor, a Mexican War hero.

In the campaign of 1848 the Whigs apparently had not deviated a hair's breadth from the dogma of presidential subserviency to Congress as proclaimed by them from the earliest days of the party. In his famous Allison letter Taylor declared that the Executive should return to a co-ordinate branch of the government, the veto power should be used to protect the Constitution and but sparingly for other purposes.[48] In that year Representative Abraham Lincoln, conforming to the policy of the Whig Congressional caucus was expounding it, both on the floor of the House[49] and on the stump. In a campaign speech delivered at Worcester, Massachusetts, September 12, he answered the charge that General Taylor had no political principles and, according to the Boston *Advertiser,* "maintained that General Taylor occupied a high and exceptional Whig ground, and took for his first instance and proof of this the statement in the Allison letter—with regard to the bank, tariff, rivers and harbors, etc.—that the will of the people should produce its own result without executive influence. This principle that the people should do what— under the Constitution—they pleased, is a Whig prin-

48 See the letter in *Niles Register,* July 8, 1848, p. 8.
49 *Cong. Globe,* July 27, 1848.

ciple. . . . It was the platform on which they had
fought all their battles, the resistance of executive influence and the principle of enabling the people to
frame the government according to their will." [50]
"Were I President," said Lincoln on the floor of the
House, "I should desire the legislation of the country
to rest with Congress, uninfluenced in its origin or
progress, and undisturbed by the veto unless in very
special and clear cases." [51] This was the Lincoln of
the 1840's not the 1860's.

President Taylor's inaugural address contained
the reassurance to Congress to be expected of a President nominated by the Whig party. "The Executive,"
said he, "has authority to recommend (not to dictate)
measures to Congress. Having performed that duty,
the Executive department of the Government cannot
rightfully control the decision of Congress on any
subject of legislation until that decision shall have
been officially submitted to the President for approval.
The check provided by the Constitution in the clause
conferring the qualified veto will never be exercised
by me except in the cases contemplated by the Fathers of the Republic. I view it as an extreme measure, to be resorted to only in extraordinary cases, as
when it may become necessary to defend the executive against encroachments of the legislative power
or to prevent hasty and inconsiderate or unconstitutional legislation" [52]

This self-denying declaration, honestly made, looks
a bit strange in the light of the history of Taylor's
short administration. He must have discovered that
it was impossible in 1850 to play a hands-off role
such as had been done by Madison and Monroe with

50 *Writings of Abraham Lincoln* (1905), pp. 115-16.
51 *Complete Works,* I, p. 134.
52 Richardson, *op. cit.,* V, p. 23.

respect to Congress. Inasmuch as no President after Jackson had pursued such a policy it had become all but impossible for any occupant of the presidential office to do so by 1849. Both Clay and Webster, the outstanding leaders in Congress, are on record as having expressed little less than contempt for the new President, and the group of southern Whigs who engineered Taylor's nomination broke with him as soon as they discovered his independence of judgment, so he fell under the influence of Senator William H. Seward [53] with the result that he became what might be called "a Southern man with Northern principles." He frankly informed southern congressional leaders that he would sign any bill he considered constitutional,[54] implying thereby the approval of the application of the Wilmot Proviso[55] to states to be admitted. When they threatened dissolution of the Union, the President is alleged to have told them he would take the field in person and hang those taken in rebellion "with as little mercy as he had hanged deserters and spies in Mexico." [56] It was becoming clear that the Whigs had elected in Taylor a President endowed with even less than John Tyler of the meekness demanded of a Whig Chief Executive. So profoundly had Jackson affected the presidency that not even a Whig president could now satisfy the party dogmas.

[53] See Thornton Kirtland Lathrop, *William Henry Seward*, p. 76; letter, Webster to Blatchford, in G. T. Curtis, *Daniel Webster*, II, p. 357; see letter of Seward to *National Intelligencer* in *Works of William H. Seward* (1853), III, pp. 443-44.

[54] Letter of Robert Toombs to J. J. Crittenden, quoted in Rhodes, *United States from the Compromise of 1850*, II, p. 134n.

[55] The Wilmot Proviso was a rider attached to an appropriation bill in the early months of the Mexican War. It stipulated that the appropriation was made on condition that slavery be excluded from any territory that might be acquired from Mexico. Its introduction precipitated the violent discussion of the slavery issue that culminated in the Civil War fifteen years later.

[56] Thurlow Weed, *Life of Thurlow Weed*, p. 117.

The Wilmot Proviso merely forecast the crisis precipitated by the post-war annexation of the vast acquisitions from Mexico. Senator Clay attempted to weave several controversial issues into an integrated pattern that would provide a balance of gains and losses between the slavery and antislavery interests. In the course of committee consideration this became the Compromise of 1850. California was to be admitted as a free state but the remainder of the acquisition from Mexico was to be organized as territories without applying the Wilmot Proviso; Texas was to receive $10,000,000 for accepting a certain western boundary line; and the slave trade was to be abolished in the District of Columbia but an extraordinarily severe fugitive slave law was to be enacted.

The chief political significance of the presidential career of Zachary Taylor is his consistent and unyielding opposition to the Compromise of 1850. Clay described the President's opposition to it as "war, open war, undisguised war . . . by the administration and its partisans against the plan of the Committee" [57] which framed the compromise. As a consequence the death of President Taylor in the midst of the debates on the compromise question takes on the character of a major political event. Fillmore had previously told Taylor that in case of a tie vote on the compromise in the Senate, he as presiding officer, would cast the deciding vote in its favor.[58] His accession to the presidency then effected an about-face in the attitude of the Executive toward the most important pending legislation. President Fillmore's message of August 6 turned the tide for the compromise by urging strongly the indemnifying of Texas for her flimsy boundary claim against New Mexico and by pleading urgently

[57] *Cong. Globe,* Speech of Clay in Senate, July 3.
[58] J. G. Wilson, *op. cit.,* II, p. 156.

for the settlement of the other questions connected
with the subject.[59] This led to the introduction of a
bill to pay Texas ten million dollars for her doubtful
claim, as a consequence of which Texas state securities appreciated nine hundred per cent and a powerful lobby consequently brought to bear the most
intense pressure on Congress.[60] That Fillmore's decisive message carried the anticompromise men
from confidence to despair is testified to in an unhappy
letter of Senator Salmon P. Chase. "The Texas Surrender Bill was passed by the influence of the new
administration which is Hunker and Compromise all
over. The message of Fillmore asserting the right
and declaring his purpose to support it and then
begging Congress of the necessity of doing so by a
Compromise—that message did the work. The message
gave the votes of Winthrop of Mass., Clark and Green
of R.I., Smith of Conn. and Phelps of Vermont to the
Bill." The effect on the lower house was no less
marked.[61] "Here," wrote Representative Horace Mann,
"were twenty, perhaps thirty men from the North in
the House, who before General Taylor's death would
have sworn, like St. Paul not to eat or drink until
they had voted the proviso [in effect the Wilmot],
who now, in the face of the world, turn about, defy
the instruction of their States, take back their declarations, a thousand times uttered, and vote against
it." [62] Such was the demonstrated influence of the
President on Congress in 1850.

Four successive, resolute men in the presidency—
Tyler, Polk, Taylor, and Fillmore—had given to the
development of that office a trend so positive that it

[59] Richardson, *op. cit.*, V, pp. 67-73.

[60] Beard and Beard, *op. cit.*, I, pp. 598, 599.

[61] *Annual Report of American Historical Association*, 1902, II,
p. 217.

[62] Letter of Sept. 6, 1850. Mrs. Mary Mann, *Life of Horace
Mann* (1865), p. 322.

could not be greatly deflected even by the next two less resolute incumbents, Pierce and Buchanan. Both of these were known as "dough faces," Northern men with Southern principles, whom the slavocracy had manipulated into the presidency in order to protect their "peculiar institution." Of these two, though not of any one of the preceding four, it can be said that they were overshadowed by their Cabinets. Pierce is reputed to have put to a vote of his Cabinet the policies of the administration and to have abided by the vote of the majority.[63] The resignation of the Southern members of Buchanan's Cabinet in mid-term meant an about-face in the general direction of the policies of his administration.

Both Pierce and Buchanan were eager to dismiss the slavery issue. Pierce in his first message to Congress joined in the chorus of those who proclaimed the final settlement of that troublesome question by the Compromise of 1850.[64] Yet before he had been in office a year he had agreed to make the Kansas-Nebraska Bill an administration measure. This Act repealed the Missouri Compromise line with its limit of 36° 30' as the northern boundary of slavery, thereby allowing new territories and states to determine for themselves whether or not to legalize slavery within them. Douglas, though not an administration Senator, had extracted from Pierce not only his approval but even the phrasing of the amendment repealing the Missouri Compromise in Pierce's own handwriting.[65] Thus on the bill the President had been forced into a position in which he felt impelled to employ patronage to insure passage because he believed defeat would damage the prestige of his

[63] Caleb Perry Patterson, *American Government*, p. 270.

[64] Richardson, *op. cit.*, V. p. 222.

[65] Correspondent of the *Missouri Republican* in that periodical, April 10, 1854. Quoted in P. O. Ray, *The Repeal of the Missouri Compromise*, p. 214.

administration.[66] The repeal of the Missouri Compromise, to Pierce's astonishment, proved furiously provocative and the result was the creation, within six months of the enactment of the Kansas-Nebraska Act, of a new political group, the Anti-Nebraska Men, who captured the lower house and signalized the revival of the slavery controversy with the most violent animosity yet aroused. Even the ineptitude of the President revealed the enormous significance of the presidency.

Just as anxious as Pierce to allay the sectional strife but taking warning from Pierce's unhappy experience with legislation, Buchanan announced in his inaugural address a new formula for the solution of the problem—a forthcoming opinion of the Supreme Court—to which, while pretending an innocence as to its nature, he pledged that he would, "in common with all good citizens . . . cheerfully submit." [67] This was a strange abdication of executive claims by a member of the party of Jackson who, a score of years earlier, had emphatically denied the right of the judiciary thus to determine public policies through the medium of court opinions. In any case Buchanan's hope of domestic concord by such means was a vain one. In what many regarded as *obiter dictum* Chief Justice Taney, speaking for the Court in the Dred Scott case, held that the Missouri Compromise, in forbidding slavery north of 36° 30′, had violated the due process clause of the Fifth Amendment by discriminating against one species of property, slaves. Whatever the merits of the reasoning, this foray of the Supreme Court into the realm of current politics, far from allaying the strife, provoked sectional discord beyond all precedent and the prestige of the Court barely escaped irreparable damage.

66 Roy F. Nichols, *Franklin Pierce*, p. 337.
67 Richardson, *op. cit.*, V, p. 431.

The Anti-Nebraska Men soon became the new Republican party, dedicated to preventing the spread of slavery into the territories in order that they might remain suitable for free state settlers. It failed to elect John C. Frémont in 1856, but four years later nominated Abraham Lincoln who won a good majority in the Electoral College that fall. His popular vote was so concentrated in populous Northern states that he would not have been defeated even if all the popular vote of his three opponents, Douglas, Breckenridge, and Bell had been cast for one candidate. However, this sectional concentration of Lincoln's vote, together with the capture of the presidency by a party unequivocally committed to resist the spread of slavery into the territories started the secession of the Southern states. During the three months between Lincoln's election and inauguration President Buchanan sought to maintain the status quo. Meanwhile the public waited with anxiety to see what the new President would do.

However irresolute, inept, or unlucky the incumbent of the office of President might now be, so weighted with significance in the popular mind had the presidency of the United States become by 1860 that it bore only slight resemblance to the office forty years before when James Monroe had been almost unanimously re-elected in the midst of a devastating depression and with the controversy raging over the then-pending Missouri Compromise not at all affecting the President's re-election. No more striking demonstration of the extraordinary importance attached to the office could be imagined than the fact that the secession of South Carolina was determined upon the certainty of the election of Lincoln, the first President utterly unsatisfactory to the slavocracy.

VI

President Lincoln
and Congress

*

PRESIDENT LINCOLN's problem from the day of his inauguration, March 4, 1861, was that of holding intact the heterogeneous group combination constituting the Republican party which had elected him in 1860 with not quite forty percent of the total popular vote. No matter how widely the constituent elements of the Republican party may have differed on other matters there was one and only one issue on which every Republican agreed—keep slavery out of the territories. Let Lincoln once give up this issue and the party would disintegrate, virtually explode and leave him a Chief Executive without a party and consequently as devoid of the indispensable prestige and power of a President as Tyler had been before him and as Johnson was to be following him. No wonder Lincoln resolutely rejected every proposal to restore the repealed Missouri Compromise which would have rededicated part of the territories to slavery.

Lincoln's only previous experience in national affairs had been an unhappy one. In Congress for a single term in the late forties he had chosen to co-operate wholeheartedly with the Whig congressional caucus in its strategy of harrassing President Polk on his Mexican War policy. But meanwhile Lincoln's constituency back home was wildy pro war. When Lincoln returned home at the close of his term in Congress he was chastened by the coolness of former friends—he was even denounced as a Benedict Arnold. He had defied the sovereign, the People, in a region where that sovereign reigned supreme. "But not again," as his biographer Beveridge[1] put it, "did he fail to express dominant popular thought and feeling. He neither led nor retarded mass movements but accurately registered them. In short Lincoln was the spokesman of the people." At the moment of Lincoln's inauguration there was a veritable confusion of tongues so far as a consensus was concerned. So Lincoln had to wait until the "Sovereign," that is to say the people who remained faithful to the Union, had made up its mind. Surely no one could have guessed that in this harrassing critic of the war policy of President Polk there lurked even the possibility of a war President who was to deal with both Congress and the Constitution at times in a manner more imperious than any President before or since.

Such executive conduct was bound sooner or later to arouse the resentment of the party that had elected Lincoln. The Republican minority in Congress be-

---

[1] A. J. Beveridge, *Abraham Lincoln,* II, p. 143. Because of his attitude toward the Mexican War he had been described as a "second Benedict Arnold," and was accused of having pleaded the cause of the enemy. *Ibid.,* I, p. 432.

came a majority only upon the withdrawal of the Southern representatives as a result of the secession movement. This Republican majority contained within its ranks many old Whig leaders of the North—men who no doubt had been deeply moved in their early and impressionable years by the "usurpations" of Andrew Jackson and the philippics of Clay and Webster against King Andrew the First. This element in the Republican party inevitably cherished the Whig tradition of jealously guarding legislative prerogative against executive invasion. Thus from its very beginning the Republican party was only a little less critical of strong Republican than of strong Democratic Executives. The genius of the party seems somehow to express itself most happily through Congress even to the present day.

No sooner had South Carolinians ascertained that Lincoln would have a majority in the Electoral College than the government of that state set in motion the machinery formally to declare its secession. By March 4, 1861, when Lincoln was inaugurated, South Carolina had been joined by Mississippi, Florida, Alabama, Georgia, Louisiana, and Texas in forming the Confederate States of America. Of all this President Lincoln took no official cognizance. Not until Lincoln's determination to defend property of the United States by re-enforcing the Federal troops at Fort Sumter had induced Confederate forces to bombard the fort and compel the capitulation of its garrison, did Lincoln prepare to enforce Federal authority by force of arms wherever it might be necessary.

The day Fort Sumter was bombarded and the garrison forced to capitulate, public opinion in the loyal states instantly responded with a dynamic consensus that gave Lincoln the mandate to enforce the supreme law of the land throughout the nation.

Thus the period of executive groping suddenly ended and was followed promptly by executive action so extraordinary as to challenge thus early in Lincoln's administration the Whig-Republican theory of the dominant place of Congress in the government. Congress, of course, was not in session. The available military forces were utterly inadequate for the vast emergency. Under long-standing authority granted the President by Congress in the administrations of Washington and Jefferson, Lincoln issued a call for 75,000 militia in order to suppress combinations too powerful to be suppressed by the ordinary course of judicial proceedings and by the United States marshals "and cause the laws to be duly executed." But no sooner had Lincoln exhausted his constitutional and statutory authority than he proceeded to exceed it. For example, by a proclamation of May 3, 1861, he ordered the regular army increased by 22,714 officers and men and the navy by 18,000 and called for 42,034 volunteers for three years.[2] This was such a palpable disregard of the clearly expressed constitutional delegation of power to Congress "to raise and support armies"[3] that it evoked, even from the temperate and loyal Republican, Senator John Sherman, the statement, "I have never met anyone who claimed that the President could, by proclamation, increase the regular army."[4]

Lincoln's conduct in this emergency has of course brought forth defenders. Notable among these was the late John W. Burgess, who based his defense on the "spirit of the Constitution," a magic principle under which the fundamental instrument can be given a more remarkable elasticity than John Marshall ever

2 Richardson, *op. cit.*, VI, pp. 15-16, 18, 19.
3 Art. I, Sec. 8, Clause 12.
4 Letter to Cincinnati *Gazette*, quoted by Randall, *Constitutional Problems Under Lincoln*, p. 38.

discovered. "It is certainly good political science," Burgess reasoned, "to acknowledge such powers in him (the President) and very bad political science not to do so. . . . The Constitution which permits the Executive under no exigencies, to call the people to his aid in upholding the government is an unscientific and impractical instrument of public law, and one which invites, and even requires, infractions in the most critical moments of a nation's existence." [5] In respect to this defense the question can be raised: Why was it necessary for Lincoln to act in disregard of law and Constitution? Why could not Congress have convened within the interval of almost three weeks between the firing on Fort Sumter and the issuing of the proclamation increasing the army? It had no doubt been prudent on the part of the President not to call Congress into session during the six weeks between inauguration and the bombardment of Sumter because they would have but added to the prevailing confusion of public opinion.

The unhappy experience of some Presidents with special sessions of Congress had led to a conviction then that calling such a session at the very beginning of an administration was in the nature of a disaster—threatening a breakdown of the administration. The month of May for a special session had come to be regarded as "a symbol of political misfortune." [6] Lincoln delayed calling Congress and then wisely set the date at July 4, six weeks after the fall of Sumter.[7] For several weeks federal troop movements to Washington were prevented so that Washington was isolated and the city no safe place for Congress.[8] There was then

5 *The Civil War and the Constitution*, I, p. 228.

6 Carl Swisher, *American Constitutional Development*, pp. 275-76.

7 Richardson, *op. cit.*, VI, pp. 14, 15.

8 See Allan Nevins *The War For the Union*, Vol. I, p. 91.

no telegraph line to the Pacific and getting the message to California and Oregon and allowing time for Senators and Representatives to make the slow journey to Washington made an earlier meeting impossible.

In his message to Congress in special session when it convened on July 4 the President invited them to grant him retroactive authority for what he had done. "These measures," said he, "whether strictly legal or not, were ventured upon under what appeared to be a popular demand and a public necessity, trusting then as now, that Congress would readily ratify them. It is believed that nothing has been done *beyond the constitutional competence of Congress.*" [9] Such engaging frankness must have proved quite disarming for on August 6, 1861, Congress passed an act providing "that all the acts, proclamations, and orders of the President respecting the army and navy of the United States, and calling out or relating to the militia or volunteers from the United States are hereby approved and in all respects made valid . . . as if they had been issued and done under the previous express authority and direction of the Congress of the United States." [10] Congress, however, appears to have been caught here under the practical necessity of ratifying the executive acts in order to save its own claim of authority. It would have availed nothing to have refused to accept accomplished facts. It could not have been expected, however, that Congress would enact this legislation without misgivings. We have competent testimony to "a certain hesitation which robbed it of the grace of spontaneous generosity and revealed even at this early day, germs of faction among the supporters of the administration." [11]

[9] Richardson, *op. cit.,* p. 24. Italics the author's.
[10] *Statutes at Large,* XII, p. 326.
[11] Nicolay and Hay, *Abraham Lincoln: A History,* IV, p. 382.

Lincoln's trepassing on the congressional sphere was not confined to the opening weeks of the war but continued throughout. Some of these invasions will be mentioned in other connections later. At this point can be noted some isolated cases of a type that were so persistent as to amount almost to a habit. The Constitution distinctly assigns to Congress the duty "to make rules for the government and regulation of the land and naval forces." [12] In disregard of this President Lincoln in 1863 issued a general order embodying the rules applicable to the federal armies in the field.[13] They consisted of an elaborate code of laws and constituted perhaps the largest case of executive legislation in American history. Can it be maintained that such a power inheres in the office of Commander in Chief when the Constitution specifically lodges it elsewhere?

The Constitution requires that "no money shall be drawn from the treasury but in consequence of appropriations made by law." [14] But because Lincoln distrusted certain governmental officials, he directed the Secretary of the Treasury to advance, without security, two million dollars of public money to three private citizens, John A. Dix, George Opdyke, and Richard H. Blatchford, for the purpose of paying for certain military and naval measures deemed necessary for the defense and support of the government. It is interesting to note in this connection that when Andrew Jackson had his way about the withdrawal of federal deposits from the Bank of the United States, he merely had his Secretary of the Treasury exercise a power assigned him by statute. Lincoln, on the other hand, directed the Secretary of the Treasury to perform an

12 Art. I, Sec. 8, Clause 14.
13 See Randall, *Constitutional Problems,* p. 38.
14 Art. I, Sec. 9, Clause 7.

act in direct violation of an unquestionable constitutional prohibition. In reporting the matter to Congress the President offered them the comforting assurance, "I am not aware that a dollar of the public funds thus confided without authority of law to unofficial persons was either lost or wasted." [15] No one questions the purity of Lincoln's motives in this episode, but its effect must have been to goad the older Republicans to incipient revolt as they no doubt recalled Jackson's highhanded but far less irregular methods in dealing with the treasury.

Such serene disregard of the constitutional powers of Congress could not possibly have gone on indefinitely without challenge. Sooner or later the countermove of Congress would come. Many of its members had grown up in the belief that Congress was the motor of the government even in its operation of the military arm. The first notable step in this direction was taken on December 20, 1861, when Congress appointed a Joint Committee on the Conduct of the War consisting of three senators and four representatives.[16] Congress was encouraged in this move by the public impatience at the slowness with which military operations against the Confederacy were proceeding. The dominant members of this famous committee were Radical Republicans who had little if any respect for Lincoln.[17] They constantly urged a more vigorous prosecution of the war and less leniency toward the institution of slavery. Designed ostensibly to aid Congress in performance of its constitutional functions, so far did the committee depart from its legitimate purpose that it became a veritable thorn in the

[15] Richardson, *op. cit.* VI, 79; Nicolay and Hay, *op. cit.*, pp. 189, 194.

[16] *Report of the Joint Committee on the Conduct of the War* (1865), p. 111.

[17] G. W. Julian, *Political Recollections*, p. 201.

flesh of the President. The members took over partial control of military operations.[18] Their investigating missions to the front undermined army discipline and discouraged the more capable commanders. Such poor judges of military competence were these deputies on mission that their favorites were Frémont, Butler, and Hooker,[19] three of the most conspicuously questionable commanders in the military service. Their first signal accomplishment was the forced resignation of Secretary of War Cameron. Then the President somehow felt impelled to permit them to dictate the appointment of the successor in that office and Edwin M. Stanton was their choice. He behaved accordingly as a creature of the committee.[20] Interrogating generals as if they were schoolboys and advising the President like military experts, the Committee sought to intimidate Lincoln by threatening to arouse Congress against him.[21]

Secession and the outbreak of the Civil War had the peculiar effect of depriving the Republican party of its original *raison d'être,* that is, resistance to the spread of slavery. Fort Sumter shattered the party alignments of 1860 and started new ones. The preservation of the Union provided the motivation and ideological nucleus of a new political aggregation. As early as September, 1861, the Republicans, as a consequence of a fusion with some war Democrats, were adopting the designation of Union party in support of the Lincoln administration. Republican, as a party designation, disappeared from contemporary newspapers and other periodicals during the war except as Democrats insisted on tarring their opponents with

18 G. W. Dimock, *Congressional Investigating Committees*, p. 112.

19 Morison, *op. cit.*, II, p. 205.

20 Nicolay and Hay, *op. cit.*, V, p. 150.

21 N. W. Stephenson, *Lincoln*, p. 205; G. W. Julian, *op. cit.*, p. 205.

the epithet "Black Republicans." Two wings of the Union party soon appeared, the Conservatives who stood firmly behind Lincoln and his moderate policies, and the Radicals, mainly abolitionists, who criticised the President for not prosecuting the war with greater vigor.[22]

As might have been expected, there began to emerge from the congressional debates, from the lips of the Radical senators and representatives the old Whig doctrine of congressional supremacy. The war was scarcely a year old when Lincoln was confronted with the bold question as to where the Constitution had placed the powers of sovereignty, particularly with respect to war. At no time would Lincoln admit that Congress possessed plenary powers in this field. But Senator Charles Sumner, in the Whig tradition emphatically asserting the congressional dogma, declared, "I claim for Congress all that belongs to any government in the exercise of the right of war," and he treated with withering contempt any contrary view. Continuing, he said, "The Government of the United States appears most clearly in an act of Congress. . . . it is by an act of Congress that the War powers are set in motion. When once in motion the President must execute them. But *he is only the instrument of Congress under the Constitution of the United States*." [23] Senator Henry Wilson thought "the policy of the Administration will be shaped by the action of the two houses of Congress, and, in my judgment, it is the duty as the representatives of the States and the people, to indicate to those who administer the laws of the country what we think the policy of the government should be. I had rather give a policy to the President of the United States than to take a

[22] On the Union party see W. E. Binkley, *op. cit.,* Chapter X.
[23] *Cong. Globe,* XXXVII, 2, p. 2972. Italics mine.

policy from the President of the United States." [24]
Senator Lyman Trumbull insisted that since the President can only execute the laws of Congress in the manner prescribed by Congress, *"He is just as much subject to our control as if we appointed him,* except that we cannot remove him and appoint another in his place." [25] Earlier in the same session Thaddeus Stevens in the lower house, having quoted the elastic clause and applied it to the congressional power to suppress insurrection, concluded that "we [Congress] possess all the powers now claimed under the Constitution even the tremendous power of dictatorship." [26]

To these bold and extravagant assertions of the doctrine of congressional supremacy Lincoln offered no direct reply. It is probable, however, that in a speech of Senator O. H. Browning, Lincoln's intimate personal friend and at that time his spokesman in the Senate,[27] is to be found Lincoln's own view of this controversy. Admitting that the "powers of the Government are unquestionably enlarged by a state of war," he propounded the question: "But is Congress the Government? . . . I think not. . . . All the powers that Congress possess are those granted in the Constitution." At this point he was taking issue with Senator William Pitt Fessenden, who had declared that "There is no limit on the power of Congress; but it is invested with the absolute power of war." "There," declared Browning, referring to Fessenden's dictum, "is as broad and deep a foundation for absolute despotism as was ever laid." The President, if he abuses the war powers, "when peace returns, is answerable to the civil power for abuse. If Congress

24 *Ibid.*, 2, p. 2734.
25 *Ibid.*, 2, p. 2973. Italics mine.
26 *Ibid.*, 2, p. 440.
27 N. W. Stephenson, *op. cit.*, p. 217.

usurps and prostitutes them the liberty of the citizen is overthrown, and he is helpless without remedy for his grievances." Citing decisions of the Supreme Court,[28] the senator showed how the judiciary had pointed out that Congress could apply the proper remedy if a President abused his power. But if Congress were to usurp war powers "there is absolutely no remedy to be found anywhere." [29] Not long afterwards Browning declared "when the Constitution made the President commander in chief of the army and navy of the United States it clothed him with the incidental powers necessary to a full, faithful, and forceful performance of the duties of that high office; and to decide what are military necessities and to devise and to execute the requisite measures to meet them, is one of these incidents. It is not legislative, but an executive function and Congress had nothing to do with it." [30] That Browning reflected Lincoln's view became increasingly apparent as the war progressed.

At this particular stage of the conflict between Congress and the Executive the grand strategy of politics was introduced by the President to determine whether he was to rule or be ruled by Congress. He made his moves with the consummate skill of a master political craftsman. Gone were the lethargy and indecision that cramped his earlier movements. It was no longer a question of constitutional assignments of power but a matter of maneuvering to preserve the prestige and prerogatives of the executive office which he considered not only constitutionally his but highly essential for the prosecution of the war and the salva-

---

[28] Luther *vs*. Borden, 7 *Howard,* pp. 43-46; Martin *vs*. Mott, 12 *Wheaton,* pp. 209-31.

[29] *Cong. Globe,* XXXVII, 2, p. 1136.

[30] *Cong. Globe,* XXXVII, 2, p. 2922.

tion of the Union. Already he had appointed military governors in the territory occupied by the army. Sumner had, by Senate resolution, attempted to compel him to revoke this action and was reasserting, meanwhile, his doctrine of the supremacy of Congress.[31]

It so happened that these Radical exponents of congressional supremacy were also abolitionists. They were eager, through congressional action, to accomplish their major objective of emancipation. Such a consummation through statutory enactment would go far toward demonstrating their claim of the plenary powers of Congress in war matters. Lincoln regarded such legislation as beyond the constitutional competence of Congress and the Radicals were gleefully making the most of the President's reputed tenderness toward slave holders.

In the closing hours of the first regular session of the Thirty-seventh Congress, boldly taking the initiative, President Lincoln submitted a message to Congress proposing compensated emancipation.[32] He fairly took their breath by the then unprecedented expedient of accompanying the message with the draft of a bill designed to carry out the proposal, which at once raised the question in the Senate of the President's right to introduce a bill.[33] In this same week the President astonished Congress with the most audacious move yet made in his dealings with it. The second confiscation bill was under consideration.[34] Certain

31 *Ibid.*, 2, p. 2596.
32 Richardson, *op. cit.*, VI, p. 84.
33 *Cong. Globe*, XXVII, 2, p. 3223.
34 The bill provided, among other things, that the President seize the property of Confederate officeholders (*Statutes at Large*, XII, pp. 589-92). Lincoln's threatened veto was aimed at the extension of the penalty beyond the life of the offenders in violation of the constitutional prohibition against the punishment of treason extending to "forfeiture except during the life of the attainted" (Art. III, Sec. 3, Cl. 2).

features of it were, in the opinion of the President, of doubtful constitutionality. Lincoln prepared in advance a veto message and let the congressmen know it was ready for use if needed. This compelled them to remove the objectionable feature. The Radicals cried out that the President was coercing them. The opposition to the President reached the height of hysteria. "No one at a distance," wrote Julian long afterward, "could form any conception of the hostility of the Republican members to Lincoln at the time of final adjournment, while it was the belief of many that our last session of Congress had been held in Washington. Senator Wade said the country was going to hell, and that the scenes witnessed in the French Revolution were nothing in comparison with what we should see here." [35]

When the bill reached the President he played his master stroke against the Radicals. Along with the approval of the bill, revised as he desired it, he sent to Congress the veto message he would have used if the bill had not been amended.[36] Andrew Jackson had never done anything just quite so audacious as this. The rage of the Radicals and their wild predictions of coming despotism and a reign of terror were but manifestations of their deep disappointment because of the President's adroit thwarting of their plans to dominate him. The confident claimants of congressional supremacy found themselves confronted by an Executive from whom they could not wrest the leadership in the government.

The discomfiture of the Radicals was not yet complete. It remained for the President to give the final blow to the claims of congressional supremacy by the boldest stroke of executive policy of the war period.

[35] G. W. Julian, *op. cit.*, p. 220.
[36] Richardson, *op. cit.*, VI, pp. 85-87.

He issued the Emancipation Proclamation[37] after Congress had adjourned and consequently when the Radicals were at the greatest disadvantage in getting their complaints conveyed to the public. Indeed, protests against his move would have been difficult for them, for he was but moving to accomplish directly what they had criticized him for not proposing that Congress do through legislation. It is a mistake to consider the Emancipation Proclamation as merely a bid for liberal sympathy abroad and abolitionists support at home. Lincoln unquestionably was aware of the discomfiture this proclamation would produce in the ranks of the claimants of congressional supremacy. It was a perplexing stroke to the malcontents. Here they were granted the emancipation of the slaves for which they had clamored. They could not refuse it, but it had come about in the wrong way without Congress having had any part in it. Where were now the plenary war powers of Congress? The most strident critics had been silenced by an astounding stroke of executive power. So complete was their defeat that when, in the next session of Congress, the Democrats ineptly introduced a resolution condemning the proclamation,[38] even Thaddeus Stevens along with the other anti-Lincoln Radical Unionists had no choice but to vote against the measure and appear to be vindicating the President.

Two days after the Emancipation Proclamation the President issued another proclamation by means of which, under an act of Congress and by the stroke of his pen, he divested the whole American people of the privilege of the writ of habeas corpus and thus proclaimed himself virtually dictator. This proclamation declared that in addition to those engaged in

37 Richardson, *op. cit.*, VI, pp. 96-98.
38 *Cong. Globe*, XXXVII, 3, p. 76.

armed insurrection and their aiders and abettors "all persons discouraging enlistments, resisting militia drafts, or persons discouraging military drafts or guilty of any disloyal practice affording aid and comfort to the rebels against the authority of the United States shall be subject to martial law and liable to trial and punishment by court-martial or military commission; second that the writ of habeas corpus is suspended in respect to all persons arrested, or who are or hereafter during the rebellion shall be imprisoned in any fort, camp, arsenal, military prison, or other place of confinement by any military authority or by sentence of any court martial or military commission." [39] Abraham Lincoln in proclaiming here what Professor Dunning considered "a perfect platform for despotism" [40] had given his answer to Thaddeus Stevens and the Radicals who claimed for Congress itself the "power of dictatorship." [41]

It must not be assumed that the congressional opposition to Lincoln had been crushed. After the disastrous Union defeat at Fredericksburg a caucus of Radical senators concluded that Secretary of State W. H. Seward was the evil genius of the administration. They accordingly sent a committee of seven Radicals to the President to demand that his Cabinet be reorganized.[42] It looked for the moment as if the President might have to relinquish the constitutional privilege of determining his own counselors as the price of congressional cooperation and the successful prosecution of the war. Lincoln courteously requested the committee to return at an appointed time for another conference. When Seward heard of the demand

[39] Richardson, *op. cit.*, VI, pp. 98, 99.
[40] "The Constitution of United States in Civil War," *Political Science Quarterly*, I, p. 188.
[41] See N. W. Stephenson, *op. cit.*, p. 280.
[42] O. H. Browning, *Diary of Orville Hickman Browning*, p. 599.

of the committee, he sent Lincoln his resignation. Now if there was in Lincoln's Cabinet at this time a marplot it was not William H. Seward but Salmon P. Chase, who was a constant informer to the congressional Radicals of reports of dissension among the members of the Cabinet.[43] When in due time the committee of senators returned they unexpectedly found themselves compelled to resume the subject of Cabinet dissension in the presence of the entire Cabinet. Under the circumstances the distressed Chase felt impelled to eat his own words of talebearing to the senators and admit that there was no Cabinet discord. Furthermore, now thoroughly discredited before the President, the Cabinet and the senators, the humiliated Secretary of the Treasury reluctantly offered his resignation.[44] This was just what the President had been maneuvering for. With resignations of both Cabinet members in his pocket he chose to accept neither, for each had a large and valuable personal following whose support Lincoln could not spare. "This," said he, "cuts the Gordian knot." He had preserved the control of his own Cabinet, avoided loss of the support of the followers of the two Cabinet members and counteracted the encroachments of the senatorial group. The escape, however, was a narrow one. Senator Browning had informed Lincoln that the Radical strategy at this time was to surround him with a Cabinet of Radicals with Chase as premier. The President replied with a good deal of emphasis that he was master and that they should not do that.[45] It is the opinion of Samuel Eliot Morison that "in the Cabinet crisis of December, 1862, only Lincoln's

43 See Lincoln's summary of Chase's conduct in Nicolay and Hay, *op. cit.*, VIII, p. 317.
44 Welles, *Diary of Gideon Welles,* I, pp. 201-02.
45 O. H. Browning, *op. cit.*, p. 604.

astuteness saved him from becoming a mere Premier instead of a President." [46]

On no matter during the war was there a more clear-cut issue respecting the powers of the President and of Congress than on reconstruction. On December 8, 1863, the President issued a proclamation of amnesty and reconstruction. The latter part of this state paper contained the famous provision by which the President made the offer to the states that had passed ordinances of secession that, whenever a number of their voters "not less than one-tenth in number of the votes cast in such State at the presidential election of the year 1860 . . . shall reestablish a State government which shall be republican, and in no wise contravening said oath (previously prescribed) such shall be recognized as the true government of the State and the State shall receive thereunder the benefits of the constitutional provision which declares that the United States shall guarantee a Republican form of government, etc." [47] The proclamation specifically recognized the right of Congress to determine the admission of Senators and Representatives from such states to the two houses. Here was an executive act pushing the powers of the President to still another extreme—reconstruction without even a gesture in the direction of congressional authorization. The Radicals chose to regard the proclamation as a distinct challenge of the constitutional powers of Congress. Accordingly there was introduced early in the session of the Congress just convening what came to be known as the Wade-Davis bill.[48] It purposed, through statute, to make reconstruction difficult and deliberately sought to transfer matters of reconstruc-

[46] *Op. Cit.*, II, p. 254.
[47] Richardson, *op. cit.*, VI, pp. 213-15.
[48] *Cong. Globe*, XXXVIII, 1, pp. 2107.

tion from the President to Congress. Instead of the one-tenth of the voters required by the President's proclamation to effect reconstruction, the bill required a majority. Lincoln, ignoring the pending measure, proceeded with his own method of reconstruction. In 1864, encouraged somewhat no doubt by the decline of presidential prestige resulting from the terrible losses of troops in Grant's Wilderness Campaign, Congress refused to seat the senators and representatives elected from the presidentially reconstructed state of Arkansas. The session of Congress was by this time drawing to a close with the Wade-Davis bill pending in the Senate. Wade and Chandler were particularly determined that the President should not handle the matter of reconstruction in his own way. The measure reached the President on the last day of the session, and contained, among other things, a provision prohibiting slavery in the reconstructed states. It should be noted that the Emancipation Proclamation did not cover these states. In the presence of a group of Radical senators and to their utter astonishment, the President took the Wade-Davis bill which they had brought to him and, after merely glancing at it, casually laid it aside. To Senator Chandler's angry protest that Congress was merely attempting to do with slavery no more than the President had done by the Proclamation of Emancipation came Lincoln's prompt rejoinder, "I conceive that I may, in an emergency, do things on military ground which cannot constitutionally be done by Congress." [49] Thus spoke the Commander-in-Chief.

After the adjournment of Congress Lincoln gave the Wade-Davis bill a pocket veto and then issued a unique proclamation accompanied by the bill and an account of the circumstances under which it was

[49] Nicolay and Hay, *op. cit.,* IX, pp. 120-21.

passed. He submitted the Wade-Davis bill to the public for their consideration. He was not absolutely committed to any one particular plan of reconstruction.[50] The President's tactics were extremely baffling to the Radicals. Even when Congress was in session the President had a great advantage over Congress in addressing the public. Now that Congress was not in session their handicap in getting their case presented to the public was overwhelming. The President practically monopolized public attention. Nevertheless, the Radicals decided to accept the challenge of the Executive to the congressional claim of authority in the matter of reconstruction.

The answer came from the proponents of the above bill in the famous and sensational Wade-Davis Manifesto, the boldest attack made at any time upon Lincoln by responsible leaders of his party in Congress. Having no other means at the time of reaching the public, the authors of the manifesto published it in the newspapers. Addressed "to the Supporters of the Government" it opened thus: "We have read with surprise and not without indignation the proclamation of the President of July, 1864. The supporters of the administration are responsible to the country for its conduct, and it is their right and duty to check the encroachments of the Executive on the authority of Congress and to require it to confine itself to its proper sphere." The Whigs had never been more explicit in their statement, Congress is responsible to the country for the conduct of the Executive, as, for example, when the Whig Congressmen disavowed responsibility for President Tyler. Continuing, in regard to the President the manifesto declared that "he must understand that our support is of a cause and not of a man; that *the authority of Congress is paramount*

[50] Richardson, *op. cit.*, IV, pp. 222-26.

and must be respected; that the whole body of Union men in Congress will not submit to be impeached by him of rash and unconstitutional legislation; and if he wishes our support he must confine himself to his executive duties—*to obey and to execute* not to make the laws—to suppress by arms armed rebellion, and leave political reorganization to Congress." The manifesto closed with an appeal to the supporters of government to "consider the remedy of these usurpations and having found it fearlessly to execute it." [51] This manifesto represents probably the most authoritative statement possible of the Radical congressmen's conception of the proper relation of the Executive to the legislature held during the Civil War. It describes perfectly the theory on which the party functioned during Johnson's administration. The fundamental idea of it can be traced more or less through Republican party doctrine to the present day.

The rank and file of the Union men failed to rally to the call of these defenders of congressional authority. "The very strength of their paper was," wrote James G. Blaine, "by one of the paradoxes that frequently recur in public affairs, its special weakness. It was so powerful an arraignment of the President that, of necessity, it rallied his friends to his support with that intense form of energy which springs from the instinct of self-preservation." [52] Lincoln's proclamation and the manifesto served to make the presidential election of 1864 in a sense a plebiscite on the issue raised. The President was re-elected and Davis lost his seat in Congress, while Wade's senatorial term had not expired. As a consequence of this election there was no other serious challenge of Lincoln's exercise

[51] Quoted by Nicolay and Hay, *op. cit.*, IX, pp. 125-27. Italics mine.
[52] *Twenty Years in Congress*, II, p. 44.

of power on reconstruction or indeed on his broad interpretation of the scope of executive power.

Unquestionably the high-water mark of the exercise of executive power in the United States is found in the administration of Abraham Lincoln. No President before or since has pushed the boundaries of executive power so far over into the legislative sphere. No one can ever know just what Lincoln conceived to be limits of his powers. Even a partial review of them presents an imposing list of daring ventures. Under the war power he proclaimed the slaves of those in rebellion emancipated. He devised and put into execution his own peculiar plan of reconstruction. In disregard of law he increased the army and navy beyond the limits set by statute. The privilege of the writ of habeas corpus was suspended wholesale and martial law declared. Public money in the sum of millions was deliberately spent without congressional appropriation. Nor was any of this done innocently. Lincoln understood his Constitution. He knew, in many cases, just how he was transgressing and his infractions were consequently deliberate. It is all the more astonishing that this audacity was the work of a minority President who performed in the presence of a bitter congressional opposition even in his own party. Of course after the election of 1864 he probably considered that his reelection constituted a vindication of his record regardless of the question of the constitutionality of his practices.

Lincoln's nearest approach to an explanation of his disregard of the constitutional prescriptions is found in his well-known letter to A. G. Hodges of April 4, 1864, in which he wrote: "My oath to preserve the Constitution imposed on me the duty of preserving by every indispensable means that government, that nation, of which the Constitution was the organic law. Was it possible to lose the nation and yet preserve the Constitution? By general law life and limb must be protected, yet often a limb must be amputated to save a life, but a life is never wisely given to save a limb. I felt that measures, otherwise unconstitutional, might become lawful by becoming indispensable to the preservation of the Constitution through the preservation of the nation. Right or wrong, I assumed this ground and now avow it. I could not feel that, to the best of my ability, I had ever tried to preserve the Constitution, if to save slavery or any minor matter, I should permit the wreck of the government, country, and Constitution altogether." [53]

[53] Nicolay and Hay, *Works of Abraham Lincoln,* X, pp. 65-68.

★ ★ ★ VII ★ ★ ★

The Reaction against
the Executive

★

THOUGH not immediately apparent the assassination of President Lincoln was to constitute a portent of a gigantic shift of the center of gravity in the federal government. The prestige of President Lincoln, recently magnified by his decisive re-election in 1864, was lifted to its pinnacle by the surrender of Lee at Appomatox and the utter collapse of armed resistance to the enforcement of the supreme law of the land by the Chief Executive. Conciliation of those lately in rebellion was the keynote of Lincoln's policy when an assassin struck him down. No longer would his consummate skill in the management of men learned in the rough and tumble of pioneer Illinois politics be available to check the Radical Unionists and hold a fretful Congress in leash.

To those who had applauded the furious blast of the Wade-Davis Manifesto against Lincoln only to see its effect nullified by his triumphant re-election it must have now seemed as if Fate, through the assassin's bullet, had at last delivered the government into their hands. Their glee was but ill concealed. Nor did their confidence under the circumstances seem unreasonable. Andrew Johnson, who would now assume the duties of Chief Executive, had been one of them. Until appointed governor of Tennessee he had been a member of the Joint Committee on the Conduct of the War—the committee which had served as a censor of the Executive in the conduct of military affairs. Now this committee with one of its former members in the office of President could constitute a board of strategy in seeing that Congress was exalted to a dominant position with respect to the Executive.

In confirmation of this we have the testimony that Lincoln had drawn his last breath only a few hours before this group of Radicals caucused and decided on an entire change of the President's Cabinet "to get rid of the last vestige of Lincolnism," [1] without consulting Johnson, however, and on the establishment of a reconstruction policy less conciliatory than that of Lincoln. The feeling among them was practically unanimous that the accession of Johnson would prove a "god-send to the country." [2] When, a day later, this Committee on the Conduct of the War called on the new President, Senator Benjamin F. Wade, president pro tem of the upper house and co-author of the famous Wade-Davis Manifesto, expressed the consensus of the group in the well-known words: "John-

[1] MS diary of G. W. Julian, Apr. 15, 1865. Quoted by Claude Bowers, *The Tragic Era*, p. 6.

[2] G. W. Julian, *op. cit.*, p. 255.

son, we have faith in you. By the gods, there will be no trouble now in running the Government." [3]

This confidence of the Radicals in President Johnson was soon to be rudely shaken. Indeed, they were quite early disturbed in his utter disregard of their caucus decision as shown by his continued retention of Lincoln's Cabinet without a break in its membership. More disconcerting still was the fact that Johnson continued without visible change the method of reconstruction devised and initiated by Lincoln. This was the very procedure to which Congress had taken exception and which had especially provoked the wrath of the Radicals against Lincoln. They had assumed that, now that the emergency of the war had passed and Lincoln with his astute strategy could no longer frustrate them, Congress could proceed with its own plans for reconstruction. But throughout the summer and autumn in 1865 President Johnson proceeded serenely on his way with the restoration of civil government in the states where Lincoln had not previously completed it.[4] The term of the Thirty-eighth Congress had expired in March, 1865. Since the President made no move to call an extra session of the new Congress he was free to carry on his work of reconstruction without interference.

This failure of President Johnson to call Congress in a special session may have been a major mistake of his executive career. Even some of his friends thought that he erred in not convening Congress when such a momentous constitutional problem was to be solved.[5] Delightful as it undoubtedly was to be reconstructing the states, free from the carping criticism and annoy-

[3] *Ibid.*, p. 255; Nicolay and Hay, *op. cit.*, X, pp. 315-16.
[4] Richardson, *op. cit.*, VI, pp. 434-38.
[5] W. A. Dunning, *Essays on the Civil War and Reconstruction*, p. 85.

ing interference of Congress, the President must have seemed to many of the finest citizens to have been treading on doubtful constitutional ground and to have been guilty of scarcely playing fair with Congress.

If fair-minded friends of Johnson were doubtful of the propriety of his conduct, the Radicals were not. As the summer advanced their consternation at his conduct turned to indignation. When the President recognized the Pierpont government in Virginia Thaddeus Stevens wrote to Sumner, "Is there no way to arrest the insane course of the President in reorganization?" [6] On July 6 he wrote the President asking him to hold his hand and await the action of Congress, saying that he found no Northern Union party man who approved the President's course.[7] Condemning the appointment of military governors as a usurpation, Sumner wrote, "If something is not done the President will be crowned king before Congress meets." [8] On the eve of the regular meeting of Congress in December about thirty of these Radical Union congressmen caucused and laid their plans for countering the President by agreeing not to seat the congressmen elected from the reconstructed Southern states.[9]

A somewhat neglected factor in the conflict between Johnson and Congress has been the Speaker of the House of Representatives, Schuyler Colfax. He had presided over the last Congress during the war and it was universally accepted that he would be reelected Speaker of the now-convening Thirty-ninth

[6] Quoted by J. F. Rhodes, *United States from the Compromise of 1850*, V, p. 531.

[7] Johnson paper, quoted by E. P. Oberholtzer, *History of the United States since the Civil War*, I, p. 41.

[8] Summer MSS, Harvard Library, quoted by Rhodes, *United States from the Compromise of 1850*, V, p. 533.

[9] Welles, *op. cit.*, II, p. 387.

Congress. J. W. Forney, Secretary of the Senate, said that "he was the embodiment of the war policy of the government." [10] We may regard him as, in a very true sense, the first of the modern type of Speaker, such as the masterful Blaine, Reed, and Cannon. His career in that position reveals indications of a survival of that early colonial American conception of the Speaker as the people's spokesman against the danger of executive encroachment. Thus he felt himself to be the mouthpiece of the body over which he presided. It has been said that "after Lincoln no one spoke with more authority than Speaker Colfax." [11] It therefore seemed to him perfectly proper to address the crowd that gathered before his lodging place in Washington a few days before the opening of Congress and to declare to them that it was the function of Congress and not the President to determine the disposition of the conquered territory.[12] "Mr. Colfax frankly proclaimed the supremacy of Congress to the Executive as a fact, as Mr. Clay had proclaimed it in Jackson's time as a principle." [13] This informal speech of Schuyler Colfax was the first public declaration of "any Congressman taking issue with Johnson's policy and Mr. Johnson always denounced it as the initiation of the Congressional policy which antagonized his." [14] A few days later Mr. Colfax, facing from the Speaker's chair the House of Representatives, which had just then re-elected him, said, "It is yours to mature and enact legislation which, with the concurrence of the Executive, shall establish them [the

[10] A. W. Moore, *Life of Colfax*, p. 178. Quoted by M. P. Follett, *The Speaker of the House of Representatives*, pp. 98-99.

[11] O. J. Hollister, *Life of Schuyler Colfax*, p. 216.

[12] Welles, *op. cit.*, II, p. 385.

[13] G. R. Brown, *The Leadership of Congress*, p. 59.

[14] A. W. Moore, *Schuyler Colfax*, p. 178, Quoted by Follett, *op. cit.*, p. 99.

States] anew." [15] This statement that Congress had before it the duty of reconstruction was particularly significant, inasmuch as it was made in the face of the already consummated reconstruction of many states by Presidents Lincoln and Johnson.

When Congress convened, the congressmen-elect from the states reconstructed by the Presidents presented themselves to take the oath of office but were deliberately ignored through the highhanded manipulation of parliamentary procedure by Thaddeus Stevens, who had ordered the clerk to omit their names from the tentative roll.[16] This took place in spite of the fact that the great body of the Union party in Congress distrusted Sumner and Stevens and at this time preferred to co-operate with the President if they could have certain assurances as to reconstruction.[17] The conservative members of the party entered heartily into a plan for a joint committee on reconstruction, hoping through it to hold the Radicals in check.[18] But the alert Radicals at once captured control of this committee and converted it from an organ of conciliation into the "Central directory" [19] of the Radicals, a powerful engine of aggression in the war against the Executive. It turned out to be no less than a virtual resurrection of the old Committee on the Conduct of the War. "By the political dexterity of the Radicals," wrote James G. Blaine, "no opportunity was afforded the Conservatives to get together and support the President though Congress was in a frame of mind at that time to do so." [20] Yet it was

---

[15] *Cong. Globe*, XXXIX, 1, p. 5.
[16] Claude Bowers, *The Tragic Era*, p. 90.
[17] Rhodes, *History of the United States from the Compromise of 1850*, V, p. 549.
[18] Dunning, *Essays*, p. 87.
[19] Welles, *op. cit.*, II, p. 494.
[20] *Op. cit.*, II, p. 80.

quite apparent that the Radicals must bide their time and not prematurely force the issue with the President. Consequently they shrewdly postponed action on the seating of the Southern congressmen on the ground that Congress lacked information on the matter. All proposed resolutions relating to reconstruction were henceforth referred to the famous Committee of Fifteen, which promptly pigeonholed them.[21]

Under the domination of the irrepressible Stevens Congress had adjourned at the end of the first day of the session without extending the courtesy of the customary committee to inform the President that Congress was ready to receive communications from him.[22] This was a bold hint that Congress was assuming independent control and needed no advice from the President regardless of the constitutional injunction to him to provide it. When in due time the message of the President reached Congress its moderation of tone pleasantly surprised the public. The President based his reconstruction on the power to pardon, to withdraw military rule, and to guarantee a republican form of government. He reported that he had already restored the reconstructed states. "The amendment to the Constitution being adopted," said the message, "it will remain for the States whose powers have been so long in abeyance to resume their places in the two branches of the national Legislature and complete the work of restoration." [23]

On December 18 Thaddeus Stevens delivered a speech in the House in which he threw at the Executive the question, "Who can reconstruct?" and

[21] Winston, R. W., *Andrew Johnson: Plebeian and Patriot*, p. 311.

[22] Welles, *op. cit.*, II, p. 388.

[23] Richardson, *op. cit.*, VI, pp. 353-71.

answered it by declaring that the seceded states were conquered territory and could be restored only under the power of Congress to readmit.[24] If this view should prevail all the reconstruction already effected by Lincoln and Johnson would be nullified.

A crisis was reached by the middle of February when Congress presented to the President for his signature a measure providing for the continuance of the Freedman's Bureau, an agency originally established under the war power of Congress. The constitutional question now became, how can this bureau be renewed in time of peace? Secretary Gideon Welles set down in his diary that the measure was a "terrific engine and reads more like a decree emanating from a despotic power than a legislative enactment by republican representatives." [25] He revealed that great pressure was brought to bear on the Cabinet to accept the doctrines of Thaddeus Stevens. "Congress," he wrote stating the Radical Union party view, "was the supreme department of the Government and must be recognized as the supreme power. Members of Congress must be permitted to exercise executive duties. The Legislative department must control the action of the Government, prescribe its policy, its measures and dictate appointments to the Executive or subordinate departments." [26] February 13 the President alluded to the "unmistakable designs of Thaddeus Stevens and his associates to take the Government in their own hands and get rid of him by declaring Tennessee out of the Union." [27] If the President would only sign the Freedman's Bureau bill they would admit representatives from Tennessee and thus make the President secure in his office.[28] But all attempts to persuade or intimidate Johnson were in vain. He vetoed the measure and it failed to pass over his veto.

The sustaining of the veto proved, however, to be but a Pyrrhic victory for the President. Although apparently a defeat for the Radicals, it nevertheless strengthened them. They lost no time in putting through the two houses a concurrent resolution that congressmen from a "seceded" state should be admitted to neither house until both houses declared the state entitled to representation.[29] "This was a formal declaration of war on the executive policy. It notified the President that Congress intended to form its own judgment upon the status of the states irrespective of any extraneous decisions." [30]

The next issue between Congress and the Executive was on the Civil Rights Bill, designed particularly to protect the civil rights of the freedmen through the exercise of national authority. Such a thoroughgoing nationalist as the late John W. Burgess considered this measure theoretically sound from the point of view of modern jurisprudence and political science.[31] But the bill made all infractions of the statute cognizable in the federal courts. To a Southern states-rights Democrat[32] like Johnson this was a brazen infraction of the Constitution, an invasion of the reserved police powers of the states. He could not accept the theory of the bill's advocates that the Thir-

28 *Ibid.*, p. 434.
29 Rhodes, *History of the United States from the Compromise of 1850,* V, p. 572.
30 Dunning, *Essays,* p. 90.
31 *Reconstruction and the Constitution,* p. 70.
32 Johnson, of course, never was a Republican. Before the War he had been a Jacksonian Democrat. Like many other Democrats he had joined the Union party and was elected Vice President on the ticket of that party in 1864.

teenth Amendment had wrought a revolution in the nature of the federal government. Such a doctrine was viewed by the President as an alarming attempt at consolidation and such, in fact, the judiciary in due time held it to be.[33]

President Johnson promptly vetoed the bill and its passage over his head became a landmark in our constitutional development. It was the first time in our history that Congress had overcome the executive veto on an important issue.[34] It was even more important as a political event. Congress had tasted blood and the battle was on in earnest. Had the President chosen to accept the measure he would have thereby made himself the undoubted leader of his party.[35] Congress, now thoroughly alarmed at the President's conduct, took steps to put the measure beyond repeal by making it a part of the fundamental law and it became in time the Fourteenth Amendment to the Constitution. Moreover, this Civil Rights Bill was but the first of a number of acts to be passed over the President's veto. This proved fatal to the balance of the Executive and Congress in the federal system. James G. Blaine put it in a single sentence. "Two thirds of each house united and stimulated to one end can practically neutralize the executive power of the government and lay down its policy in defiance of the efforts and opposition of the President." [36] From the day of the passage of the Civil Rights Bill over the President's head Congress was master of the government and the President's initiative and usefulness as a constructive leader was at an end.

The congressional elections of 1866 were, in a

33 United States *vs* Rhodes, 1 Abbott, *U. S. Reports*, p. 50.
34 Rhodes, *History of the United States from the Compromise of 1850*, V, p. 586.
35 J. W. Burgess, *Reconstruction*, p. 71.
36 *Op. cit.*, II, p. 185.

sense, a referendum on the question of congressional versus presidential reconstruction. To the leaders of the contending groups it was also a contest for victory between two conflicting theories of the nature of the government. In the spring President Johnson had expressed succinctly his conception of his office in terms suggestive of Jacksonian Democracy. ". . . when that body [Congress] ventured on oppressive acts, he was clothed with power to say 'Veto, I forbid.' . . . Your President is now the Tribune of the people, and, thank God, I am, and intend to assert the power which the people have placed in me. . . . Tyranny and despotism can be exercised by many more rigorously, more vigorously, and more severely than by one." [37] In the midst of the campaign the chief of the Radicals, Thaddeus Stevens himself, gave an authoritative statement of the opposite doctrine. "Congress is the sovereign power, because the people speak through them; and Andrew Johnson must learn that he is your servant and that as Congress shall order he must obey. There is no escape from it. God forbid that he should have one tittle of power except what he derives through Congress and the Constitution. This is the whole question." [38] The dogmas that Lincoln had prevented the Radicals from getting established had now been translated into facts.

But what were the stakes for which the denouncers of the President were really playing? Let it not be forgotten that Andrew Johnson was a true Jacksonian Democrat, a champion of the underdog and consequently a menace to some of the most powerful economic interests in America. Here was a President determined that the public domain should go to actual

[37] Speech on occasion of a serenade, April 18, 1866, Johnson MS, XCIII, quoted, H. K. Beale, *The Critical Year*, p. 214.
[38] Speech at Lancaster, New York *Herald*, Sept. 29, 1866.

settlers instead of land speculators who had been
fraudulently acquiring vast tracts and railroad promoters seeking million-acre grants. He alarmed manufacturers by condemning high tariffs and government
bond holders by deliberately proposing to pare down
the debt by what amounted to partial repudiation.[39]

Whatever its significance as to issues, the verdict of
the electorate was overwhelmingly in favor of the
Radicals. The President's followers were so thoroughly defeated that the next House of Representatives would stand almost three to one against him. The
people seemed to have given Congress a mandate to
take up the matter of reconstruction de novo. The
electorate had been influenced strongly by the unanimous rejection of the Fourteenth Amendment by the
states which had been reconstructed by presidential
proclamation. That rejection had been made upon
the advice of the President.[40] The public came to
look upon Congress as practically the government of
the United States.[41] Stevens had the House of Representatives in his pocket. A reconstruction bill was
passed, abolishing the state governments established
by Johnson and dividing the South into military districts subject to military commanders, who must, however, under a rider attached to an appropriation
measure, take orders from General Grant and not the
Constitutional Commander-in-Chief.[42] In the opinion

39 See L. M. Hacker, *Triumph of American Capitalism*, p. 375.

40 See Chase Correspondence, American Historical Association,
Annual Report (1902), p. 516.

41 New York *Nation*, Nov. 29, 1866. In a message protesting
against this provision, President Johnson said: "If the executive trust vested in the President is to be taken from him and
vested in a subordinate officer the responsibility will be with Congress in clothing the subordinate with unconstitutional power
and with the officer who assumes to exercise it." Richardson,
op. cit., p. 544.

42 *Statutes at Large*, XIV, pp. 486, 487.

of a distinguished political scientist, a former Union soldier, this provision was "the most brutal proposition ever introduced into Congress by a responsible committee. . . ." [43] More astonishing still is the fact that this arrangement, so humiliating to the President, was devised by a member of President Johnson's Cabinet, Edwin M. Stanton, the Secretary of War. Congressman G. S. Boutwell took it down as the terms of the measure were secretly dictated to him by Stanton.[44]

Stanton's initiating the move to have General Grant put in charge of the military free from President Johnson's command, calls for an explanation since it was in a sense done in self defense. President Lincoln had used his reconstruction proclamation based on his power to pardon as a means of luring southern whites away from the Confederacy. He used the federal army then occupying recovered southern territory to support his reconstruction plan and had never failed to use his authority to sustain and protect federal soldiers even in the reconstructed states. Secretary of War Stanton and General Grant under whom the post-war army of occupation operated expected President Johnson likewise to protect the military. In this they were to be disappointed.

Under President Johnson's reconstruction procedure southern state courts were restored and began to function. At once former rebels began initiating scores of damage suits against federal military personnel, even against soldiers acting under the martial law that had been authorized. Officers quite naturally became afraid to exercise their authority because they would have little chance of being ex-

---

[43] J. W. Burgess, *Reconstruction*, p. 114.
[44] G. S. Boutwell, *Reminiscences of Sixty Years in Public Affairs*, II, p. 108.

onerated before a southern jury. Late in 1865 Stanton himself was sued by a disloyal northern citizen in a case instigated by President Johnson's legal advisers in an attempt to drive Stanton from public life. As instances of outrages in the South against the military accumulated, the animosity of Stanton and Grant against Johnson grew apace. Under the circumstances Congress naturally assumed the role of protector of the army putting Grant in charge of it. Grant appears not to have questioned Congress's authority to do this and he is believed to have carried into the presidency later this exaggerated conception of Congress's authority.[45]

Not only was Congress the chief organ of the government, no longer checked by the President, but it no longer regarded itself subject even to constitutional provisions. Not only was the Commander-in-Chief not to have command of the army, but by an ingenious provision the President was prevented from the possibility of the employment of the pocket veto which cannot be overridden because it is possible only after an adjournment. A new act provided "for the meeting of the fortieth and all succeeding Congresses immediately after the adjournment of the next preceding one." [46] This nullified the constitutional privilege of the President, enabling him to decide whether or not to call special sessions of Congress. Many Presidents anticipate with relief the season when Congress will not be in session. This privilege was permanently to be denied to Johnson. Accordingly, the Fortieth Congress convened on March 4, the chamber of the House having been

45 See Harold M. Hyman, "Johnson, Stanton and Grant" *The American Historical Review.* Vol. LXVI, No. 1 (October, 1960), pp. 85-100.
46 *Statutes at Large,* XIV, p. 378.

kept occupied by vigilant congressmen even throughout Sunday. These men were almost hysterical with
the baseless fear that the President might seek to employ military force to compel a recess. Without any
call by the President, as the Constitution requires,
there were three extra sessions of Congress in a
single year, that body remaining in almost continuous session to prevent the President from interfering
with the congressional reconstruction policy.

Having deprived the President absolutely of his
constitutional discretion as to the calling of extra
sessions of Congress and having made a mockery of
the constitutional provision that the President shall
be Commander-in-Chief of the army and navy,[47] Congress proceeded next to divest the Chief Executive of
control over the personnel of the executive branch of
the government. The debates of the First Congress had
revealed the then prevailing opinion that the power
of dismissal was incidental to the power of appointment because essential for efficient administration. By
construction this had come to be considered an established constitutional principle. It was to be respected by the Radicals no more than the explicit
prescriptions of the Constitution. Here they felt themselves to be confronted by a stern fact rather than
just a theory. The assassination of Lincoln had suddenly thrown the patronage of the President, swollen
by four years of intense war activity, into the hands
of Andrew Johnson, a Southerner and a Democrat of
the old states-rights school. There were those congressmen who were deeply concerned lest this President,
through the power to remove from office and fill
the vacancies with pliant tools, might have his way
in reconstruction despite all legislation of Congress.
Then there was that immense army of spoilsmen to

[47] *Supra,* p. 167.

whom the struggle was primarily one of getting control of patronage. Johnson, like Lincoln, was versed in the arts of the practical politician and the days of civil service reform were yet far in the future. Johnson knew how to wield the weapon of patronage in the conflict with Congress and had not refrained wholly from employing it.[48] Representative George S. Boutwell, one of the managers who prosecuted the President in the impeachment trial, betrayed rather too much of the grievance of the Radicals when he naïvely enumerated the number of officers and the millions of patronage in the hands of President Johnson.[49] The "cohesive power of public plunder" hoped for unquestionably helped cement the opposition to the President into a powerfully motivated group.

James G. Blaine, who was a Conservative Unionist, said that toward the end of the closing session of the Thirty-ninth Congress "the belief became general, that, as soon as Congress should adjourn, there would be a removal of all Federal officers throughout the Union who were not faithful to the principles, and did not respond to the exactions, of the Administration." [50] Accordingly there was enacted, vetoed by the President, and passed over his veto the Tenure of Office Act which went into effect March 2, 1867. President Johnson was convinced that the act was unconstitutional and he was consequently eager to get it in the courts for the purpose of a test. This was his avowed purpose nearly a year later in dismissing Secretary of War Stanton, who in spite of being a member of Johnson's official family was regularly

---

48 Rhodes, *History of the United States from the Compromise of 1850*, VI, p. 47; *Atlantic Monthly*, June, 1901, p. 824; Dunning, *Civil War and Reconstruction*, p. 255; J. G. Blaine, *op. cit.*, II, p. 267.

49 *Cong. Globe*, XL, supplement, p. 269.

50 *Op. cit.*, II, p. 267.

conspiring with the President's enemies in Congress, the Radical Unionists. The Radicals at first made a rash tactical blunder by having the newly appointed Secretary of War ad interim, General Lorenzo Thomas, arrested. Then it suddenly occurred to them that this would be playing into the hands of the President by giving the courts a chance to pass on the constitutionality of the Tenure of Office Act. Fearful of the result of such a test, they withdrew the charges against Thomas and he was accordingly released. Stanton insisted on retaining the office despite the President's removal of him. The Radicals made the most of the President's breaking a law to test its constitutionality and proceeded to prepare the articles of impeachment.

It will be recalled that as late as the reign of William III the Parliament of Great Britain had been unable to think of any device other than impeachment for effecting ministerial responsibility to Parliament. It was even at that early date rejected as an antiquated device unsuited for the purpose. It is one of the amazing anachronisms of history that in the middle of the nineteenth century these Radicals revived this ancient and outmoded device—revived it, moreover, for the very purpose of compelling ministerial responsibility of the Executive to the legislature. Benjamin F. Butler, who had assumed the leadership of the managers of the prosecution of the President in behalf of the House of Representatives, perhaps unconsciously revealed this purpose in the breadth he sought to give to the definition of an impeachable offense. He put it thus in his opening address to the Senate: "We define, therefore, an impeachable crime or misdemeanor to be one in its nature or consequence subversive of some fundamental or essential principle of government, or highly prejudicial to the public interest and this may consist of a violation of the Constitution, of law, of an official oath or duty, by an act committed or omitted, or, without violating a positive law, by the abuse of discretionary power from improper motives or for any improper motives." [51] He was but expressing the prevailing opinion of the majority of both houses of Congress when, as he continued, he maintained that the Senate during the impeachment "had none of the attributes of a judicial court. . . . As a constitutional tribunal solely you are bound by no law either statute or common, which may limit your constitutional prerogatives. . . . You are a law unto yourselves, bound only by natural principles of equity and justice and that *salus populi suprema lex*." [52]

When one brushes aside the surplus verbiage and gets at the essential idea in Butler's address he finds that it was not so much a judicial trial they were conducting as an awkward improvisation of a constitutional device to get from the Senate a vote of lack of confidence and the consequent removal of what the Radicals conceived to be Congress's chief minister, the President of the United States. Never did Butler come closer to revealing the real objective of the impeachers than when he countered the claim of the President's counsel that the Constitution vested exclusively in the President the power of removal from office. To this he pompously replied that "the momentous question, here and now is raised *whether the Presidential office (if it bears the prerogatives and power claimed for it) ought, in fact, to exist, as a part of the constitutional government of a free people*." [53]

A corollary of the proposition that the Senate, in

[51] *Cong. Globe*, XL, 2, supplement, p. 29.
[52] *Ibid.*, p. 30.
[53] Quoted by D. M. DeWitt, *The Impeachment and Trial of Andrew Johnson*, pp. 410-11. Italics mine.

an impeachment trial, was not a court was the idea, prevalent among the Radicals, that the senators were not obligated to confine themselves to the evidence presented at the trial. They were free to be influenced by any information they possessed from whatever source derived. The responsibility of the senator to his constituents' opinions was stressed and the tremendous pressure of well-organized propaganda against the President was brought to bear on the senators suspected of wavering on the vote for conviction. The way was being cleared for the establishment of a precedent looking to the permanent subordination of the Executive to Congress. Not through the parliamentary method of a vote of a lack of confidence in the popular branch of the legislature but by the irresistible pressure of popular opinion to compel the Senate to convict and thereby remove the President and, in this case, elevate one of its own members to the vacated office, was obedience to the legislature to be enforced. Thaddeus Stevens was but expressing the opinion of his group when he insisted that the Senate sitting on an impeachment case under the Constitution was performing a political and not a judicial function.[54]

The only one of the eleven articles of impeachment on which the managers approached making a case against the President was the one charging him with violating the Tenure of Office Act. This only recently enacted statute was another bit of evidence of the strong reaction against the executive power Lincoln had exercised during the war and, moreover, of a more or less deliberate determination to establish a

---

[54] *Cong. Globe*, Apr. 27. Stevens argued that "in order to sustain impeachment under the Constitution it is not necessary to prove a crime as an indictable offense, or any act *malum in se*. It is purely *political* proceeding."

governmental system centered in Congress. The first section of the Tenure of Office Act, after declaring that every civil officer appointed with the consent of the Senate should be entitled to hold such office until a successor shall have been in a like manner appointed and qualified, continued with this exception:

> "Provided, that the secretaries of state, of the treasury, of war, of the navy, and of the interior, the postmaster general, and the attorney general shall hold their offices respectively for and during the term of the President by whom appointed and for one month thereafter, subject to removal by and with the advice and consent of the Senate." [55]

When this bill had reached the President, the Cabinet members had all agreed with him that it ought to be vetoed and Stanton himself had assisted Seward in the preparation of the veto message. Stanton at this meeting of the Cabinet recognized that the act could not possibly apply to those members who, like himself, had been appointed by Lincoln.[56]

And now when the impeachment trial was on, it was the dismissal of this same Stanton who, in spite of all he had said, clung tenaciously to the office, that constituted the one point that had a semblance of validity. The hysterical Radicals had selected an almost impossible case on which to convict the President of a violation of the act. Nevertheless the managers centered the prosecution on Johnson's alleged defiance of the law. He had had no right to take even the steps he did to get the matter before the courts to

[55] *Statutes at Large*, XIV, pp. 430-32.

[56] Wells, *op. cit.*, III, p. 54. In a message to the Senate, Dec. 12, 1867, President Johnson said: "Every member of my Cabinet advised me that the proposed law was unconstitutional. All spoke without doubt or reservation, but Mr. Stanton's condemnation of the law was the most elaborate and emphatic." Richardson, *op. cit.*, VI, p. 587.

test the constitutionality of the act. Congress assumed itself to be the master of the nation.

Just how close we came to a radical revolution in our constitutional system we shall never know. In the opinion of a competent authority the trial barely failed to suspend the federal system.[57] If they had succeeded in convicting Johnson, the irrepressible Radicals would scarcely have spared Chief Justice Chase, whose efforts to maintain a judicial conduct of the trial had infuriated the congressmen, who regarded it as a political procedure. They were no doubt prepared to strike viciously at the head of the system of federal courts. It remained for one of the most naïve of the Radicals, General Grant, who had fallen into their hands, to confess years later the contempt for the Constitution entertained by the President's prosecutors. ". . . the legislation enacted during the reconstruction period to stay the hand of the President," he wrote, ". . . much of it, no doubt, was unconstitutional, but it was hoped that the laws enacted would serve their purpose before the question of constitutionality could be submitted to the judiciary and a decision obtained. These laws did serve their purpose. . . ." Congress was not only above the Executive and the judiciary, it was even superior to the Constitution.[58]

It was an open secret during the impeachment trial that Senator Benjamin F. Wade, who as president pro tem of the Senate would become President in case of Johnson's conviction, had ready a Cabinet hand-picked by the Radical caucus, with Benjamin F. Butler slated for Secretary of State.[59] Thus the Executive once again in our history would have been

[57] Morison, *op. cit.,* II, p. 342.
[58] U. S. Grant, *Personal Memoirs,* II, pp. 523-24.
[59] Adam Badeau, *Grant in Peace,* pp. 136, 137.

the choice of the national legislature, a revival of the conditions obtaining during the Virginia dynasty. General Grant's busy movements among the senators, soliciting their votes against the President, was all a part of the grand conspiracy. The Radical caucus had secured the services of Grant as a lobbyist for conviction of Johnson in return for the promise to support him for the presidency *provided he would, when elected, retain Wade's Cabinet intact.*[60] Thus the Executive would be mortgaged to Congress for some years in the future at least.

The prospective promotion of Wade and Butler to these eminences was, in fact, an important factor in defeating conviction. Wade had alarmed conservative interests by advocating free distribution of land to Negroes and by championing the interests of farmers and working men against capitalists, not even hesitating at woman's suffrage. Even the utterly unvindictive Lincoln had said that the notorious Benjamin F. Butler was "as full of poison gas as a dead dog." There were even Radical senators who paused at the thought of such a perilous consummation as the elevation of such an extremist as Wade and such a charlatan as Butler to the most important two offices in the government. The opinions expressed by the seven Republicans who voted for acquittal indicate that they feared the threat to the balance in the federal system.[61] By a single vote the system established by the Constitution had been saved from suspension if not destruction.

[60] Senator John B. Henderson, "Emancipation and Impeachment," *The Century Magazine,* Dec., 1912. LXXXV, No. 2; Hugh McCulloch, *Men and Measures of Half a Century,* p. 403; Badeau, *op. cit.,* pp. 136-37.

[61] See Dunning, *Essays,* p. 300.

The Hegemony of the Senate

★

WE HAVE seen that the firing on Fort Sumter resulted in a rally of Northern support to the Lincoln administration without too much regard to party affiliation, and out of this evolved the Union party. The movement attracted many Democrats including a notable galaxy of future Republican leaders. During the postwar conflict between the President and Congress the Union party disintegrated and by the late 1860's there was emerging a reincarnated Republican party with a personnel quite different from that which had elected Lincoln in 1860. Indeed one scholar has discovered that out of thirty-four outstanding Republican congressional leaders in the late sixties, nineteen, that is, more than half, were former Democrats.[1] Significantly enough, a Douglas Democrat, General

[1] L. K. Bowersox, *Reconstruction of the Republican Party, 1867-1870*, unpublished doctoral dissertation, Ohio State University, p. 22.

John A. Logan, in the National Republican Convention of 1868, made the speech nominating Ulysses S. Grant, who had been a Buchanan Democrat and who was elected President that fall.

The congressional elections during President Johnson's administration, as well as editorial comment and other indices of public opinion, all clearly indicate that the American electorate had lost faith in their Chief Executive. Congress had won their confidence and fairly accurately reflected prevailing public opinion.[2] It would, however, be a misinterpretation of the situation to assume that the American people desired a permanent subordination of the Executive to Congress. Without clearly thinking it out they had, nevertheless, apparently come to regard the positive leadership of the President since Jackson's administration as a permanent constitutional development.[3] Johnson was President by accident and his administration represented, they thought, a departure from the normal functioning of the system. "Soon," they seemed to say, "we shall elect a President whom we can trust and then Congress will return to its proper place in the governmental system."

This is what the American people evidently thought they were doing in the autumn of 1868. In the election of Ulysses S. Grant to the presidency they believed they had found a new tribune of the people and they looked to him as an earlier generation had looked to Andrew Jackson.[4] Henry Adams wrote of "Nordhoff, Murat Halstead, Henry Watterson, Sam Bowles—all reformers, and all mixed and jumbled together in a tidal wave of expectation, waiting for General Grant

2 See C. E. Merriam, *American Political Ideas,* p. 108.

3 See editorial, "The Movement for General Grant," *Harper's Weekly,* Jan. 11, 1868, p. 19.

4 Editorial, "The Men Inside Politics," *New York Nation,* Mar. 4, 1868.

to give orders." [5] Nor ought their faith be regarded so unreasonable as it now appears in the perspective of history. General Grant's military career had been one, on the whole, to justify a belief that he possessed unusual executive ability.[6] The brain that had conceived, planned, and executed the Vicksburg campaign surely represented no mean intellect. Primarily an engineer, he had displayed throughout his campaigns rare administrative skill in directing the enormous apparatus of his armies. His judgment of military men was generally sound. Except for occasional puzzling lapses, now overlooked by the public, he had assumed responsibility for his vast military duties and conducted affairs in a masterful manner.[7] At any rate this was the popular conception of General Grant's military record when he was inaugurated. Could not such ability be transferred over into the office of the presidency?[8] Andrew Jackson had done as much. So statesman and scholar joined the rank and file of the electorate in elevating the hero of Appomattox to the chief executiveship of the republic.[9]

By this time the public had come to feel that the balance of the departments prescribed in the Constitution could be restored only through a popular President, capable of assuming charge of the government and disposed to do so. The more thoughtful even believed that the first year of Grant's administration would be a critical one in this respect.[10] Unless the

---

[5] *The Education of Henry Adams*, p. 255.

[6] See editorial, *New York Nation*, Oct. 29, 1868, p. 344.

[7] See "The Intellectual Character of General Grant," *Atlantic Monthly*, May 1869, pp. 625-35.

[8] See "Our New President," *Atlantic Monthly*, Mar. 1869, pp. 378-83.

[9] See Henry Adams, "The Session," *North American Review*, CXI, pp. 31-33; Park Godwin, *Life of William Cullen Bryant*, II, p. 276; Henry Adams, *The Education of Henry Adams*, p. 260.

[10] Henry Adams, "The Session," *North American Review*, CXI, p. 40.

President acted promptly, congressional aggrandizement would continue and the system might be stabilized with a titular head, who neither reigned nor ruled. The courts, it was feared, might not recover their self-confidence, the Senate would continue its encroachments, the House of Representatives would grow ever less efficient. Only prompt and vigorous executive leadership could challenge and bring to an end the prevailing hegemony of the Senate.

This executive leadership which the public confidently expected of President Grant was just as certainly feared by the Senate.[11] Neither public nor Senate had to wait long for the revelation of the striking difference between Grant, the General, and Grant, the President. He seems never to have adjusted himself to the fact that, although a military commander must defer to civil authority, the President of the United States is himself a civil officer.[12] Mingling as he had been with the congressional clique that sought to convict Andrew Johnson and reduce the presidency to a congressional agency, he readily absorbed their philosophy without understanding its implications. For example, Grant had accepted serenely Congress's ignoring the Constitution's making the President Commander-in-Chief and instead vesting independent command of the army in Grant himself. Apparently Grant had accepted this as a proper exercise of Congressional authority and he apparently carried this conception of Congressional supremacy into the presidency. Except on rare occasions he was, as President, disposed to accept without question the work of Congress as the authoritative expression of the will of the American people. Not having divested himself of the military mentality, he would now dutifully defer to the civil authority vested in Congress.

11 See *The Education of Henry Adams*, p. 261.
12 Henry Adams, "The Session," p. 40.

Such appears to have been the intention with which Grant assumed his presidential duties.

President Grant's innocence of the nature of American government was astounding. The senators discovered it as soon as he assumed the duties of the office. No sooner had he been inaugurated than one of them returned from an interview with him to relate to his colleagues the story of an amazing but significant episode. The new President had disclosed to the senator his determination to remove a federal territorial judge. Since territorial judges are under the direct authority of Congress they do not necessarily have the tenure the Constitution gives other federal judges. The senator knew the judge to be a capable official and he promptly protested against the proposed removal unless there were good reasons for it. Whereupon the President replied that he did not question the judge's fitness but "the Governor of the territory writes that he cannot get along with that judge at all, and is very anxious to be rid of him, and I think the Governor is entitled to have control of his staff." Only with difficulty had the senator convinced the President that the relation of a general to his staff was in no way similar to that of a territorial governor to a federal judge.[13]

It was no slight relief to the leaders of the Senate majority to discover the new President's innocence, ineptitude, and eventually even his considerable indifference concerning governmental affairs. They had looked forward with deep concern to the inauguration of a President-elect to restore the office of Chief Executive. The maintenance of their hegemony ought not to be so difficult now. Grant might have strengthened his position by surrounding himself with a group of able counsellors in his Cabinet, leaders

[13] Carl Schurz, *Reminiscences*, III, p. 306.

with political experience and strong followings in the Republican party. Thus he might have fortified himself against the senatorial clique. Instead he chose mostly nonentities and the few capable men in the Cabinet were eventually either dismissed or disregarded by the President under the influence of the senators. Starting out to isolate himself in the presidency, he was before long in the hands of that group of designing politicians.

Fortunately we have the testimony of a very trustworthy eyewitness of the results of the setup of the government under the presidency of Ulysses S. Grant. "In both houses all trace of responsibility is lost," wrote Henry Brook Adams at the close of the first session of Congress in Grant's administration, "and while the Executive fumes with impatience or resigns himself with the significant consolation that this is the people's government, and the people may accept the responsibility, the members of the lower house are equally ready with the excuse that they are not responsible for the action of the Senators and the Senators, being responsible to no power under Heaven except their party organizations, which they control, are able to obtain precisely what legislation answers their personal objects or their individual conception of the public good." [14] The Senate had ignored the recommendations of the President's message, wrecked his reconstruction policy in the face of a feeble opposition by the House, and Conkling had led a Senate attack on Grant's capable Attorney General, Judge Hoar, for whose resignation the President would soon ask at the behest of the senatorial clique.

When President Grant did make a sporadic effort at taking the initiative early in his first term he chose a foolish and almost impossible project. He presented

14 "The Session," p. 60.

his treaty of annexation of Santo Domingo in the confident expectation of immediate ratification by the Senate. To his astonishment the Committee on Foreign Affairs recommended refusal of consent.[15] Then ensued a struggle to obtain the Senate's approval, during which the President descended almost to the level of a common lobbyist, stopping only short of the Senate's floor. Senator Sumner, chairman of the Committee on Foreign Affairs, defeated the desires of the President on annexation, indeed dominated the foreign policy of the government and "issued orders with almost the authority of a Roman triumvir." [16] Although the President later succeeded, through the senatorial clique, in having Sumner deposed from the chairmanship of the Committee on Foreign Affairs, it was a costly victory. The public was disposed to regard it as a piece of petty vengeance unbecoming the Chief Executive of the Republic.

One of the ablest of the Republican senators has left his expression of satisfaction concerning this relationship between Congress and the Executive. "The executive department of a republic like ours," wrote John Sherman, commenting on the Grant administration, "should be subordinate to the legislative department. The President should obey and enforce the laws, leaving to the people the duty of correcting any errors committed by their representatives in Congress." [17] For the first time in the history of the Republican party its most influential members had found in Grant a man who approached their ideal of a President. Lincoln's masterful executive conduct had driven the leaders of the House and the Senate to the violent protest of the Wade-Davis Manifesto.[18] A coura-

---

15 J. W. Burgess, *Reconstruction*, p. 324.
16 Henry Adams, "The Session," p. 58.
17 *Recollections*, p. 375.
18 *Supra* pp. 150-51.

geous but less adroit executive, President Johnson, following the Lincoln pattern, had been impeached by the Radicals and almost removed from office. Grant, however, was manageable. George F. Hoar, a faithful Republican who had just become a member of the lower house, has given us an authoritative view of the attitude of the Senate with respect to the Executive during Grant's administration. "The most eminent Senators," he wrote, "Sumner, Conkling, Sherman, Edmunds, Carpenter, Frelinghuysen, Simon Cameron, Anthony, Logan—would have received as a personal affront a private message from the White House expressing a desire that they should adopt any course in the discharge of their legislative duties that they did not approve. If they visited the White House, it was to give, not to receive advice. Any little company or coterie who had undertaken to arrange public policies with the President and to report to their associates what the President thought would have rapidly come to grief. . . . Each of these stars kept his own orbit and shone in his sphere within which he tolerated no intrusion from the President or from anybody else." [19]

It may indeed be true, as one of his contemporaries believed, that Ulysses S. Grant in complacently accepting the situation and serenely letting events take their own course missed the greatest opportunity since the inauguration of George Washington.[20] The intelligent opinion of the country was ready and even eager to line up behind him had he but raised the rallying cry. The prestige of his great name constituted a mighty political resource capable of being exploited for the salvation of good government. Exploited indeed it finally was, but only by the most sinister forces in the body politic. Blind to the great

[19] *Autobiography*, II, p. 46.
[20] Henry Adams, "The Session," *North Am. Rev.* CXIX, p. 45.

emergency confronting him and incapable of dealing with it even if he could have seen it, he became little more than the political puppet of his flatterers and consequently he stands today in our history as the most pathetic figure that ever occupied the office of President of the United States.

The Senate attained the pinnacle of its power by the end of Grant's administration.[21] Senators even claimed a place at the dinner table above the President's Cabinet whose members had hitherto outranked them at social functions.[22] They no doubt regarded the position of the upper house secure in its mastery over the Executive. Their conduct was soon to show that they believed the Senate's place in the government then to be the culmination of its constitutional development. It was the opinion of the late John W. Burgess that since the Civil War the Senate had been proceeding "to the overturning of the check and balance system and the substitution of the parliamentary system for it."[23] When Grant retired from the presidency no one, in or out of the Senate, could have believed it possible that within the following decade the Executive would four times successfully challenge and decisively repulse the Senate in its pretension of control over the Executive.

Grant would have welcomed a third term but the omens were certainly not auspicious in 1876 for him, or indeed for any candidate the Republicans might nominate. The scandals of his administration, pitilessly exposed by Congressional committees with Democratic majorities, had been damaging enough. More potent, however, in reducing the prestige of Grant and his party had been the now deepening economic depres-

[21] G. F. Hoar, *op. cit.*, II, p. 45.
[22] Horace Davis, "The Relation of the Three Departments as Adjusted by a Century," Johns Hopkins Studies in Historical and Political Science, III (1885), p. 494.
[23] *The Administration of President Hayes*, p. 11.

.ion following the panic that broke in the first year
of his second term. Somehow the Republican Convention managed to circumvent the odium attaching
to the maladministration under Grant by nominating
for the presidency the thrice-elected Governor of
Ohio, Rutherford B. Hayes, who had an irreproach-
able personal character and an exceptional official
courage. Because of election irregularities the counting of the electoral votes was long delayed and finally
decided in Hayes's favor by a single vote just in
time for his inauguration. The long deadlock on the
counting of the vote had indeed been broken as the
result of an understanding on the part of the Southern Democrats that if Hayes were elected President he
would relieve them of military rule by ordering federal troops withdrawn from the Southern states.

In the pride of power the senatorial oligarchy deliberately prepared to dictate the appointment of
Hayes's Cabinet. His prestige had not been enhanced
by the disputed election, his fame was not at all comparable to Grant's, and he ought to be easier to
subordinate than the victor of Appomattox. Senator
Conkling, chief of the spoilsmen, would have planted
his lieutenant, Thomas C. Platt, in that strategic
position of the politicians, the headship of the Post
Office Department, and Senator Simon Cameron, boss
of Pennsylvania, wanted his son Don continued at
the head of the War Department. A new senator, James
G. Blaine, with scarcely veiled threats if denied his
demand, expected to put William P. Frye in the
Cabinet. The impecunious John A. Logan, having
suddenly become an ex-senator, needed and expected
the salary of a Cabinet officer.[24] None of them could,
of course, be aware of the entry that Hayes, with inflexible resolution, had set down in his diary—"to
appoint no member of Grant's Cabinet, no Presiden-

24 E. P. Oberholtzer, *op. cit.*, III, p. 332.

tial candidate and to make no appointment to take care of anybody." [25]

To the amazement of these senators Hayes prepared his own list of Cabinet nominations in utter disregard of their wishes. Their patriotic indignation was aroused by the appearance on his list of the name of the "rebel" David M. Key, nominated, of all places, for that key position of the spoils system, the postmaster generalship. But the severest blow of all to these spoilsmen was the nomination of that hated political renegade and civil service reformer, Carl Schurz, who, from the vantage point of the Interior Department, would impress his heretical doctrines on the President and wage war on the spoilsmen. Disregarding Conkling's wishes as to a New York man in the Cabinet, the President chose instead an outstanding anti-Conkling man from that state, William M. Evarts, whom he put at the very head of his cabinet as Secretary of State. President Hayes had embarrassed these senators by the sheer fitness of his nominees. Senator Hoar, who was just then entering the Senate, declared long afterward, "There has hardly been a stronger cabinet since Washington than that of President Hayes." [26] Burgess praised it in even less qualified terms.[27]

Decisively challenged, the senatorial oligarchy manifested no hesitation in going into this conflict with the new President of whom they knew but little and for whom they entertained a profound contempt. They, who had broken the power of Andrew Johnson and easily overawed such a popular idol as General Grant, would promptly crush this political amateur and pious fanatic who proposed to elevate and reform the public service. Accordingly, when the Cabi-

25 Feb. 19, 1877.
26 *Op. cit.*, II, p. 7.
27 *Administration of President Hayes*, p. 65.

net nominations were submitted to the Senate the entire list was referred to committees for examination and report. They distinctly violated custom when they did not even make an exception of their fellow senator, John Sherman, nominated for Secretary of the Treasury and eminently qualified for the position. Customarily fellow senators were confirmed without investigation.[28] In this case, however, the new President was to be disciplined and put in his proper place because he had not permitted senators to dictate his Cabinet appointments.

This unprecedented move of the Senate in delaying confirmation of an entire list of Cabinet nominations astounded the nation. It was quite naturally inferred that the Senate planned to reject some or even all of them. The excellence of the nominations had elicited the enthusiastic approval of the country and a storm of public condemnation promptly fell upon the astonished Senate. The President's office was flooded with telegrams and letters urging him to stand firm. Editorial support rallied on the side of the President and condemned the Senate's assumption of dictatorial power.[29] Then the Senate decided to yield a bit and the nomination of Sherman was confirmed. Embarrassed by the rising tide of public indignation, the senatorial leaders grew desperate and vainly sought a combination with the Democrats against confirmation.[30] The Southern Democrats would not conspire to embarrass a President pledged to deliver them from military rule.

Presently the senators began hearing from mass meetings in New York, Philadelphia, and elsewhere, all commending the President and condemning the

28 *Ibid.*, p. 66.
29 C. S. Williams, *Dairy of Hayes,* Mar. 14, 1877.
30 C. S. Williams, *The Life of Rutherford B. Hayes,* II, pp. 26-29.

Senate. Telegrams from party men, political clubs, and commercial bodies in all parts of the country came pouring in, demanding prompt confirmation.[31] The press was almost unanimously with the President.[32] Within seventy hours the Senate had been overwhelmed by the tide of public opinion and felt impelled to confirm the whole list of Cabinet nominations with practical unanimity.[33] What Grant had not even attempted to do Hayes had accomplished with signal success. He had checked the Senate by rallying the people once more around the President. For the first time since the Civil War the Senate had been vanquished on a clear-cut issue between it and the President. The upper House had passed its zenith. Power had been checked by power even as Montesquieu had said it must be.

President Hayes had intended it as no mere perfunctory remark when in his inaugural address he had said: "I ask the attention of the public to the paramount necessity of reform in our civil service . . . a reform that shall be thorough, radical, and complete." [34] As soon as the federal troops had been recalled from the South he recorded in his diary the next major objective, "Now for Civil Service Reform." [35] The New York Custom House, however, stood, a veritable citadel of the spoilsmen, in the path to reform. Its personnel from Chester A. Arthur,[36] collector of the port, and Alonzo B. Cornell, naval officer, down to the rank and file constituted a part of

---

[31] C. S. Williams, *Diary and Letters of Rutherford B. Hayes,* Mar. 14, 1877.

[32] C. S. Williams, *Life of Hayes,* II, p. 27.

[33] *Ibid.,* II, p. 28.

[34] Richardson, *op. cit.,* VI, p. 4396.

[35] April 22, 1877.

[36] While Arthur was personally incorruptible and conducted his office honestly he was nevertheless a Conkling machine politician. See Fred Lewis Pattee, "Chester Alan Arthur," *Dictionary of American Biography,* I, p. 373.

he state political machine of Senator Conkling. The
President did not hesitate. An investigating committee
of distinguished citizens appointed by the Secretary of
the Treasury revealed all the inefficiency and unnecessary personnel suspected.[37] Hayes issued an executive order forbidding federal office-holders to participate in party politics.[38] Alonzo B. Cornell defied the
President by presiding over a New York Republican
convention.[39] Then the President informed Cornell
that he had decided upon a change in the three
principal officers of the New York Custom House. The
incumbents refused to resign.[40]

The President's next move was to send to the Senate
the nominations of successors of the occupants of the
offices. The nominations were greeted in the Senate
with derisive laughter.[41] The Senate Republicans in
caucus considered turning the President out of the
party as the Whigs had done with Tyler. The nominations were referred to a committee of which the
chairman was Senator Conkling, who invoked the
power of the Senate over removals under the Tenure
of Office Act, and the special session closed without
confirmation of the nominations. President Hayes
recorded in his diary, "In the language of the press,
Senator Conkling has won a great victory over the
administration. My New York nominations were rejected 31-25. But the end is not yet. I am right and I
shall not give up the contest." [42]

Conkling could not have invoked the Tenure of
Office Act had Congress heeded President Grant's request for its repeal. Even before Grant's inauguration
Representative Benjamin F. Butler had pressed for the

37 C. S. Williams, *Life of Hayes,* II, p. 77.
38 Richardson, *op. cit.,* VI, pp. 4402-03.
39 *Harper's Weekly,* Nov. 10, 1877, p. 878, column 4.
40 John Sherman, *op. cit.,* II, p. 679.
41 Philadelphia *Inquirer,* Oct. 30.
42 Dec. 3, 1877.

repeal of the measure which had been designed specifically to tie the hands of President Johnson. The Senate had refused to surrender its advantage. When Grant became President, in his first message to Congress he declared the Tenure of Office Act "inconsistent with a faithful and efficient administration of the Government. . . . What faith can an Executive put in officials forced upon him, and those too whom he has suspended for reason?" [43] Grant obtained action on this recommendation by one of the few effective moves of his dealings with Congress. He simply let it be known that as long as the Tenure of Office Act remained in force he would make no nominations. This declaration threw consternation into the ranks of the spoilsmen, for it left the Johnson appointees secure in their government positions. Soon the representatives who had been loudest in condemning Johnson's violation of the Tenure of Office Act, led by Benjamin F. Butler, voted for repeal. Again the Senate resisted but a meausre was finally enacted into law after a compromise framed in the conference committee and understood differently by the two houses.[44] Grant could easily have won by standing his ground and insisting on repeal but the senatorial oligarchy was already closing in upon him and they persuaded him to accept the mongrel measure. The lawyers of the Senate had taken the Executive into camp.[45] In effect the new law practically compelled the President to keep submitting nominations until the Senate confirmed one and in the meantime the incumbent retained the office.[46]

President Hayes was firm in his belief that the "senatorial usurpation" was doomed. "In the end, the

[43] Richardson, op. cit., VII, p. 138.

[44] Blaine, op. cit., II, p. 405.

[45] Welles, op. cit., pp. 553, 556, 557, 558, 560, 564, 567-69, 571.

[46] Cong. Globe, 41st Cong., 1st Session, p. 395.

claim of a single Senator to control all nominations in his state will be found so preposterous that it will fall of its own weight." [47] In the next regular session following, the Senate again rejected these nominations and the three incumbents were apparently secure in their offices. The Senate seemed virtually to have extinguished the President's power of removal. Many citizens looked upon the matter as finally settled.

The invincible determination of the President was demonstrated the following summer. Summarily dismissing the three officials in question, he filled the vacancies thus created with recess appointments. Upon the reassembling of the Senate in December the three nominations were again presented for confirmation. Once more they were referred to Senator Conkling's committee. Several weeks of parliamentary maneuverings followed, during which it began to dawn upon the proud Senator that he was fighting a losing battle. In the frenzy of his fear that his state machine was about to lose the highly essential patronage of the Custom House he resorted to an unspeakably bitter speech against the administration in which he alienated friends by stooping to the reading of the private correspondence of Cabinet members.[48] Meanwhile Secretary Sherman had been busy among his erstwhile senatorial colleagues and had let them understand that he would resign if the nominations were not confirmed. "I would not hold office," he afterwards wrote, "when my political friends forced me to act through unfriendly subordinates." [49] He persuaded some of them to desert Conkling. Thus the Executive was using direct influence to restore its power. This time Senator Conkling had invoked senatorial courtesy in

[47] Letter to Henry Smith Williams. See C. S. Williams, *Life of Hayes*, p. 87n.

[48] V. L. Shores, *The Hayes-Conkling Controversy*, Smith College Studies in History, IV, pp. 250-63.

[49] *Recollections*, II, p. 683; New York *World*, Feb. 4, 1879.

vain, for confirmation soon followed. Well indeed has
E. P. Oberholtzer observed that the President "had
broken the power of the Senatorial group which for
so long had been dictatorially directing the government and had accomplished . . . a return to the
principles enunciated in the Constitution." [50] The decisive effect of the President's victory was noted in
his diary a year later: "The end I have chiefly
aimed at has been to break down Congressional patronage and especially Senatorial patronage. . . . I
have had great success. No member of either House
now attempts even to dictate appointments. My sole
right to make appointments is tacitly conceded." [51]

Hayes had pledged himself in advance to a single
term. In 1880 the Republicans nominated and succeeded in electing to the presidency James A. Garfield. It might have been supposed that the defeats
administered to Senator Conkling by President Hayes
had settled the question of the President's power of
removal and established a precedent for future administrations. The first weeks of President Garfield's
administration were, however, to witness a renewal of
the conflict with savage ferocity. It has long been assumed that Garfield blundered into this controversy.
This view is quite evidently erroneous. The studious
habits of the new President together with his long
experience as a congressional leader had afforded him
a grasp of the situation he faced unsurpassed by that
of any previous President.[52] He was familiar with
almost every man with whom he had to deal. His
letters revealed that he understood as well as did
Hayes that the constitutional independence of the
Executive could be preserved only by a sharp chal-

---

[50] *Op. cit.*, III, p. 360; see Eckenrode, *op. cit.*, p. 275.
[51] July 14, 1880.
[52] W. R. Thayer, *Life and Letters of John Hay*, II, p. 59; T. C.
Smith, *Life and Letters of James A. Garfield*, II, p. 1101.

lenge of the pretensions of the Senate and a duel to the finish with the most militant champion of senatorial courtesy.[53] When Garfield nominated William H. Robertson as collector of the port of New York he was leaving no doubt as to the challenge. Robertson, though a member of the New York delegation at the recent Republican National Convention, had been an anti-Grant man while Conkling was the leader of the Grant delegates. This was even a more distinct challenge to the New York senator than President Hayes had ever given. "This [nomination]," wrote President Garfield to B. A. Hinsdale, "brings on the contest at once and will settle the question whether the President is registering clerk of the Senate or the Executive of the United States. Summed up in a single sentence this is the question: shall the principal port of entry in which more than ninety per cent of all our customs duties are collected be under the control of the administration or under the local control of the factional senator?" [54]

The enormous weight of Senator Conkling's political machine was promptly brought to bear against the President to compel him to yield. Senator Platt, Vice President Arthur, Governor Cornell and even Postmaster General James sought to move Garfield, but in vain.[55] For the third time in his conflicts with the President, Senator Conkling sought an alliance with Democratic senators. Party leaders pleaded for a compromise to save the party. On this proposition the President wrote to John Hay: "If it were a difference between individuals there could be some sense in such advice. But the one represents a whole independent function of the government. The other is

[53] T. C. Smith, *op. cit.*, II, p. 1104.
[54] *Ibid.*, II, p. 1109.
[55] H. C. Thomas, *The Return of the Democratic Party to Power in 1884*, p. 58.

$\frac{1}{76}$ of $\frac{1}{2}$ of another independent branch of the government with which compound vulgar fractions the President is asked to compromise. If this demand is acceded to, its effect upon the independence of the Executive is too plain for comment." [56]

Soon it became evident that the senators under Conkling had devised a stratagem to outwit the President. They would confirm all the nominations except the one over which the controversy raged and then adjourn.[57] At Blaine's suggestion Garfield then withdrew all the nominations except that of Robertson. There would be no appointments of any kind until the major issue was settled. It was a breath-taking stroke and left the senators practically helpless.[58] The brilliant move electrified the President's friends. The constitutional issue involved was stated perfectly in an editorial in the *Baltimore American:* "At last President Garfield has answered the question: 'Who is President?' " [59]

Seeing that the confirmation of Robertson was now inevitable, Conkling and his colleague, Platt, resigned to seek vindication through re-election by the legislature of New York. When the legislature chose others in their stead, the President's victory was complete. The repudiation of the senators by the legislature of New York assumed an unusual importance in the development of our constitutional system. "If they had been returned," wrote John Sherman, "the President would have been powerless to appoint anyone in New York without consulting the Senators, practically transferring to them his constitutional power." [60]

[56] T. C. Smith, *op. cit.,* II, p. 1127; cf. G. F. Hoar, *op. cit.,* II, p. 57.

[57] *Ibid.,* II, p. 1125.

[58] Appleton's *Annual Cyclopedia,* 1884, p. 194.

[59] May 6, 1881. Quoted by T. C. Smith, *op. cit.,* II, p. 1126.

[60] *Op. cit.,* II, p. 817.

An intensely interested follower of this contest was ex-President Hayes, who summarized in his diary the conflict of the Senate and the Executive thus far: "If the boss system is to go down, as it now seems probable, I can say I struck the first and most difficult blows. It is based on Congressional patronage and Senatorial prerogative or courtesy. . . . The principal steps have been (1) The appointment of the Cabinet in 1877, (2) The defeat of Conkling in the Custom House conflict which made a business house institution of the New York Custom House, (3) The defeat of Conkling and Platt and their dismissal from Public Life in 1881." [61] It was a disappointed office seeker, inflamed by the bitter controversy between the President and the New York senators, that assassinated Garfield, who was, consequently, President only six months. Vice President Chester A. Arthur then succeeded to the presidency and conducted the office with dignity and courage, as we shall see later.

The fourth one of these conflicts of the Executive with the Senate over the appointing power took place early in the first term of President Cleveland. After a long period of control of the executive branch of the government the Republican party in 1884 lost the presidency and along with it the lower house. In due time, however, it became apparent that the Republican party strategy was to be to retain a degree of control over administration through the provisions of the Tenure of Office Act. The party would thus intrench itself in the Senate as the Federalist party had long before done in the Judiciary. Previous repulses of the Senate had left them unabashed and unless checked again perhaps they "would have turned the Presidency into an office like that of the Doge of Venice, one of ceremonial dignity without real

61 May 17, 1881.

power." [62] The confidence of these veterans of the Senate was fortified by the fact that the new President was unfamiliar with the federal government. When Grover Cleveland went to Washington to be inaugurated it was but the second time he had seen the national capital.[63] The new President may have had a presentiment of the impending conflict if we may judge by a theme touched upon in his first message to Congress. An intensely practical man, he seldom ventured on any excursion into the field of political philosophy. However, both in his conduct and in his writings he manifested a profound veneration for the dogma of separated powers. Accordingly in his first annual message Grover Cleveland struck a note of warning which the Senate might well have heeded. "It is well for us to bear in mind," said he, "that our usefulness to the people's interest will be promoted by a constant appreciation of the scope and character of our respective bodies as they relate to Federal legislation. Contemplation of the grave and responsible functions assigned to the respective branches of the Government under the Constitution will disclose the partition of power between our respective departments and their necessary independence, and also the need for the exercise of all the powers in that spirit of comity and co-operation which is essential to the proper fulfillment of the patriotic obligation which rests upon us as faithful servants of the people." [64]

Between the date of his inauguration and the opening of the regular session of Congress President Cleveland made 634 suspensions from and corresponding appointments to offices.[65] In strict compliance with the revised Tenure of Office Act (1869) he sent these

---

[62] H. J. Ford, *The Cleveland Era*, p. 54.
[63] William Allen White, *Masks in a Pageant*, p. 110.
[64] Richardson, *op. cit.*, VIII, p. 325.
[65] Grover Cleveland, *Presidential Problems*, p. 45.

recess nominations to the Senate as soon as Congress convened. The committees to which they were referred at once began bombarding the executive departments with requests for the reasons for the suspensions. "These requests," wrote the President long afterwards, foreshadowed what the Senatorial construction of the Law of 1869 might be, and indicated that the Senate, notwithstanding constitutional limitations, and even in the face of the repeal of statutory provisions giving it the right to pass upon suspensions by the President, was still inclined to insist, directly or indirectly, upon that right.[66] Amateur though he may have been in matters of the national government, Cleveland was quick enough to see this. To answer the requests concerning suspensions would give the Senate its initial grip on the new administration. Accordingly, despite the urgent advice of his friend, ex-Senator Schurz,[67] that he must not become involved in a controversy with the Senate, the President simply had his department heads return the stereotyped reply to requests concerning suspensions "that the public interest would not be thereby promoted" or that "the reasons related to purely administrative acts." [68]

The Senate countered with a policy of delay and at the end of three months only 17 out of 643 nominations had been considered and only 15 had been confirmed.[69] This convinced the President that the Senate's committees, in addressing the department heads for information, were preparing "to lay a foundation for the contention that not only the Senate but its committees had a right to control these heads of departments as against the President in mat-

66 *Ibid.,* p. 46.
67 R. M. McElroy, *Grover Cleveland,* I, p. 179.
68 Grover Cleveland, *op. cit.,* p. 46.
69 *Ibid.,* p. 48.

ters of executive duty." [70] Here was a situation reminiscent of Jackson's controversy with the Senate that led to the famous resolution censuring the President. Besides, President Cleveland's hallowed doctrine of separated powers was in jeopardy.

Before long the issue between the Executive and Senate was clarified by being concentrated on a specific nomination. Among the recess suspensions had been that of one George M. Duskin from the office of District Attorney of Alabama, in whose stead President Cleveland had submitted the nomination of John D. Burnett. The Senate committee asked the Department of Justice for all the papers and information touching the nomination of Burnett and also "all papers touching the suspension and proposed removal from office of George M. Duskin." [71] The Attorney General promptly complied with the first part of the request, which pertained to the unquestioned constitutional power of the Senate, but concerning the suspension he informed the Senate committee "that he has as yet received no direction from the President in relation to their transmission."

Thus far the controversy had involved only Senate committees and department heads and the President was content to remain in the background. But the refusal of information just related provoked the Senate as a whole to inject itself into the controversy with the resolution adopted in executive session: "Resolved that the Attorney-General be, and he hereby is, directed to transmit to the Senate copies of all documents and papers that have been filed in the Department of Justice since the first day of January, A.D., 1885 in relation to the conduct of the Office of District Attorney of the United States for the Southern Dis-

70 *Ibid.*, p. 49.
71 *Ibid.*, p. 51.

trict of Alabama." [72] This was but an adroit subterfuge for obtaining what had previously been refused. The Attorney General replied that "the President of the United States directs me to say . . . It is not considered that the public interests will be promoted by a compliance with said resolution and the transmission of papers and documents therein mentioned to the Senate in executive session." [73]

The issue was now clearly defined between the Senate and the President. The President's refusal of compliance had hurt the Senate's pride and they responded with a resolution expressing their "condemnation of the refusal of the Attorney-General under whatever influence, to send to the Senate copies of the papers called for in its resolution of the 25th of January . . . as in violation of his official duty and subversive of the principles of Government and good administration thereof." Furthermore, it was declared to be the duty of the Senate "to refuse its advice and consent to the proposed removals of officers when such papers are denied." [74] The successors of the Whigs of the thirties once more challenged the powers of the Executive now directed by a Jacksonian Democrat.

The Senate's resolution condemning the conduct of the Attorney General elicited the President's prompt assumption of responsibility for the refusal to deliver the information and papers requested. In his statement he quoted the report of the Senate committee upon whose recommendation the vote of censure had been passed and which had contained the declaration that "the important question then, is whether it is within the constitutional competence of either House of Congress to have access to the official papers and

[72] Cleveland, *op. cit.*, p. 52.
[73] *Ibid.*, p. 56.
[74] *Ibid.*, p. 67.

documents in the various public offices of the United States created by laws enacted by themselves." [75] Perhaps it never occurred to the Senators that anybody would have the temerity to question the right of Congress to supervise the conduct of the agencies they had created. Should the President be so bold as to do so they had no doubt he would be delivering himself into their hands. With a fatuity reminiscent of that of the Whigs in respect to Jackson's Bank veto these Senators assumed that the public would join in condemning such folly on the part of the inexperienced Cleveland.

Nor was the Senate wholly to blame for such a view of the situation. The most realistic analysis of the national government made in that day considered congressional domination of administration as thoroughly established. "It [Congress] does not domineer over the President himself," wrote young Woodrow Wilson, "but it makes the Secretaries its humble servants. Not that it would hesitate, upon occasion, to deal directly with the chief magistrate himself; but it has few calls to do so, because our latter day Presidents live by proxy; they are executives in theory but the secretaries are executives in fact." [76]

To the utter astonishment of the Senate the President sent them a message in which, referring to the executive departments, he pointed out that "these instrumentalities were created for the benefit of the people and to answer the general purposes of the Government under the Constitution and the laws; and that they are unencumbered by any lien in favor of either branch of Congress growing out of their construction and unembarrassed by any obligation to the Senate as the price of their creation." The President denied the right of the Senate to any of the papers

[75] Richardson, *op. cit.*, VIII, p. 376.
[76] *Congressional Government*, p. 45.

relating to the suspension. They consisted of letters and communications of various kinds, unofficial in their nature and merely kept in the files of the departments for convenience. "I suppose," continued the President, "if I desired to take them into my custody, I might do so with entire propriety, and if I saw fit to destroy them no one could complain." [77]

Proceeding, the President soon came to the heart of the matter with the declaration that the requests and demands with which the Senate had plied the departments "have but one complexion. They assume the right of the Senate to sit in judgment upon the exercise of my exclusive discretion and executive function." He closed the message with these ringing words: "Neither the discontent of party friends, nor the allurements constantly offered of confirmation of appointees conditioned upon the avowal that suspensions have been made on party grounds alone, nor the threat proposed in the resolutions now before the Senate that no confirmation will be complied with, are sufficient to discourage or deter me from following in the way I am convinced leads to better government for the people." [78]

Public opinion responded promptly but not as the Senate expected. The President's courageous message had dramatized the issue with the Senate and it promptly caught the attention of the nation, which manifested its intense enjoyment of the predicament into which the sophisticated Senators had maneuvered themselves. President Cleveland began to realize the truth he long afterwards expressed that "the Presidency is pre-eminently the people's office." [79] The Senate's vote on the resolution of censure had been a strictly party one of 30 to 26. On the resolution to

77 Richardson, *op. cit.*, VIII, pp. 376-78.
78 Richardson, *op. cit.*, pp. 381-83.
79 *Presidential Problems*, p. 10.

refuse consent to removal without information, lines broke and a bare majority of a single vote was obtained. It was just as the Republican ranks were breaking that President Cleveland dealt the fatal stroke to the Senate's pretensions. He pointed out what had hitherto escaped everybody's notice; namely, that Duskin's term had expired long before the controversy started. The Senate could consequently have no possible concern over removal. Once again, just as in the impeachment of Johnson, the Senate had selected an impossible case with which to test its power over removal. Their experience with the Tenure of Office acts was altogether unlucky. The only question now before the Senate was the confirmation of the nomination of a successor to Duskin. Presently Burnett was soon confirmed and the Senate challenged no further the President's power of removal.[80]

The President's discovery of the fact that Duskin's term had expired gave to the heroics of the Senate the effect of a pathetic anticlimax. He was soon to behold the vindication of his position by the repeal of the Tenure of Office Act, the bill originating in the Senate, proposed by a Republican and receiving but a single adverse Republican vote in that house.[81] The Senate had at last come to realize that in every one of these four great conflicts with the Executive the people promptly aligned themselves with the Executive. The Republicans at long last had begun to suspect what the Whigs never could comprehend; namely, that the people did seem to regard the President as a tribune.

80 *Ibid.*, p. 69.
81 Hoar, *op. cit.*, II, pp. 143-44.

IX

Congressional Government

★

UNDER THE IRREPRESSIBLE LEADERSHIP of Thaddeus Stevens the House of Representatives had seized the initiative in shaping the reconstruction policy and for a while it overshadowed the Senate. After the death of Stevens, which followed hard upon the acquittal of the President in the impeachment trial, however, the House declined rapidly in prestige. Its clashes with the Senate, noted in the chapter immediately preceding, were but rear-guard actions in its retreat before the imperious upper house. Yet it did not submit to subordination without two or three notable efforts to maintain its prestige.

The lethargy and ineptitude of President Grant and the consequent inefficiency and corruption of his administrative personnel aroused the lower house after the "tidal wave" of 1874 had given the Democrats a heavy majority, and it resorted once more to the time-honored device of the investigating committee. Only blind partisans or political purists, fearful of the violation of the doctrine of separated powers, could question the propriety of the practice. It would seem strange indeed if Congress, whose function it is to determine what policies the government is to undertake to perform, could not later take the necessary steps to discover whether the legislative determinations had been adequately and properly executed. Congress, moreover, provides the agencies to carry out the policies it decides upon and determines with what personnel the agencies shall be provided, as well as the procedures in the performance of the functions. Congress provides the necessary financial support. It prescribes the means for the supervision and control of the various agencies to the end that the execution may be orderly and efficient. Since all governmental agencies are in their very nature experimental, modification and improvement are inevitably called for. In order that such revision may be intelligently done, Congress must act in the light of the accumulating experience of administrative officials. If Congress is in a sense, as Professor Willoughby has suggested, a "Board of Directors of the Government Corporation," [1] then it must be free to investigate the administration of its enactments.

We have already seen how the first generation of statesmen under the Constitution regarded the apparatus for administration as little more than a group of congressional agencies. Quite naturally, then, the employment of the investigating committee started in the administration of the very first President. Up to 1925 there had been about 285 of these investigations and only three Congresses had completely refrained from them. Largely through them Congress

[1] See W. F. Willoughby, *The Government of Modern States,* pp. 301-02.

has maintained contact with the expanding functions of the Executive until in the opinion of Mr. George B. Galloway they constituted in conjunction with the standing committees "the buckle that binds, the hyphen that joins the legislature and the executive." [2]

It is indicative of the incompetency of President Grant that the congressional investigating committee reached its high-water mark during his administration. Presidents like Grant and Harding who are not circumspect in their choice of Cabinet heads inevitably provoke outbursts of investigation by congressional committees. The astonishing range of the investigations in the latter part of Grant's administration is revealed by the resolution passed in the first session of the Forty-fourth Congress:

"Resolved that the several committees of this house having in charge matters pertaining to appropriations, foreign affairs, military affairs, post offices and post roads, public lands, public buildings and grounds, claims and war claims, be and they are hereby, instructed to inquire, so far as the same may properly be before their respective committees, into any errors, abuses, or frauds that may exist in the administration and execution of existing laws affecting said branches of the public service, with a view to ascertaining what change and reformation can be made so as to promote integrity, economy and efficiency therein . . . to report whether the expenditures of the various departments are justified by law." [3]

Why did not the congressional investigations of this period enhance the prestige of the lower house? The answer is found in the fact that, bad as the administration was proved to be, Congress itself could

---

[2] George B. Galloway, "The Investigative Function of Congress," *Am. Pol. Sci. Rev.*, XXI, p. 47.

[3] *Cong. Record*, 44th Cong., 1st Session, p. 414.

not come with clean hands to the task of correcting the evils. Disappointed as the public may have been with the failure of Grant to measure up to their expectations of a great Executive who would restore leadership in the government, still they could not turn with confidence to a Congress discredited with the revelations of the Credit Mobilier investigation, which had damaged the reputations of some of its outstanding members.[4] The prestige of the lower house had suffered from the revelations of the Mulligan letters which indicated that its speaker, James G. Blaine, had used his position imprudently if not corruptly.[5] Moreover, the House could not point with pride to its record as an investigator of the Executive, since its activities as such were so largely confined to the last two years of Grant's administration, when the Democratic party had obtained control of it. In the public mind it could not escape the charge that it displayed activity over maladministration mainly when there was an opportunity to make political capital by discrediting political opponents. Then, even as later, administration leaders held in check the lower house when a President of the same party as the majority might be mismanaging or neglecting public services.

In no respect is the contrast between Grant and Hayes more strikingly revealed than in the cessation of the investigation of administrative agencies during the presidential term of the latter. Congressional investigations there were, it is true, but such was the character of Hayes's Cabinet and the exceptional administrative honesty and efficiency that small opportu-

---

[4] The Credit Mobilier was a promoter's scheme to make a "killing" out of the construction of the Union Pacific Railroad. The public was shocked when a congressional investigation revealed that prominent congressmen had been given stock to silence inquiry.

[5] See Claude G. Bowers, *The Tragic Era*, pp. 477-81.

nity was afforded the Democratic lower house on that line during his four years in the presidency. Even the investigations of the House Committee attempting to discredit the election of Hayes backfired when Tilden at his own request appeared before the Committee and answered clearly every question that helped his cause but was evasive on all others.[6]

The Democratic House of Representatives did, however, attempt, by parliamentary coup, to enhance its prestige and reduce the power of President Hayes. It was difficult for them to reconcile themselves to the occupancy of the presidential office by a man who had been elected by a minority of the popular vote and whose title was assumed by many of them to be tainted with fraud. In the Forty-sixth Congress the Democrats had a majority of thirteen in the lower house and the Republicans controlled the Senate by a bare majority of three. Late in the last session of this Congress the strategy of the Democratic congressional leaders began to be apparent. Taking advantage of the exclusive right of the lower house to originate revenue measures, the Democratic majority confidently planned to obtain control of the government in certain matters by withholding financial support from the Executive unless they were permitted to have their way. They would thus abolish the juror's test oath which disqualified participants in the recent rebellion and render illegal the further employment of federal troops at the polls on election day. The device for accomplishing this purpose was to be the rider attached to appropriation bills. It had often been employed before but never for the purpose of coercing a co-ordinate branch of the government into pursuing a definite line of policy determined by the lower house. The Republican Senate would

6 See H. T. Peck: *Twenty Years of the Republic*, pp. 117-18.

not approve the House bills with the attached riders and the Forty-fifth Congress consequently came to an end with important services of the government unprovided with indispensable financial support. This was exactly the situation desired by the majority of the lower house. Now, thought they, the President will be compelled to call a special session of the new Congress in which he would face a Democratic majority in both houses.[7]

There was a touch of historic irony in the spectacle of the disciples of Andrew Jackson invoking the prerogatives of the legislature in the presence of a Chief Executive belonging to the party that, since the mantle of the Whigs had fallen upon their shoulders, had never accepted the doctrine of executive leadership. Since Jackson's day the Democratic party had applauded as one Democratic President after another had expounded the theory that the Chief Executive bears a mandate direct from the sovereign people who elect him. They criticized Lincoln, but he had been a minority President, guilty of usurpation of power, in the opinion even of members of the party that had nominated and elected him. Now Hayes likewise was a minority President with a clouded title to office, as they saw it. Congress, particularly the people's House, must rescue the government for the people. Hayes was to be subordinated to Congress as Johnson had been, though by the employment of somewhat different methods.

The fact that the strategy of the Democrats in this case proved abortive gives to the episode a trivial appearance as viewed in the perspective of time. But in its day it seemed to raise an issue fraught with the possibility of a constitutional revolution. Who can say

[7] See C. S. Williams. *Life of Hayes,* II, Chap. XXXIV.

with assurance that the circumstances then obtaining were not implicit with such a possibility? What if Hayes had given in and the precedent had been established? When in due time the expected special session was called and convened, and when the appropriation bills carrying the riders were again introduced, the President's diary discloses the constitutional crisis as viewed by his discerning eye. "They [Congress] will stop the wheels—block the wheels of Government if I do not yield my convictions in favor of the election laws. It will be severe, perhaps a long contest. I do not fear it. I do not even dread it. The people will not allow this revolutionary cause to triumph.[8] . . . No precedent shall be established which is tantamount to coercion of the Executive. I stand for 'the equal' and constitutional independence of the Executive. The independence of the different departments of the Government is essential to the progress and the existence of good government."[9] A little more than a week later the President records more specifically his conviction that only his veto can prevent the revolution. "To consent to it is to make a radical change in the character of the Government . . . and with the doctrine established that the House may legitimately refuse to act unless the other branches of the Government obey its commands, the House of Representatives becomes a despotism."[10] March 27 he was writing to William Henry Smith that "the dangerous doctrine that a bare majority of the two houses can absorb all the powers of all the departments cannot under any circumstances be approved when embodied in legislation. They mean to obtain and establish a precedent for the consolidation of all the powers of

8 C. S. Williams, *Diary of Hayes,* Mar. 9, 1879.
9 *Ibid.,* Mar. 18, 1879.
10 *Ibid.,* Mar. 23, 1879.

the government in the hands of a majority of the House of Representatives." [11]

These quotations indicate that Rutherford B. Hayes had strong convictions concerning the nature of the national government. The late John W. Burgess, who knew him intimately, declared him to have been "a political scientist and statesman as well as a party man." [12] At any rate as a young law student at Harvard Hayes had sat entranced at the feet of Professor Joseph Story and imbibed his philosophy and interpretation of the Constitution as it fell fresh from the lips of that renowned commentator.[13] One can see the faithful disciple of Story in the message of April 29, 1879, vetoing the army appropriation bill with rider attached. "But no single branch or department of the Government," he explained, "has exclusive authority to speak for the American people. The most authentic and solemn expression of their will is contained in the Constitution of the United States. By that Constitution they have ordained and established a government whose powers are distributed among co-ordinated branches, and as far as possible consistent with a harmonious co-operation, are absolutely independent of each other. The people of this country are unwilling to see the supremacy of the Constitution replaced by the omnipotence of any department of the Government." [14]

Among other things the President's veto message was designed to answer a novel argument advanced by the Democratic majority to justify their use of the riders in order to restrict the President's use of the army. They contended that they were merely em-

---

[11] Quoted in C. S. Williams, *Life of Hayes,* II, p. 179n.
[12] *The Administration of President Hayes,* p. 123.
[13] See C. S. Williams, *Diary of Hayes,* I, Chap. 6.
[14] Richardson, *op. cit.,* VII, p. 531.

ploying the time-honored parliamentary practice of the English Commons, that of insisting on the satisfaction of "grievance before supply" and that the House of Representatives was peculiarly the popular agency, the sole representatives of the people. This is one reason for President Hayes's clear and precise restatement of the American principle of separated powers. The message continued with a specific denial of the validity of the doctrine of "grievance before supply" in our system: "The House alone will be the sole judge of what constitutes a grievance, also of the means and measures of redress. An act to control the elections is now the grievance complained of. But the House may on the same principle determine that any other act of Congress, a treaty made by the President, with the advice and consent of the Senate, a nomination or appointment to office, or that a decision or opinion of the Supreme Court is a grievance, and that the measure of redress is to withhold appropriations required for the support of the offending branch of the Government." [15]

The floor leader of the Republican minority, James A. Garfield, had struck the keynote of the opposition to the Democratic method of seeking to encroach on the Executive. "We are ready," he declared, "to pass these bills for the support of the Government at any hour when you will offer them in the ordinary way by the methods prescribed by the Constitution. If you will offer those other propositions of legislation in the fraternal spirit of fair debate we will meet you and discuss their merits. . . . But you shall not coerce any independent branch of the government by the threat of starvation to consent to surrender its voluntary powers until the question has been appealed to the sovereign and decided in your favor. On this

[15] *Ibid.,* pp. 531, 532.

ground we plant ourselves and here we will stand to the end." [16]

The President had to employ the veto seven times to defeat these riders attached to appropriation bills. So well reasoned were his veto messages that they struck a popular chord. "I am congratulated by Senators and Representatives and by people of all sorts," he recorded in his diary.[17] The Democratic House seemed to violate the American tradition of fair play and its tactics came to be regarded as revolutionary.[18]

Burgess may have been somewhat extravagant in claiming that these vetoes had "prevented the parliamentary system, the system of the sovereignty of the lower house of the legislature, the system which finally extinguishes all constitutional immunities of the individual from displacing the check and balance system provided by the Constitution for the purpose of maintaining and protecting those immunities." [19] Be that as it may, it cannot be denied that once again both Senate and House were confronted with a Chief Executive who jealously guarded the independence of his office against encroachments by them. For the first time since the Civil War the veto power was wielded intelligently, decisively, even persistently to maintain "the peoples' office." Hayes had checked the decline in dignity and prestige of the presidential office.

While the administration of Hayes is something of a landmark in the history of the presidency, it is because of a successful defense and not because of any

16 *Cong. Record,* 46th Cong., 1st Session, p. 118.

17 C. S. Williams, *Diary of Hayes,* May 12.

18 See article by General J. D. Cox, "The Hayes Administration," *Atlantic Monthly,* LXXI, p. 831.

19 *Op. cit.,* p. 123.

great constructive accomplishment in the character of the office. In the middle of this administration Woodrow Wilson uttered the lament that the President "is merely the executor of the sovereign legislative will." [20] Here was a stubborn fact that Hayes was powerless to change. Rather he was not aware of it and, had he been, would not have been disposed to change it. Hayes retired from the presidency only a few years before Woodrow Wilson published his penetrating analysis of the national government under the significant title of *Congressional Government*.

Years afterwards Woodrow Wilson was to declare that "the President is at liberty both in law and conscience to be as big a man as he can"; and that "the Constitution explicitly authorizes the President to recommend to Congress 'such measures as he shall deem necessary and expedient'" and that such recommendations need not be merely perfunctory.[21] This would have been regarded as an impractical and preposterous doctrine in the eighties. The experience of President Chester A. Arthur who succeeded to the office upon the death of Garfield did not make the idea look at all plausible. For example, in his first message to Congress he sought authority to deal with a band of from fifty to one hundred cowboys who had been engaged for months in committing acts of lawlessness and brutality which the territorial authorities were powerless to repress. These depredations extended into Mexico, which the marauders reached from Arizona territory, an area subject to the exclusive control of Congress. "With every disposition to meet the exigencies of the case," wrote the perplexed President in his message to Congress, "I am embarrassed by

20 "The Presidency in 1879," *International Review*, VI, p. 46.
21 *Constitutional Government in the United States*, pp. 70-71.

the lack of authority to deal with them effectively." [22]
Congress had left the territorial laws so defective that
the President was thus compelled to beg for authority.
But this request was ignored, as was another one three
months later. This time he made his appeal in a special
message in which he informed Congress "that an alarming state of disorder continues to exist within the territory of Arizona. . . . The governor of the Territory
. . . reports that violence and anarchy prevail—that
robbery, murder, and resistance to law have become so
common as to cease causing surprise." [23] In his second
annual message President Arthur repeated his appeal
to Congress once more, only to be met again with utter
indifference and the lawlessness continued unhamp-
ered until it had spent its force.

Nor was the treatment of these recommendations
exceptional. President Arthur's third message to Congress contained eight important recommendations:
(1) the maintenance of United States Bank notes; (2)
the retirement of the trade dollar; (3) the enlarge-
ment of the navy; (4) territorial government for
Alaska; (5) federal aid for education; (6) a presidential succession law; (7) control of interstate commerce; (8) forest preservation.[24] At the end of the
session Congress had provided government for Alaska
but nothing else that had been recommended. No
wonder James Bryce was even then recording the
observation that "the expression of his [the President's] wishes conveyed in a message has not necessarily any more effect on Congress than an article in a
prominent party newspaper . . . ; and in fact the
suggestions which he makes year after year, are usually neglected, even when his party has a majority in

22 Richardson, *op. cit.*, VIII, p. 54.
23 *Ibid.*, pp. 101-02.
24 *Ibid.*, pp. 179-88.

both Houses, or when the subject lies outside party lines." [25]

In the absence of positive leadership on the part of the Chief Executive the congressional aggrandizement went on apace. No trace of the methods later employed by Wilson and the two Roosevelts to coordinate the political branches of the government to achieve a common end can be detected in the eighties. Cleveland seems to have been almost obsessed with a veneration for the dogma of separated powers. His favorite political theme was the "Independence of the Executive." [26] In the contemporary opinion of Woodrow Wilson ". . . he [Cleveland] thought it no part of his proper function to press his preference in any other way [than by recommendation in a message] upon the acceptance of Congress. . . . But he deemed his duty done when he had thus used the only initiative given him by the Constitution and expressly declined to use any other means of pressing his views on his party. He meant to be aloof and to be President with a certain separateness as the Constitution seemed to suggest." [27] Though Cleveland now and then in his first term raised a clarion call that aroused the public and stirred Congress, he possessed neither the philosophic insight nor the political technique that gave such effectiveness to some of his distinguished successors in their dealings with Congress.

So persistent had the intervention in even matters of detail in administration by Congress now become that congressional sovereignty was becoming, as has been already implied, the theme of a rising school of

[25] *American Commonwealth* (Commonwealth ed.), I, pp. 230-31.

[26] Grover Cleveland, *op. cit.*, pp. 3-76.

[27] *Atlantic Monthly*, LXXIX, p. 292.

political realists. There was, however, something almost tragic in the situation. The culmination of this vast assumption of power by Congress in the 1880's coincided almost exactly with the decline of the lower house to almost the nadir of incompetence. Despite its assumption of sovereign power in the government, it lay floundering in a confusion of warring committees. Spurning all suggestion of external leadership, it yet found no trace of leadership within. Each succeeding census was swelling its membership and compelling an increasing reliance upon committees, the chairmen of which were of chief significance. These were then, as indeed they still are, mainly elderly men who had attained their eminence by leisurely ascent under the seniority rule rather than by a process of natural selection. Each of these chairmen scrimmaged for an opportunity to have the measures reported from his committee considered by the House. The cause of the confusion lay in the fact that no rational system had been devised for sifting bills for consideration by the House. Consequently among the tens of thousands of measures introduced during a session something like sheer caprice had come to determine which should reach the floor for consideration and vote.

Although these committees had been created by the House to act as its servants, in the prevailing confusion the creatures had become accustomed to lord it over their helpless creator. Because of the apparent impossibility of control by the House over these committees in the matter of reporting bills committed to them, the committees had come to be regarded as legislative cemeteries. Even when bills were eventually reported to the House from committees they were placed in the calendars where "they became for them," in the words of Representative Charles B. Lore of Delaware, "the tomb of the Capulets and most

of them were never heard of afterwards." [28] In one
session of the Forty-eighth Congress the calendars
were never once reached.[29] All business was done
either under unanimous consent or on a motion to
suspend the rules by a two-thirds vote, which in practice enabled a minority to prevent legislation. The
situation drew from Representative Thomas B. Reed
the caustic remark that the "only way to do business
inside the rules is to suspend the rules. . . . The object of the rules appears to be to prevent the transaction of business." [30] One member had computed
that to follow the calendar and allow each member of
the House only one minute of debate on each measure
on the calendar would require sixty-six years to dispose
of the measures listed there.[31]

So far as subject matter was concerned, the most
perplexing problem was that of dealing with national
finance. The suggestion of a budget system seems
never to have occurred to any congressman of that
generation. This would have enabled the House to
have had laid before it immediately upon assembling
a definite proposal for a financial program formulated by the Executive. Such an innovation in that
day would have been looked upon as a piece of perilous executive usurpation of the constitutional powers
of Congress. Here, however, was the means by which
might have been broken the autocratic power of the
appropriations committees whose proposals took prece-
dence over those of all other committees and consequently threw into confusion the plans of numerous other committees.

No one would deny President Cleveland full credit

[28] *Cong. Record,* XVII, Part 1, p. 285.
[29] Statement of Representative Springer, *Cong. Record,* XVII,
Part 1, p. 149.
[30] See Woodrow Wilson, *Congressional Government,* p. 61.
[31] See H. J. Ford, *The Cleveland Era,* p. 91.

for his laborious scrutinizing of special pension bills and vetoing them whenever he discovered irregularities. To solve this problem he proposed "The most generous treatment of the disabled, aged, and needy among the veterans" by general laws. But when the Pension Committee of the House, endeavoring to comply with this recommendation, framed a general pension bill that passed both houses, Cleveland promptly vetoed it with the charge that it was "so ambiguous that it would put a further premium on dishonesty and mendacity" and reaffirmed his approval of a general measure. The perplexed Pension Committee then declared "their hearty accord with these views of the President and, largely in accordance with his suggestions, they framed the bill which they thought and still continue to think will best accomplish the ends proposed." "Such a fiasco," wrote the late Henry Jones Ford, "amounted to a demonstration of the lack of intelligent leadership. If the President and his party were cooperating for the furtherance of the same objects, as they both averred, it was discreditable all around that there should have been such a complete misunderstanding as to procedure." [32]

What if every President had been as independent as Cleveland in disregarding his party and the complex of social forces in the nation that determined when to act and when not to act? Lincoln, according to an intimate and observing friend, "managed his campaigns by ignoring men and ignoring all small causes but by closely calculating the tendency of events and the great forces producing logical results." Thus President Lincoln told his friend Sweet: "I can see emancipation coming; whoever can wait for it will see it; whoever stands in its way will be run over." [33]

[32] See H. J. Ford, *The Cleveland Era*, p. 122.
[33] E. Hertz, *The Hidden Lincoln*, p. 298.

It is difficult to find in Cleveland's ways a trace of Lincoln's wisdom. Seldom did he show a sense of timing as to raising issues. Against the unanimous advice of seasoned politicians he devoted his annual message of December, 1887, exclusively to a demand for tariff revisions with the consequence that he demoralized his party and delivered the government into the hands of the extreme protectionists certainly without benefit to the presidency. "Perhaps I made a mistake from the party standpoint," he said after the election, "but damn it, it was right." Concerning which we can imagine the late Mr. Justice Oliver Wendell Holmes remarking, as he once spoke to his cocksure associates: "We must remember that we are not God."

If Cleveland abdicated leadership of Congress, even more so did his successor. Benjamin Harrison was nominated by the Republicans and elected in 1888 and occupied the presidential office during the four years between Cleveland's two terms. Perhaps the Republican party never came nearer getting its type of president than in Harrison. Like Harding later he came from the dominant group in the Senate, although he was far superior to Harding in intellect and in his judgment of men. He had sat in the Senate when it clashed with Cleveland on the President's power of removal. He understood perfectly their conception of the proper place of the Executive in the federal government. Only a few weeks after his election he wrote to his fellow senator, John Sherman, a rival candidate for the presidential nomination in the convention that had nominated Harrison: "I wish you would feel that I desire you to deal with me in the utmost frankness, without any restraint at all, and, in the assurance that all you say will be received and will have the weight which your long experience in public life and your friendship for me entitled you to." [34] Senator Sherman's frank reply contains what may be considered the classic statement of the Republican party's conception of the proper subordination of the Executive to the legislature. "The President," he wrote, "should have no policy distinct from that of his party and that is better represented in Congress than in the Executive. Cleveland made a cardinal mistake in dictating a tariff policy to Congress. Grant also failed to cultivate friendly relations with Congress and was constantly thwarted by it. Lincoln had a happy faculty of dealing with members and Senators." [35]

John Sherman had originally been a Whig and he no doubt cherished boyhood memories of the days of Webster's and Clay's heroic battles against the "executive usurpation" of "King Andrew the First." Despite his gracious reference to Lincoln, he had been among the very first to criticize the war President because of his usurpations of the powers of Congress.[36] No doubt he had frequently heard with approval the proverb current to this day among faithful Republicans: "The party is bigger than any man." Harrison needed no urging on the matter of Sherman's letter. Even if he had had the desire, he lacked the aptitude and peculiar capacity necessary to lead Congress. His conduct of his office leaves the distinct impression that he regarded the President as little more than an agent of Congress, particularly of a Republican Congress, such as had just been elected.

The first half of Harrison's administration affords us one of the finest examples of party government according to the Republican model that that party has

34 John Sherman, *op. cit.*, II, p. 1031.
35 *Ibid.*, II, p. 1032.
36 *Supra*, p. 136.

ever provided. It would hardly be an exaggeration to say that the Republican party organization ran the government. Harrison's vetoes did not pertain to outstanding matters. The spoilsmen were given a free hand in the unclassified service, the President seeming to invite it in his inaugural address with the statement that "honorable party service will certainly not be esteemed by me a disqualification for public office." [37] John Wanamaker, who as party treasurer had "fried the fat out of the manufacturers" to obtain campaign funds by raising the dread specter of "free trade" under a possibly re-elected Cleveland, became Postmaster General. Platt and Quay, who had been active in the campaign to elect Harrison, shared in the distribution of the spoils. The complacent type of President for whom the Whigs had sought in vain the Republicans found in the person of Benjamin Harrison. "Harrison," wrote James Ford Rhodes, "left no particular impress upon the office." [38]

Now that President Harrison made not even a gesture in the direction of leadership and accepted instead the Republican doctrine of congressional sovereignty, it behooved that branch of the government, particularly the lower house, to put its house in order and prepare for the efficient performance of its functions. In the utter absence of presidential leadership, internal leadership needed to be established. The man for the task came to the speakership in the person of Thomas B. Reed. He was confronted with the chaotic conditions in Congress described above. Dilatory motions were being persistently presented and members of the minority party were from time to time refusing to answer "present" at roll calls, thereby preventing the official establishing of a quorum. Reed,

[37] Richardson, *op. cit.,* IX, p. 11.
[38] *Historical Essays,* p. 222.

uncertain of the support of his own party and without consulting his party caucus, secretly laid his plans to break the legislative deadlock. He decided to count a quorum whenever sufficient members were present, regardless of refusals to answer "present" to roll calls. So slender was the Republican majority that the placing on record of the presence of some few Democratic members was usually necessary to carry on the business of the House. The Democrats were planning to take advantage of this fact and render the Fifty-first Congress as impotent as the Fiftieth had been.

Accordingly when on July 29, 1890, a roll call disclosed that only 163 members had answered present, two less than the number necessary for a quorum, Reed provoked a tremendous furore by calmly directing the clerk to record the names of several Democrats as present and refusing to vote.[39] When order had been restored Reed explained that he interpreted the Constitution as intending that members actually present were to be counted present for the purpose of establishing a quorum whether they voted or refused to vote. The Constitution authorized Congress to take steps to compel the attendance of members. "If members can be present and refuse to exercise their function, to wit, not be counted as a quorum, that provision would seem to be nugatory. Inasmuch as the Constitution only provides for their attendance, that attendance is enough. If more was needed the Constitution would have provided more." [40] On the next demand for a roll call the Democrats rushed to the doors to escape from the chamber only to discover that Speaker Reed had ordered them locked. In time the Supreme Court sustained Reed's rule of counting present those who re-

[39] S. W. McCall, *The Life of Thomas B. Reed,* p. 167.
[40] *Cong. Record,* Jan. 29, 1890, p. 950.

fused to answer present. At the next Democratic Congress Reed and the Republicans sat silent at the roll calls until the Democratic majority also had to adopt Reed's Rule. The immediately preceding Congress had been bedeviled by dilatory motions. It had once remained in continuous session for eight days and nights during which there were over one hundred roll calls on dilatory motions to adjourn and to take recess and amendments to these motions. In the Fifty-first Congress Reed peremptorily brought these obstructive tactics to an end by simply refusing to entertain dilatory motions.[41] Once more the House of Representatives began to take on some semblance of a deliberative body.

The intimate touch with the common man that Cleveland had developed as he climbed from Buffalo ward politician through the offices of sheriff, mayor, and governor to the presidency atrophied during his four years between terms as he was affiliated with his Wall Street law partners. Here was no place to ascertain the agrarian discontent that was about to set the South and West aflame with populism. During his first term Cleveland had apparently not cared what forces played upon the presidency. During his second term it is to be doubted whether he understood what they were or how substantial was the basis of the all-pervading social unrest. It was in the face of this that his first important step of the second term was to be the calling of Congress in special session in order to obtain the repeal of the Silver Purchase Act which was draining the federal treasury of its gold reserve. Here he gave one of his few instances of leadership by pleading with Democratic Senators for the repeal measure and he was humiliated by the necessity of purchasing the support of a Democratic member of

41 *Cong. Record*, 51st Cong., 2nd Session, pp. 998-1001.

the finance committee of the upper house, Senator Voorhees, by the use of patronage.[42] One irate Senator protesting to the President that Hell would freeze over before the Silver Purchase Act would be repealed received from Cleveland, who had dispensed the necessary patronage, the reply, "Then it will freeze over in exactly twenty-four hours."

Cleveland's leadership, however, stopped short of the accomplishment of positive, constructive legislation to meet the treasury crisis. His success in compelling repeal of the Silver Purchase Act had so offended Congress that they stubbornly refused Secretary Carlisle's request for authority to sell bonds at three per cent instead of the four per cent specified by the old Resumption Act of 1876. Neither house manifested any sense of responsibility in the crisis and left the President to resort to whatever means might be employed under existing law.[43] Even when J. P. Morgan, making his famous gold loan, offered to reduce the rate to three per cent if the bonds were made specifically payable in gold, the lower house under the leadership of Congressman William J. Bryan resented the insult to the silver men and the public burden was consequently increased $16,000,000.[44] Later pleas of the President were met with similar indifference even in the face of apparently impending national bankruptcy.[45] Cleveland left his party disorganized by alienating the elements within it that had constituted original Jacksonian Democracy and still largely makes up its rank and file. He left the presidency on March 4, 1897, at one of its lowest points in prestige.

There can be little doubt that Cleveland was again

---

[42] J. F. Rhodes, *Historical Essays*, p. 224.
[43] Horace White, *Money and Banking*, p. 182.
[44] R. M. McElroy, *op. cit.*, II, p. 36.
[45] H. White, *op. cit.*, p. 186.

hampered in handling these problems by his theory of separated powers. He compromised with this theory somewhat when he was securing the repeal of the purchase act. Later, when the Wilson-Gorman Tariff Act was being framed, he played no effective part in shaping the measure. When the Senate had utterly mutilated the fairly reasonable bill prepared by the House, the President could repress his fury no longer. Through a letter read by his spokesman on the floor of the House he declared, "Every true Democrat knows that this bill in its present form is not the consummation for which we have long looked. . . . Our abandonment of the cause or principles upon which it rests means party perfidy and party dishonor." [46] Here was a blast of righteous indignation better calculated to relieve the pent-up wrath of the President than to placate the proud Senate and accomplish the results desired. This was done at a time when there could have been no possible hope that public opinion would compel appropriate congressional action because there was then no sufficient consensus on the tariff question. The nation had to await the advent of a President who, like McKinley, could with rare tact restore the harmony of the political branches of the government without abdicating executive leadership; or Presidents who, like Wilson and the two Roosevelts, as the mouthpieces of an aroused public could compel the translation of its consensus into legislative enactments and governmental policies.

[46] Quoted by H. T. Peck, *Twenty Years of the Republic*, p. 366.

X

The Leadership
of William McKinley and
Theodore Roosevelt

*

IT IS INDICATIVE of the caliber of William McKinley as a legislator that only three years after entering Congress he had attained the top committee chairmanship of the House—that of the Ways and Means Committee. He succeeded to this post James A. Garfield who had just been elected President of the United States. McKinley did not align himself with the Old Guard. We have the competent testimony of his fellow member on the Ways and Means Committee and devoted admirer Robert M. LaFollette that McKinley represented "the newer view," and "on the great questions arising was generally on the side of the public

against the private interests." [1] Congress was Mc-
Kinley's school of politics and here he mastered the
perplexing art. So when McKinley moved into the
White House in 1897 few of his predecessors could
have been so adroit in dealing with Congress. No
other President has begun his duties after as long and
able a service in Congress except Garfield who was
not to live long enough to utilize such an experience
in dealing with Congress.

The inauguration of William McKinley marked
the beginning of a new era in the operation of the
national government. Not since the presidency of
Thomas Jefferson, had there been achieved such an
integration of the political branches of the federal
government and such consequent coherence and sense
of direction in its functioning. Only once since the
second inauguration of Grant had the political party
of a President succeeded in carrying the mid-term congressional elections. Only during two of these twenty-
two years had the Senate, the House, and the Executive been in the control of one and the same party.
The accession of William McKinley, however, marked
the beginning of a period of fourteen years of uninter-
rupted Republican control of the national government. It was fortunate for that party and the nation
that during that period two Chief Executives, each
in his own different way an exceptional political
leader, occupied the presidential office.

Several factors combined to make the administration of President McKinley a peculiarly harmonious
one. The President entered the White House supported by a vast personal following whose devotion
to him had accumulated almost the strength of a
messianic faith. His courtesy, dignity, tact, and con-

[1] *Autobiography*, p. 127.

vincing sincerity captivated all who came in contact with him. Moreover, there had not been elected in a generation a President who represented a broader and more distinct consensus. "Mr. McKinley," wrote Herbert Croly, "represented, on the whole, a group of ideas and interests as nearly national as could any political leader of his generation." [2] Henry Adams believed that "Mr. McKinley brought to the problem of American government a solution . . . which seemed to be at least practical and American. He undertook to pool interests in a general trust into which every interest should be taken, more or less at its own valuation, and whose mass should, under his management, create efficiency. He achieved very remarkable results." [3]

The flattering words of President Benjamin Ide Wheeler of the University of California in conferring upon President McKinley the degree of Doctor of Laws represent the sober judgment of the historian a generation later: "A statesman singularly gifted to unite the discordant forces of government and mould the diverse purposes of men toward progressive and salutary action." [4] What was the method by which President McKinley exercised his leadership in the government?

In the first place it must be kept in mind that McKinley, like Garfield, came to the presidency after a long apprenticeship in political leadership in the House of Representatives. He was a regular Republican with a firm conviction that good government could come only through party organization.[5] He car-

---

[2] *Marcus A. Hanna*, p. 187.

[3] *Education of Henry Adams,* pp. 373-74.

[4] See David Saville Muzzey, *The United States of America,* II, p. 374.

[5] F. L. Paxson, "William McKinley," *Dictionary of American Biography,* XII, p. 107.

ried into the Presidential office a sympathetic understanding of the viewpoint of the legislator and a
profound respect for the prerogatives which Congress
so jealously guarded against executive encroachment. Yet he did not, like Harrison, permit the executive branch to suffer a decline. One is compelled to
go back almost a century to President Jefferson, to
find the prototype of President McKinley as the gentle but undoubted leader of Congress.[6] "We never had
a President who had more influence with Congress
than McKinley," was the opinion of Senator Shelby
M. Cullom. "I have never heard of even the slightest
friction between him and the party leaders in Senate
and House." [7] After a long service in the Senate, Senator George F. Hoar expressed the opinion that no
other President, with the possible exception of Jackson, had exercised such influence over the Senate as
President McKinley.[8] Anyone who will review the experience of the Presidents from Lincoln to McKinley
must admit that the latter was the first Republican
President to exercise any considerable initiative
without arousing the resentment of his party in Congress. And no President since McKinley has been as
happy as he in dealing with a Republican Congress.

Because McKinley did not manifest toward Congress the sometimes pugnacious stubbornness of his
predecessor, Cleveland, and was incapable of the theatrical leadership of his immediate successor he has
sometimes been considered a weak President. We have
the unanimous testimony to the contrary from unquestionably strong men who knew him intimately
such as John Hay, Elihu Root, and Jules Cambon.

[6] See J. F. Rhodes, "The Presidential Office," *Scribner's,* Feb.,
1903.

[7] *Fifty Years of Public Service,* p. 275.

[8] *Op. cit.,* II, p. 47. See also opinion of Elihu Root in Olcott,
William McKinley, II, pp. 346-47.

"We who know him regard him as a man of extraordinary ability, integrity, and force of character," wrote his intimate friend Hay before his election, and two weeks later added to his estimate, "There are idiots who think Mark Hanna will run him." [9] The charge that Mark Hanna dominated him becomes ridiculous in the light of Hanna's frank admission that McKinley repeatedly repulsed his suggestions that he might gain political advantage by compromising with his conscience. Hanna admitted that he had been made a better man by McKinley's insisting that there were things a presidential candidate must not do even to win the presidency.[10] Herman Kohlsaat was present in a small group in 1896 that heard candidate McKinley resolutely refuse to come to terms with the disreputable boss of Pennsylvania, Senator Matthew Quay, and Hanna did not criticize his candidate for it.[11]

It has to be admitted that President McKinley ultimately did not have his way in his opposition to war with Spain, even though a powerful group of senators supported him in his desire for peace. But the President of the United States is no dictator. He certainly cannot lead a people where they do not want to go. None knew better than Speaker Thomas B. Reed the irresistible war frenzy of Congress. When ex-Governor Morton of New York wrote urging him to dissuade members of Congress against war, Reed said, "He might as well ask me to stand out in the middle of a Kansas waste and dissuade a cyclone." [12] Indeed Congress could not possibly have withstood the demand for war and would have repassed a declaration of war over McKinley's veto. And a war the President

[9] Quotations by Tyler Dennett, *John Hay*, pp. 175, 178.
[10] Herbert Croly, *op. cit.*, p. 363.
[11] Thomas Beer, *The Mauve Decade* (Overseas Edition), p. 80.
[12] Margaret Leech, *In the Days of McKinley*, p. 185.

does not believe in to the extent of a veto is unthinkable.

In connection with the wild debate on the declaration of war a combination of Democrats and Republicans argued for days in favor of a resolution to recognize the "Republic of Cuba." Such a flagrant usurpation of the President's constitutional control of foreign relations spurred McKinley to prepare a tentative veto of such a resolution if passed in both houses.[13] This possible Congressional-Executive impasse brought the Senate to its senses and the resolution was dropped. President McKinley no doubt reasoned that he was but an instrument of public opinion in this matter. The fact that the opinion was artificially created by strident propaganda made the pressure on President and Congress not one whit less severe than if it had developed naturally. In the spring of 1898, as never before in our history, there was a popular demand for war. The vote of 324 to 19 in the House of Representatives on the resolution of the declaration of war is fairly representative of public sentiment. Madison, Polk, Lincoln, Wilson—each in his day yielded to a less universal cry for war than did William McKinley in 1898. For thirteen anxious months he held a restless Congress in leash until their constituents could apparently be restrained no longer.

As another instance of the irony of history, this war, which McKinley did not want, served to increase enormously his power. The conflict was so brief, the victory so complete, and the public so dazzled and flattered by the resulting territorial expansion that no reaction against executive aggrandizement set in as it had after the Civil War. No such congressional revolt as threatened Lincoln and almost paralyzed the ex-

13 *Ibid.*, p. 188.

ecutive branch under Johnson rose to annoy Mc-
Kinley. The reason for this is apparent enough. The
entrance of the United States into world affairs tended
to obliterate party lines. The President's conscious-
ness of this fact was revealed when he said to his
secretary, "I can no longer be called the President of
a party; I am now the President of the whole people." [14] Suddenly our domestic affairs had been overshadowed by the problems of war and treaties and
newly acquired territories even in the uttermost parts
of the planet. Our participation in the intervention in
China during the Boxer uprising and our successful
insistence upon the "open door" thrilled the public
at our new position in world affairs. Thus the Spanish-
American War became in a very real sense a landmark in the constitutional development of the Executive.[15]

At this juncture an assassin removed McKinley and
elevated to the presidency Theodore Roosevelt. Here
was a man whose profound faith in our "manifest
destiny" made it certain that the President's constitutional duties in respect to foreign policy would be
freely exercised and expanded through the interpretation of a daring enthusiast for nationalism. Moreover,
in domestic matters the young President held most
extraordinary views regarding the range of authority
permitted the President under the Constitution. John
Marshall was a strict constructionist in comparison
with Theodore Roosevelt. "The most important factor
in getting the right spirit in my administration,"
he explained many years later ". . . was my insistence
upon the theory that the executive power was limited
only by specific restrictions and prohibitions appearing in the Constitution or imposed by Congress under

14 Olcott, *op. cit.*, II, p. 296.
15 See Woodrow Wilson, *Constitutional Government*, p. 59.

its constitutional powers. My view was that every executive officer, and above all every executive officer in high position was a steward of the people bound actively and affirmatively to do all he could for the people. . . . I declined to adopt the view that what was imperatively necessary for the Nation could not be done by the President unless he could find some specific authorization to do it. . . . Under this interpretation of executive power I did and caused to be done many things not previously done by the President and the heads of the departments. I did not usurp power but I did greatly broaden the use of executive power." [16]

Theodore Roosevelt believed that in his theory of the scope of presidential power he was a disciple of Jackson and of Lincoln.[17] It is doubtful whether he was correct with respect to either of these two predecessors in his office. He was not a painstaking student either of constitutional theory or constitutional history. So far as Lincoln is concerned it is impossible to say what he regarded as the limits of executive power and in the stress of war he of course went farther than Roosevelt in the realm of executive prerogative. Moreover, as above noted, he frankly confessed disregard of constitutional details. Jackson, in the preparation of his state papers, was usually careful to employ the talents of capable constitutional lawyers whose logic was baffling to the Whig opponents who had raised the issue of constitutionality with respect to his executive acts. On the whole, Jackson's executive conduct conforms to prevailing constitutional interpretation today while Theodore Roosevelt's does not.

In one respect Theodore Roosevelt was uncon-

16 *An Autobiography,* p. 389.
17 *Ibid.,* p. 395.

sciously a disciple of Jackson. To a greater extent than
any of the intervening Presidents he believed that he
bore a special mandate from the people.[18] In this respect he was the least Republican of all the Presidents
elected by his party. Roosevelt would have found
comfort in the exposition of executive prerogative
written by Alexander Hamilton in 1793 under the
pen name of "Pacificus." One can imagine the glee
with which the irrepressible Theodore would have
seized upon this bit of constitutional doctrine by
means of which he could have rationalized his conduct as Chief Executive. "The general doctrine of
our constitution, then," wrote Hamilton, "is that the
Executive power of the nation is vested in the President, subject only to the exceptions and qualifications which are expressed in the instrument." [19]

President Roosevelt countered every effort of Congress to confine him to definite constitutional and
legal limits. His practice conformed to his theory. For
example, he appointed a number of extralegal, unsal-
aried commissions. When his commission on country
life had completed its work he asked Congress for an
appropriation of $25,000 to print and distribute its
findings. The Congress responded with a refusal of
the appropriation and a positive prohibition against
the appointment of any other commission without
specific congressional authorization. Roosevelt signed
the bill containing the restrictive amendment but
frankly declared he would disregard the restriction,
declaring "Congress cannot prevent the President from
seeking advice" nor prevent citizens he might desig-

18 F. L. Paxson, "Theodore Roosevelt," *Dictionary of American Biography,* XVI, p. 140.
19 *Works of Alexander Hamilton* (Lodge ed.), IV, pp. 142-44.

nate from giving their service to the people." [20] Even in his first term congressional concern over the young President's executive conduct took the form of a resolution calling upon him to file a copy of every executive order accompanied by a citation of the law under which it was issued and, furthermore, providing for the creation of a commission of distinguished lawyers to pass on the executive acts and orders.[21]

At the same time that Roosevelt ranged freely in the exercise of what he considered his powers he could brook no thought of congressional interference with executive duties except with respect to the Senate's constitutional power to refuse confirmation of nominations. "My secretaries and their subordinates were responsible to me and I accepted the responsibility for all their deeds . . . and as for getting Congress to make up my mind for me the thought would have been inconceivable to me." [22] As an ex-President he was later stirred to indignation by the deference his successor, Taft, paid to Congress in the Ballinger controversy. "The charges [against Ballinger]," he declared, "were made to the President. The President had the facts before him and could get at them at any time, and he alone had power to act if the charges were true. However, he permitted and requested Congress to investigate Mr. Ballinger. . . . The President abode by the majority. Of course one who believes in the Jackson-Lincoln theory of the Presidency would not be content with this town-meeting majority and minority method of determining by another branch of the government what it seems the especial duty of

20 *Autobiography*, pp. 416-17.
21 C. G. Washburn, *Theodore Roosevelt, the Logic of His Career*, pp. 138-39.
22 *Autobiography*, p. 396.

the President himself to determine for himself in dealing with his own subordinates in his own department." [23]

In the number and importance of legislative accomplishments Roosevelt's seven years stands unsurpassed by any previous administration. S. E. Morison's statement that "Roosevelt gave the Presidency an organic connection with Congress" [24] goes far toward explaining how it happened. The President was not in doubt as to what the American people expected of their Chief Executive. "In theory," he set down in his *Autobiography* years later, "the Executive has nothing to do with legislation. In practice, as things now are, the Executive is or ought to be peculiarly representative of the people as a whole. . . . Therefore a good Executive under present conditions of American life must take a very active interest in getting the right kind of legislation in addition to performing his Executive duties with an eye single to the public welfare." [25] A perusal of Roosevelt's messages reveals the fact that, while they are addressed to Congress, the President had in mind the larger audience, the American people, through the pressure of whose opinion he frequently was able to get his legislative program enacted.[26]

Theodore Roosevelt came to the presidency thoroughly seasoned in practical politics. His essays and public utterances generally revealed his profound belief in political parties and party organizations.[27] His experience as a legislator and later as governor of

[23] *Idem*, p. 397.

[24] *Op. cit.*, II, p. 449.

[25] P. 292.

[26] See H. C. Black, *op. cit.*, pp. 22-24; also Chas. G. Washburn, *op. cit.*, p. 127.

[27] See "The Duties of American Citizenship," *Works*, XIII, pp. 281 ff.

New York had afforded him a fine apprenticeship
for the presidency. He manifested a quick understanding and realistic grasp of the value of the Speaker of
the House as the medium through whom executive
leadership in legislation might be exercised. No
sooner had Joseph G. Cannon been elected to the
speakership than the President asked him to call at
the White House. So frequent did these visits become
that before long they were occasioning comment.[28]
The two men lost no time in arriving at a good working understanding of their respective roles in the government. Perfect harmony would have been impossible between two such individualists. Cannon long
afterwards admitted "we did not always agree; in
fact we more often disagreed, but seldom in principle
and usually as to practical methods. Roosevelt had
the outlook of the Executive and the ambition to do
things. I had the more confined outlook of the legislator who had to consider ways of meeting the expenditures of new departments and expansions in
Government." [29]

The lower house was at this time perhaps better
organized and probably functioned more smoothly
than at any other time in its history. Its esprit de
corps had been raised largely through the personality
and leadership of its Speaker and it was proud of its
place in the federal system. It was on its guard against
senatorial encroachment. President Roosevelt paid a
high tribute to the House of Representatives in a
letter to the Republican whip, Representative James
E. Watson, written in 1906: "I feel that all good
citizens who have the welfare of America at heart
should appreciate the immense amount that has been
accomplished by the present House, organized as it is

and the urgent need of keeping this organization in power. With Mr. Cannon as Speaker, the House has literally accomplished a phenomenal amount of good work." [30]

Roosevelt recognized the Speaker as the duly authorized agent of the majority of the House. Since it was impractical to confer personally with the members to ascertain the sentiment of the majority, the President consulted instead their Speaker, as the spokesman of the majority of the House as well as the master of its procedure. As Cannon has explained it, "The chairmen of Committees conferred with the Speaker as to legislation before their committees, and the Speaker's room became a clearing house where the views of the majority were freely discussed, and the Speaker could intelligently present the majority opinion to the President. It was a workable plan and Roosevelt, whatever he may have permitted the Insurgents to think, conferred with the Speaker on all proposed legislation throughout his administration.

"I think Mr. Roosevelt talked over with me virtually every serious recommendation to Congress before he made it and requested me to sound out the leaders in the House, for he did not want to recommend legislation simply to write messages. He wanted results and he wanted to know how to secure results with the least friction. He was a good sportsman and accepted what he could get so long as the legislation conformed even in part to his recommendations." [31] Even after discounting Speaker Cannon's somewhat idealized description of the system, there remains the essential truth that explains how such remarkable legislative results were obtained by the practical in-

[30] *Cong. Record,* 61st Cong., 2nd Session, p. 3303.
[31] L. W. Busbey, *op. cit.,* p. 219. See G. R. Brown, *The Leadership of Congress,* pp. 122, 123, 127.

tegration of the legislative and executive branches of the federal government in the first decade of the twentieth century.

Let no one assume that Theodore Roosevelt was not compelled, now and then, to make sacrifices to attain his major objectives. The intensely practical character of his leadership is revealed in the means by which he got the railroad legislation he recommended. Success crowned his efforts in the end but not without the payment of a price to obtain it. He was reinforced in his efforts by the long accumulating public indignation against the outrages committed by the common carriers. But only by coming to an understanding with the House organization was the President enabled to accomplish this crowning achievement of his administration. Though long an advocate of a protective tariff, Roosevelt had caught something of the vision of McKinley, revealed in his last public address at Buffalo, and he was ready to lead a crusade for tariff reform. Here he met the stubborn opposition of Speaker Cannon. On one occasion a message to Congress containing a recommendation for tariff revision had already been written, printed, and even circulated when the President consented to withdraw the recommendation and thereby won Speaker Cannon's backing on the Hepburn Railroad Rate Bill, which then passed the House with only seven dissenting votes. As a legislator Roosevelt had learned how to create situations for the sheer purpose of getting bargaining advantages.

When the Hepburn Bill reached the Senate it encountered the determined opposition of leaders of the President's own party. Presently the nation was witnessing the almost unprecedented spectacle of a major administration measure being championed by a leader of the opposition, Senator Tillman, who reported the measure from the Interstate Commerce Committee. The minority report was presented by the Republican chairman of the committee and four outstanding Republican senators. The bill become a law on June 29, 1906, and three days later came the most striking testimony as to the success of Roosevelt's leadership in legislation, testimony from the editorial page of the New York *World,* a persistent and often bitter critic of the President. "Mr. Roosevelt would be more than human," wrote the editor, "if he could conceal his elation over the achievements of a Congress that has evidenced almost phonographic fidelity to the wishes of the President. The sentiment of the country is undoubtedly in accord with him in praising Congress for what it has done—concerning which Roosevelt might say, 'All of which I saw and a great part of which I was.' " [32]

It is not surprising that the continuous success of Roosevelt in securing legislation led to a reaction on the part of Congress in the latter part of his second term. He had given them but little rest in the persistent pushing of his program and the popular tendency to give the President credit for legislation left the congressmen more or less resentful and even frustrated at the seeming subordinate role. Indeed the last session of Congress during his presidency, sitting after his successor, William Howard Taft, had already been elected, was embittered by a foolish quarrel precipitated by the President's objection to an amendment in an appropriation bill forbidding the use of the Secret Service in investigating congressmen.[33] "I had not been consulted," said Speaker Cannon, "on President Roosevelt's last annual message, nor had it

[32] Quoted by J. B. Bishop, *Theodore Roosevelt and His Times,* II, pp. 17, 18.

[33] H. F. Pringle, *Theodore Roosevelt, a Biography,* p. 483.

been submitted to me in advance of publication as had all the former messages of Mr. Roosevelt. I was as much surprised as anyone when I found that this message contained an assault upon Congress, and especially upon the House of Representatives because of the amendment limiting the activities of the Secret Service." [34] Nothing of consequence resulted more than a furious outburst of indignation against the President on the floors of the two Houses in which even the President's friends joined.[35] A month later, upon the eve of Taft's inauguration, the President wrote to his eldest son, "I have entered on the last month of my Presidency and I think I can hold Congress down so that no disastrous break can occur during that period. . . . I have a very strong feeling that it is a President's duty to get on with Congress if he possibly can and that it is a reflection upon him if he and Congress come to a complete break. For seven sessions I have been able to prevent such a break. This session, however, they felt it was safe utterly to disregard me because I was going out and my successor had been selected. . . ." [36]

As Secretary of War William Howard Taft had been President Roosevelt's most trusted Cabinet member. Apparently he saw eye to eye with his chief on administration policies. In 1908 Roosevelt threw the weight of his office behind Taft's candidacy and he was easily nominated and elected. The new President entered the office with an exceptionally high prestige and many believed he might administer his duties with greater efficiency than his immediate predecessor.

William Howard Taft entered upon the duties of the presidency at a juncture in public affairs when

34 L. W. Busbey, *op. cit.*, pp. 231, 232.
35 H. F. Pringle, *op. cit.*, p. 483.
36 J. B. Bishop, *op. cit.*, II, p. 134.

his office was bound to be an exceptionally trying one. Van Buren had found it difficult to take up the duties of the presidency after picturesque old Andrew Jackson had just laid them down. Taft had to follow a colorful President, Theodore Roosevelt, who had dazzled the American people with his dynamic personality. It was expected that Taft too would be an exponent of the progressive movement and while his program was certainly forward looking he did not quite keep step with the tempo of public opinion.

Taft seems not to have caught the vision of the presidency as primarily a political office. While he said nothing about the matter under Roosevelt he never sympathized with his chief's theory that it is the President's duty "to do anything that the needs of the nation demand, unless such action is forbidden by the Constitution or the laws." [37] President Taft, on the contrary, held that, as he expressed it later, "The true view of the executive function is, as I conceive it, that the President can exercise no power which cannot be reasonably and fairly traced to some specific grant of power or justly implied or included within such express grant as necessary and proper to its exercise. Such specific grant must be either in the Constitution or in an act of Congress passed in pursuance thereof. There is no undefined residuum of power which he can exercise because it seems to him to be in the public interest." [38]

This juristic conception of the presidency is not surprising in one whose education was fundamentally legal. Early in his career he had taught law at the University of Cincinnati and upon retirement from the presidency he became a professor of law at Yale University. It perhaps never occurred to Taft that

[37] *Supra*, p. 234.
[38] *Our Chief Magistrate and His Powers*, pp. 139-42.

the country would be prompt to notice that he had filled every Cabinet position with a lawyer except the two in which he had retained members of Roosevelt's official family. His Cabinet seemed to him to be his trusted group of personal advisers. The fact is that his experience before reaching the presidency had been so exclusively administrative—in the courts, in the Philippines as governor general, and in the Cabinet—that he came, like Herbert Hoover later, to the chief political office of the nation relatively inexperienced in political functions.

He got off with an unfortunate start on the revision of the tariff by delaying taking a hand in its passage through Congress until it was too late. Unlike his predecessor, he established no organic connection of the Executive and the Congress through the Speaker of the House. In any case this would have been difficult. Speaker Cannon was personally so disagreeable to Taft that we cannot think of their sitting down together in the White House to map out a legislative program. Even if he could have overcome his personal aversion to Cannon, the Speaker was now so unpopular that the President's prestige suffered from a few occasions when he was photographed with Cannon. Before Taft had been President a year Cannon was deprived of his position on the Rules Committee and of the power to appoint committees, after which he was no longer possible as the liaison agent between the President and the Congress.

Early in Taft's administration progressive Republicans who had looked to him for leadership were dismayed to see him fraternizing with reactionaries and neglecting them. A party cleavage developed during the debates on the Payne-Aldrich Tariff that degenerated into factional warfare during the Ballinger-Pinchot clash over conservation of natural resources.

In 1910 came the tidal wave that gave the Democrats control of the lower house for the first time in sixteen years. Convinced that the progressive cause he had promoted during his presidency would be doomed if Taft were re-elected, Theodore Roosevelt sought the Republican nomination in 1912. Failing to obtain it, his followers organized the Progressive party and made him its candidate for President. The Democratic nominee, Governor Woodrow Wilson of New Jersey, won the election over Taft and Roosevelt.

Cleveland, as a devotee of the dogma of checks and balances, had twice left the presidency locked in futile combat with Congress. McKinley, attaining the presidency after a long legislative career, integrated the two branches by cordial and conciliatory relations with Congress. Theodore Roosevelt, through the give and take of conferences with the imperious Speaker of the House, had accomplished comparable results. Now that the Speaker had been "dethroned" it remained to be seen how Woodrow Wilson, a political scientist in the presidential office, might utilize new methods of bringing together the political branches of the government.

XI

The Theory and Practice
of Woodrow Wilson

★

THE CONCEPTION of the presidency that Woodrow Wilson carried into the White House was no well-worn political theory of his. Instead it represented the culmination of a generation-long ideological evolution, influenced mainly by his reflection on the course of political events. It started in his undergraduate days, at Princeton, 1875-79, when he decided that he was predestined for a political career. This appears to have been a persisting conviction and if we can believe his campaign manager, William Combs, Wilson at a conference the day following his election in 1912 coldly informed him: "Whether you did little or much, remember that God ordained that I should be the next President of the United States. Neither you nor any other mortal or mortals could have prevented that." But such was the low estate of the presidency in Wilson's college student days that he did not then at all aspire to it. It was suffering from its decline under the presidencies of Johnson and Grant. This was the era of the hegemony of the Senate. So it is a curious but significant fact that the young student purchased a pack of calling cards and inscribed on each one, "Thomas Woodrow Wilson, Senator from Virginia."

In 1879 Henry Cabot Lodge, then editor of the *International Review,* received and accepted a manuscript submitted by the twenty-three-year-old student, Woodrow Wilson. The article is significant because it reveals that, despite his youth, he was already a keen observer of the functioning of the national government. Viewing public affairs in the midst of the Hayes administration with a mind already remarkably free from the prevailing conventional conceptions of American government, he detected what he believed to be radical defects in our constitutional system. "The President can seldom make himself recognized as a leader," he wrote. "He is merely the executor of the sovereign legislative will; his cabinet officers are little more than the chief clerks or superintendents in the executive departments, who advise the President as to matters in most of which he has no power of action independently of the concurrence of the Senate." This article reveals the fact that Woodrow Wilson was already pondering upon a theory of executive not necessarily presidential leadership that was to become the outstanding contribution of his pedagogic and political career. Even at that early date he was proposing "to give the heads of the Executive departments—the members of the Cabinet—seats in Congress, with the privilege of the initiative in legislation and some part in the unbounded privileges now commanded by the Standing Committees." [1]

A few years later he was writing his doctoral dissertation on "Congressional Government" and in it he was condemning control of the government in the secret meetings of irresponsible committees. There is no indication yet that the presidency is considered a significant office, one to which Wilson could aspire. The focus of power in the federal government is still in Congress and, as we have seen, in Chapter IX, it is a distressingly unsatisfactory organ. But a curious omission in Wilson's *Congressional Government* (1884) indicated that a fundamental change was taking place in his conception of the federal government. There is in it no suggestion of cabinet government. It can be suspected that the rise of Grover Cleveland who was then running for President may account for Wilson's change.

In April, 1893, he thought that circumstances gave the recently inaugurated President, Grover Cleveland, an opportunity to bring order out of the governmental chaos. He courteously but vigorously urged the President to assume leadership. For the first time in many years the same party was in control of the House, the Senate, and the Executive. Let the President now assume the role of prime minister with the Cabinet as the agency of co-ordination to accomplish the popular will.[2] The hope was a vain one. Dogmatic President Cleveland entertained no such novel conception of the operation of the government. Even if he had, the season was not opportune. The furious controversies over the repeal of the Silver Purchase Act and the re-

[1] "Cabinet Government in the United States," *International Review*, Aug., 1879, VI, pp. 46-163.
[2] *Review of Reviews*, April, 1893.

vision of the tariff indicated an absence of a definite popular will and independent-minded Cleveland made no search for unifying ideologies or possible points of equilibrium among conflicting interests. Moreover, the devastating depression of the 1890's was drastically reducing Cleveland's prestige.

Shortly after the inauguration of President McKinley, Mr. Wilson again analyzed the situation. He saw no hope of a solution under the new President. But once more he stated the problem and proposed his solution. "We must find or make somewhere in our system," he said, "a group of men to lead us, who represent the nation in the origin and responsibility of their power; who shall draw the Executive, which makes the choice of foreign policy and upon whose ability and good faith and honorable execution of law depends, into cordial co-operation with the legislature, which under whatever form of government, must sanction law and policy." [3]

Not until the death of McKinley and the succession to the presidency of Theodore Roosevelt did Woodrow Wilson see much he could commend in the relationship of the President to Congress. In spite of the incompatibility of temperament between these two men Wilson did not altogether withhold credit from the President in this matter. "Whatever else we may think or say of Theodore Roosevelt," he said, "we must admit that he is an aggressive leader. He led Congress—he was not driven by Congress. We may not approve his methods but we must concede that he made Congress follow him." [4]

The comment on Theodore Roosevelt's leadership was made only a few weeks after the inauguration of

[3] Woodrow Wilson, *College and State Papers*. Edited by R. S. Baker and W. E. Dodd, II, p. 335.
[4] David Lawrence, *The True Story of Woodrow Wilson*, p. 39.

William Howard Taft. Wilson had already published his lectures on *Constitutional Government in the United States*. They represented his mature judgment on the matters discussed and contain the key to explain his career as an Executive. "Leadership and control must be lodged somewhere," he declared. "The whole art of statesmanship is the art of bringing the several parts of government into effective co-operation for the accomplishment of common objects and daily objects at that." [5] When he had first raised his voice against the governmental confusion prevailing in 1879 it had been as one crying in the wilderness. Since then there had been a growing popular tendency toward the recognition of the President "as the unifying force in our complex system, the leader both of his party and the nation." [6]

It must be kept in mind that Woodrow Wilson was a party man. This would seem inevitable in such an enthusiast for the English parliamentary system where the party becomes practically a part of the governmental system, serving to focus public opinion and translate its agreements into public policies. Moreover, the President is the head of his party. "He cannot escape being the leader of his party except by incapacity and lack of personal force because he is at once the choice of the party and the nation." [7] Wilson's political mentor, Walter Bagehot, had once declared that the American President was the choice of the wire-pullers and the product of a complicated system of caucuses, which made the office hardly worth holding.[8] Consequently in 1897 Wilson concluded that the national nominating convention ren-

---

5 *Constitutional Government*, p. 54.
6 *Ibid.*, p. 60.
7 *Ibid.*, p. 67.
8 *Works and Life of Walter Bagehot*, V, p. 177.

dered it "in the highest degree unlikely that our Presidents should ever again be leaders of men." [9] Conventions had been instrumental in separating Congress and the President even more than the framers of the Constitution intended. But in 1907 Wilson rejected this view. "What is it that the nominating convention wants in the man it is to present to the country for its suffrages?" he inquired and then provided the answer. "A man who will be and who will seem to the country in some sort an embodiment of the character and purposes it wishes its government to have—a man who understands his own day and the needs of the country, and who has the personality and the initiative to enforce his views both upon the people and upon Congress." [10] This interpretation is significant, no matter how idealized or romantic it may be in its ignoring of the delegates' one great purpose of finding a candidate who can attract enough votes to capture for the party the control of patronage and policy inherent in the presidency.

So the President carries a mandate from his party which consists of a majority of the nation. Within the party councils he can control its program through his position as leader and through his personal force. [11] "The President is at liberty, both in law and conscience, to be as big a man as he can. His capacity will set the limit." If Congress is overborne by him it will be "because the President has the nation behind him and Congress has not. He has no means of compelling Congress except through public opinion." [12] The reign of public opinion through presidential leadership was unquestionably the dream of Woodrow Wilson, a

9 *Atlantic Monthly* LXXV, (July, 1897) pp. 1-14.
10 *Constitutional Government*, p. 65.
11 *Ibid.*, p. 69.
12 *Ibid.*, pp. 70-71.

dream that was to turn into the nightmare of the debacle of his attempt to pressure the Senate into ratifying the Covenant of the League of Nations.

In the clause of the Constitution, hitherto neglected by the commentators, Woodrow Wilson found the authority for the exercise of the presidential leadership of Congress. As he dwelt upon it he employed methods suggestive of Marshall's in extracting its hidden meaning. "And yet," he points out, "the Constitution explicitly authorizes the President to recommend to Congress 'such measures as he shall deem necessary and expedient' and it is not necessary to the integrity of even the literary theory of the Constitution to insist that recommendations should be merely perfunctory. . . . The Constitution bids him speak and times of stress must more and more thrust upon him the attitude of originator of policies." [13]

After election and just a few weeks before inauguration he felt impelled once again to make clear his conception of the executive office. This was done in a letter to Representative A. Mitchell Palmer, soon to be appointed Attorney General of the United States. Palmer had suggested to the President-elect the advisability of an amendment to the Constitution limiting the President to a single term, which had been declared to be the policy of the party in the platform on which Wilson had been elected. From such a proposition he vigorously dissented. The President, he argued, "is expected by the nation to be the leader of his party as well as the chief executive officer of the Government and the country will take no excuses from him. He must play the part and play it successfully or lose the country's confidence. He must be Prime Minister, as much concerned with the guidance of legislation as with just and orderly execution of law; and he

[13] *Constitutional Government*, pp. 72, 73.

is the spokesman of the nation in everything, even the most momentous and most delicate dealings of the Government in foreign affairs." He was certain that the President ought not to be hampered by denial of the strength derived from the possibility of re-election. Turning again to his old hope of a parliamentary system, he continued: "Sooner or later it would seem he must be made answerable to opinion in a somewhat more informal and intimate fashion, answerable, it may be, to the Houses whom he seeks to lead, either personally or through a cabinet, as well as to the people for whom they speak. But that is a matter to be worked out—as it will inevitably be in some natural American way which we cannot yet even predict." [14]

Vestiges of Wilson's early pattern of parliamentary government crop out again and again in Wilson's conduct after inauguration. So eager was he after the idea that he saw analogies between the American and English governmental systems where most students of government never suspected them. If one reads between the lines of that ill-starred appeal for a Democratic Congress in October, 1918, there can be seen the prime minister's appeal to the country for a vote of confidence in the government.[15] The "solemn referendum" on the Treaty of Versailles, particularly the Covenant of the League of Nations asked for in the presidential election of 1920, reflects a similar conception. He even hoped his health would be restored so that he might be candidate for a third term in 1920. The prime minister, we might say, would "go to the country" on the major issue, the ratification of the treaty. The President's most trusted friends were at the San

[14] The letter in reply to Mitchell is printed in the appendix to H. J. Ford, *Woodrow Wilson, the Man and his Work.*
[15] The appeal is printed in J. P. Tumulty, *Woodrow Wilson as I Knew Him,* pp. 130-32.

Francisco Convention, ready to execute the master stroke. Bainbridge Colby was to have made the motion to suspend the rules and nominate by acclamation. Of course they found such a move inopportune.[16] It should be remembered that the "Big Four" of the Versailles Conference was a group of premiers. President Wilson saw that any head of an American delegation he might send to the conference would be outranked by these actual heads of foreign governments and the only way that America's dignity, prestige, and power could be maintained would be for the American "prime minister" to appear in person.

One step in the process of parliamentary government, the resignation of the prime minister on an adverse vote on one of his important measures, Wilson never carried out, but there is no doubt that he thought of such a move on two occasions. The first was but a few weeks after his inauguration, when he urged the repeal of the exemption of American vessels from the payment of tolls when they passed through the Panama Canal. He had difficulty controlling his own party on this issue and for a while was threatened with defeat. "In case of failure in this matter," he wrote, "I shall go to the country, after my resignation is tendered, and ask it whether America is to stand before the world as a nation that violates its contracts as mere matters of convenience, upon a basis of expediency." [17]

The second occasion when President Wilson considered resignation in case of possible defeat was when the McLemore Resolution sought, in the face of the President's opposition, to warn American citizens against traveling on armed vessels of the belligerents.

16 David Lawrence, *op. cit.*, p. 320.
17 From a letter of J. P. Tumulty to H. F. Gunnison, quoting the President's remarks to him. See Ray Stannard Baker, *Woodrow Wilson, Life and Letters*, IX, p. 415; also David Lawrence, *op. cit.*, p. 311.

When informed that this proposal might pass in spite of his opposition he again thought of resigning.[18] Whether, in either case, the President would have carried out his intention can never be known, because he won both contests, but it would seem doubtful. Would he not have seen before the irrevocable step was taken that such a device as resignation would operate unsatisfactorily in a system where Congress would not at the same time be dissolved to give the nation an opportunity to pass judgment on the issue presented?

Just how President Wilson would have procured the Constitutional changes to get a presidential election when needed has not been revealed. Nevertheless, his was a rationalization of the American political process in terms of an alien system and, however far-fetched the interpretation may have been, the very intensity of conviction of his confessedly single-track mind produced remarkably successful results in his first term.

Now that we have ascertained the theory of executive leadership propounded by Woodrow Wilson let us investigate the technique by which he put it in operation when inauguration to the presidency afforded him his great opportunity. A revolution was indeed due in 1913. In the opinion of the late Henry Jones Ford, "the ship of state seemed to have become a derelict swinging on the tides and veering with the winds, but incapable of settled course and direction. . . . To digest plans for the public welfare and bring them to determination seemed beyond the ability of the government." [19] This seems to characterize adequately the unhappy administration of President Taft. The most striking example of the disintegration of the system

18 David Lawrence, *op. cit.*, pp. 310, 311.
19 *Woodrow Wilson, the Man and His Works,* p. 316.

that McKinley and Roosevelt had found workable was the Congressional Revolution, 1910-11.

We have noticed that Speaker Reed, in what has sometimes been called the Congressional Revolution of 1890, had resolved the then-prevailing confusion in the House by refusing to recognize members bent on filibustering and by counting "present," for the purpose of establishing a quorum, members who refused to answer a roll call. Twenty years later, under Speaker Joseph G. Cannon, the office had developed into a reactionary dictatorship through the Speaker's membership on the Rules Committee and his power to appoint all committees. Cannon ignored the seniority rule in order to prevent the committee's advancement of such Progressives as George W. Norris and others. Catching Cannon's following off-guard in 1909 when the House had just rejected a particularly arbitrary change of the rules by the Rules Committee, Norris introduced a resolution, long held in reserve, requiring the removal of the Speaker from the Rules Committee and depriving him of the power to appoint the committees of the House. After thirty hours of vain attempts by the organization to rally Cannon's following, which was widely scattered throughout the country, the resolution was passed and the Speaker's imperious control of the House was ended.

We have seen how neatly Theodore Roosevelt integrated the legislative and executive branches by coming to a working understanding with Speaker Cannon. By Wilson's time the "czar" had been dethroned and power had gravitated toward the floor leader and even been dispersed among the chairmen of the several committees. The day, of course, had passed when the President and the Speaker of the House were to sit down cozily before the blazing fireplace of the

White House and plan a legislative program. The new day called for new methods and a President ideologically equipped for the change was at hand.

His first move was almost theatrical in its nature. As early as 1889, in reference to Jefferson's abandoning the presidential practice of addressing Congress in person, Wilson had written, "Possibly had the President not so closed the matter against new adjustments, this clause of the Constitution [Art. II, Sec. 3] might legitimately have been the foundation for a much more habitual and informal and yet at the same time more public responsible interchange of opinion between the Executive and Congress." [20] After some hesitation on the matter he decided to revive the early practice. It was impossible to foretell just how the innovation would be received. The Cabinet was a "trifle shaky about the venture." [21] The Senate is said to have been quite unhappy about the plan and Democratic Senator John Sharp Williams spoke sarcastically of it as "the speech from the throne." Democrats more than Republicans were concerned over the peril to the "separation of powers." Senator Henry Cabot Lodge even approved of it.[22]

When at length on the appointed day the President stood face to face with Congress his opening sentence made clear his purpose. "I am very glad indeed," he said, "to have this opportunity to address the two Houses directly and to verify for myself the impression that the President of the United States is a person, not a mere department of the Government hailing Congress from some isolated island of jealous power, sending messages, not speaking naturally and with his own

20 *The State,* p. 566.
21 David F. Houston, *Eight Years with the Wilson Cabinet,* I, p. 52.
22 R. S. Baker, *op. cit.,* IV, pp. 104-05.

voice—that he is a human being trying to co-operate with other human beings in a common service.'' [23]

The message itself was short and crisp and dealt with a single topic. As an oral communication it contrasted almost of necessity with the conventional lengthy and frequently perfunctory written messages of previous Presidents. When a friendly critic had taken Theodore Roosevelt to task for the lack of definiteness in his exceedingly long addresses to Congress, with their miscellaneous topics, often outside the range of federal functions, he replied with the question, "Are you aware also of the extreme unwisdom of irritating Congress by fixing the details of a bill concerning which they are very sensitive instead of laying down a general policy?" [24]

President Wilson's strategy called for the dismissing of all such fears concerning congressional jealousy. His immediate object was the revision of the tariff in a thoroughgoing fashion. The Committee on Ways and Means had begun work on this measure before the inauguration of President Wilson and by March 25 they placed the complete draft in the President's hands and he was prepared to support it with the influence of his office.[25] Oscar W. Underwood, the floor leader of the Democrats and the chairman of the Ways and Means Committee, took nearly everything to the caucus. From there, after thorough discussion and bound by the two-thirds rule of the Democratic caucus, the party membership went forth to the floor of the House completely organized for united action.[26] So compact was the party organization that without the use of closure or even a motion to limit debate the

23 Message of April 8, 1913.
24 J. B. Bishop, *op. cit.*, I, p. 233.
25 H. J. Ford, *Woodrow Wilson, the Man and His Work*, p. 182.
26 O. W. Underwood, *Drifting Sands of Party Politics*, p. 171.
G. R. Brown, *The Leadership of Congress*, pp. 185, 186.

bill passed the House without material change and by a large majority.[27] Not even the well-disciplined Republican organization had ever done anything like that on a tariff bill.

The President's astute leadership was felt no less in the Senate than in the House. A few hours after his address to Congress on the tariff he appeared in the President's room just off the Senate chamber and conferred with the Finance Committee on the matter of the tariff. This had been done by no President since Lincoln's time and then only in time of war. When the House bill reached the Senate, he returned frequently to his room at the Capitol and also conferred with delegations of senators at the White House.[28] To obtain harmonious party action on this measure in the upper house seemed impossible. Every proposal for a caucus of the party was rejected until June 20, when "the first caucus of Democratic Senators that anyone can remember" was held. Red-hot sessions of the caucus on the bill continued and then came the President's victory. On July 7 the Senate Democratic caucus declared the tariff bill to be a party measure and urged the duty of all Democrats to support it.[29] As Professor F. W. Taussig put it: "President Wilson had quietly but unhesitatingly assumed leadership and secured a hold on his associates and followers which astonished friend and enemy." [30] For the first time since James K. Polk was President the tariff had been revised under the effective leadership of a Democratic President. Wilson's leadership contrasts strikingly with the experience of Cleveland with the Wilson-

27 O. W. Underwood, *op. cit.*, p. 172.
28 R. S. Baker, *op. cit.*, IV, p. 123.
29 *Ibid.*, IV, p. 124.
30 Quoted by H. J. Ford, *Woodrow Wilson*, p. 185.

Gorman Tariff, which the President permitted to become a law without his signature after bitterly condemning it in a letter to a member of the House of Representatives.

The bill providing for the Federal Reserve System was worked out by the President and several party leaders, most of whom were not members of Congress. There was at first some difficulty with William Jennings Bryan, who feared that Wall Street was influencing the President, but his suspicions were allayed and he pledged his support.[31] The President was convinced that the monetary situation called for prompt action. When the proposal had taken shape he invited the members of the Banking and Currency Committee of the House to a conference at the White House. The members accepted, but one of them could not "conceive any service that I or any other member of the committee can render as the President already has committed himself on the principles and policies of the bill you [Glass], Owens, and McAdoo are said to have drafted." [32]

Again the President addressed Congress, saying, "I have come to you as the head of the Government, and the responsible leader of the party in power, to urge action now, while there is time to serve the country deliberately in the clear air of common counsel." [33] August 11 the Democratic caucus of the House began a series of stormy sessions on the measure. "No such scenes were ever witnessed before, nor have any been enacted since." [34] Bryan's followers attacked the bill with great vigor and were silenced only by the shrewd

31 J. E. Tumulty, *op. cit.*, pp. 179, 180, 181.
32 Carter Glass, *An Adventure in Constructive Finance*, p. 130.
33 Message of June 23, 1913.
34 Carter Glass, *op. cit.*, p. 133.

device of a letter from Bryan to Glass urging all to stand by the President on the bill." [35] The measure passed the House, September 18, by an overwhelming vote, only three Democrats voting with the opponents of the measure. As usual the Senate was less tractable but under the influence of the President's lieutenants, Bryan, McAdoo, and Colonel House, recruits were mustered. The stubborn opposition broke down when the President refused to consent to a holiday recess unless the bill was first passed. December 19 the Senate passed the measure by a vote of 54 to 34, *every Democratic senator voting in favor of it.* Woodrow Wilson's formula for responsible government was working as planned.[36]

The entrance of America into the World War marked the end of the distinctively Wilsonian government. In July, 1917, there was a movement in Congress to set up a bipartisan committee of both Houses on the conduct of the war. It would have been a revival of the strange arrangement that had proved such an annoyance to President Lincoln. Wilson's protest against the plan was effectual. Then there was a strong move for a Coalition Cabinet to be headed by Theodore Roosevelt.[37] The idea was fostered that the regular government had broken down. Senator Chamberlain of Oregon, a Democrat, led in the movement, asserting that the military establishment of the country had "broken down and almost stopped functioning because of inefficiency in every bureau and every department of the government." [38] Just as the Asquith government in England had failed, only to be suc-

[35] *Ibid.*, pp. 138-39.

[36] R. S. Baker, *op. cit.*, IV, pp. 174 ff.

[37] W. E. Dodd, *Woodrow Wilson and His Works*, p. 253. Lindsay Rogers, "Presidential Dictatorship," *Quarterly Review*, CCXXXI, p. 141.

[38] D. S. Muzzey, *op. cit.*, II, p. 651.

ceeded by the Lloyd George Coalition Cabinet, so was Theodore Rossevelt heralded as the potential savior of the United States and destined to head a Coalition Cabinet here.[39] President Wilson countered the movement with Lincolnian strategy by sending to Congress a bill asking for all the powers suggested for the proposed War Cabinet. The result was the Overman Act giving the President practically the powers of a dictator in redistributing the functions, duties, powers, administrative agencies, and personnel of the federal government as he might deem necessary for the successful prosecution of the war. The movement against the President collapsed and his prestige increased as a result.[40] When American troops began to enter the trenches in France and the clash of arms grew furious, the American people gave their almost undivided support to the President. Opposition to the Executive was silenced as never before in wartime. An unprecedented hysteria against criticism spread from the populace to the Department of Justice and even to the courts where severe penalties were laid for what today appears to be considered legitimate discussion of public affairs. Official authority combined with social terror to drive criticism of the Executive underground. "Senators of sovereign states, and leaders of parties, groveled in their marble corridors, so terrified were they of public opinion." [41] To doubt Wilson was to invite proscription as pro-German.

This superficial appearance of complete unanimity of support apparently misled President Wilson. It may account for his ill-timed appeal for the election of a Democratic Congress, made late in the war and not too long after he had uttered the slogan "Politics is

39 See W. E. Dodd, *op. cit.*, pp. 259-60.
40 *Ibid.*, p. 263.
41 G. R. Brown, *The Leadership of Congress*, p. 187.

adjourned." In the ensuing election, held a few days before the armistice, Republican candidates not only captured control of Congress but received 1,200,000 more votes than their Democratic opponents. So President Wilson went to Versailles to frame the Covenant of the League of Nations with his prestige seriously impaired. In the light of this political reverse it is puzzling to find him in his final "swing around the circle" a year later saying: "I had gone over with, so to say, explicit instructions." It was on this speaking trip during his futile effort to arouse the nation in support of the Covenant of the League that he became ill, was soon stricken with paralysis, and completed his term an invalid.

It fell to the lot of his second wife to ascertain the irreducible minimum of matters to be brought to the attention of the enfeebled President. Inevitably this selection involved some control of policies so that, in a sense, Mrs. Wilson became virtually Acting President. Once again was encountered that curious hiatus in our Constitution, the result of the failure of the framers to designate the authority for determining in precisely what degree of "inability to discharge the duties of said office the same shall devolve upon the Vice President."

XII

A Renaissance of
Congressional Government

★

ONLY THOSE who witnessed or experienced it can visualize the startling reaction of the war-weary electorate in November, 1918, against the Democratic party. The emotional exaltation of the Crusade to "make the world safe for democracy" as President Wilson had phrased it culminated in the frantic emotional binge of armistice day followed soon by a historic moral letdown. The accumulated frustrations of the war years were vented on Woodrow Wilson and the Democratic party with the consequent election of the Republican presidential candidate Warren G. Harding by the largest percentage of the popular vote ever given a presidential candidate since records of popular votes for President have been available. The selection of Senator Harding as presidential candidate by a little coterie of Republican Senators in the historic "smoke filled room" proved to be the most irresponsible act in the history of selecting presidential candidates. Yet in the next two years the magic of American journalism had created a myth so convincing that Bishop William Manning delivering the Harding funeral address in the Cathedral of St. John the Divine could say, "May God ever give our country leaders as wise, as noble in spirit as the one whom we now mourn."

So the Republican party resumed command of the ship of state, confident and determined to vest control in the directorate of the party, not in the new President. One of the senatorial clique responsible for the selection of Harding had recommended him as one who "would, when elected, sign whatever bill the Senate sent him and not send bills for the Senate to pass." [1] Harding was a seasoned politician, a somewhat naïve devotee of the Republican party and its traditions, and a master of the art of compromise and composing party differences.[2] Now and then there would fall from his lips that favorite Republican maxim, "The party is bigger than any man." Benjamin Harrison had not been more ready to make the President the willing servant of the Republican party than was Warren G. Harding in 1921.

Heartily co-operating in the Republican campaign strategy of 1920, Candidate Harding had capitalized the popular reaction against executive autocracy. Meanwhile President Wilson, on his bed of affliction, had been playing into the hands of his political enemies. Before Congress had adjourned in the summer of 1920 they had, in accordance with public opinion, passed a bill repealing sixty wartime measures vesting

[1] N. M. Butler, *Across the Busy Years,* quoted by W. A. White, *Puritan in Babylon,* p. 207n.
[2] See P. W. Slosson, "Warren G. Harding, A Revised Estimate," *Current-History,* XXXIII, pp. 174-79.

extraordinary powers in the Executive. This legislation had passed the House of Representatives by a vote of 343 to 3 and the Senate unanimously. Nevertheless, after Congress adjourned, the stricken President gave the repealing act a pocket veto, thereby retaining the war powers two years after the close of hostilities and at the same time providing the Republican campaigners additional ammunition against "executive dictatorship." [3]

Candidate Harding accordingly pledged that, when elected, he would restore "party government as distinguished from personal government, individual, dictatorial, autocratic, or what not." [4] "Constitutional" government would be resumed of a type that would do no violence to the ancient dogma of separated powers. The President would announce his program, which the Constitution directed him to do, but after that, legislation would be the work of Congress.[5] Harding was always disturbed by threatened differences with Congress and was disposed to modify his course as a consequence.[6] President McKinley was his model, as he gave advance notice in a Senate speech delivered after his election but before his inauguration,[7] but Harding proved to be no McKinley.

There were puzzled citizens who wondered how the government would function under such executive self-denial, particularly when momentous problems of public policy both domestic and foreign were thrusting themselves upon the attention of the nation.

[3] See William Starr Myers, *The Republican Party*, p. 441.

[4] Speech of Acceptance, *Republican Campaign Textbook*, 1920, p. 35.

[5] See P. W. Slosson, *op. cit.*, pp. 176-77.

[6] Allan Nevins, "Warren G. Harding," *Dictionary of American Biography*, VIII, p. 52.

[7] Judson C. Welliver, "President Harding," in A. B. Hart, *American History Told by Contemporaries*, V, p. 831.

"How can he lead when he does not know where he is going?" asked embittered Woodrow Wilson. It was soon apparent that Congress would hold President Harding strictly to his pre-election pledge of a hands-off policy with respect to legislation. The Senate manifested resentment even at mild suggestions from the Executive and the senatorial group that had engineered his nomination would brook no leadership at his hands, one of them, Senator Brandegee, having rather betrayed the strategy of the group that nominated Harding by saying that the time did not require a first-rater as President.[8] In the special session of Congress called soon after the inauguration the President chose to appear before the Senate and urge the keeping of appropriations within the limits of income. It must have seemed innocent enough to him to appear thus to speak face to face with his erstwhile colleagues. But the constitutional purists of the upper house were deeply disturbed at what they chose to consider executive participation in debate and "veto by argument." The President's appearance in the Senate on this occasion was denounced as a "pitiable, intolerable, and indefensible spectacle . . . simply deplorable." One might have supposed he was back in the days when Henry Clay thundered against the dictator, Andrew Jackson, to hear a senator raising such questions about Harding's appearance before the Senate as: "Who legislated? What became of the greatest legislative body in the world? It has become the amanuensis to record the vote of one man." [9] Although some senators approved the President's action, the significant fact remains that the Senate fresh from its conquest of Wilson on the issue of the League of Nations was

[8] *Dictionary of American Biography*, VIII, p. 254.
[9] *Cong. Record*, July 14, 1921, p. 3748; Aug. 22, 1921, pp. 5421, 5422.

not going to tolerate executive leadership. When the House of Representatives resented Harding's addressing the Senate on a money bill the President could no longer have the least doubt that he had committed a faux pas in the eyes of his fellow Republicans. Henceforth he must be more circumspect. So blind had Republican leadership become to the historical transformation of the presidency in the twentieth century, the fact that it had become as never before the focal point of a major party's strength, that they could not see how their emasculation of the great office was impairing if not even imperiling their party's future.

President Harding lived to regret his pre-election pledge not to be a leader in legislation. Perhaps he never intended it to be taken as seriously as it was.[10] In his heart he had never planned to abdicate absolutely executive leadership, for that would not have been McKinley-like. But the technique of legislative leadership available to McKinley and Theodore Roosevelt was now out of the question. The day was past and gone when the President of the United States and the Speaker of the House of Representatives in the quiet seclusion of the Executive Mansion could confer, compose differences, and bring together the departments the fathers had taken such pains to separate. Harding was the first Republican President to begin an administration confronted with the problem of co-operating with Congress since the Congressional Revolution of 1910 had dethroned the Speaker and thus deprived the lower house of that authentic spokesman in dealing with the President. Harding's political philosophy of checks and balances,[11] his party's traditions, and the popular revolt against the

10 L. Rogers, "American Government and Politics," *Am. Pol. Sci. Rev.*, XVI, pp. 41, 42.

11 Allan Nevins, *op. cit.*, p. 254.

methods of his predecessor all precluded the employment of any such bold methods as Woodrow Wilson had at first found so effective.

President Harding must have longed fervently for just such a liaison official as a Reed or Cannon would have afforded him when he put his budget system into operation. In submitting to Congress his first estimates, which he regarded as an executive budget, he made the mistake of letting it be known that he expected Congress not to make "any substantial changes in the estimates." [12] This was contrary to the traditional concepts of the congressmen, concepts that had their roots as far back as the colonial legislatures' conflicts with the royal governors. The people's representatives in the nineteen-twenties would maintain intact their ancient guardianship of the public purse against executive usurpation. So the House, after abolishing several committees dealing with appropriation, established a single Appropriations Committee of thirty-five members. This re-organization enhanced its efficiency and soon the House of Representatives was challenging the primacy of the Senate despite the immense prestige of the upper house due to its recent triumph in its conflict with President Woodrow Wilson over the treaty.

No matter if the estimates of the Budget Bureau submitted by the President had been carefully prepared, the Committee on Appropriations re-examined the items minutely, taking twenty thousand pages of printed testimony. They even reduced the estimates more than three hundred million dollars. [13] The quizzing of the administrative agencies, in this case by the various subcommittees of the Committee on Appropriations, is the American counterpart of the ques-

12 New York *Tribune*, Dec. 14, 1921.
13 *Cong. Record*, 67th Cong., 2nd Session, p. 11,065.

tions and interpellations of a parliamentary system. Unfortunately the attention is here focused on prospective legislation while in the American Congress the committee hearings function only crudely as a check on the Executive.

The committee resisted successfully President Harding's pressure to relax their urge for economy in respect to the army and navy. The chairman of the Appropriations Committee developed a prestige suggestive of the old Speaker before 1910. "For the first time since Joseph G. Cannon had been tumbled from the throne of Blaine and Reed," wrote George Rothwell Brown, "there was an individual in the House who could put on his hat and walk to the other end of Pennsylvania Avenue and talk to the President of the United States eye to eye and man to man in the plain blunt language of 'yes' and 'no.' " [14]

President Harding was a man versed in the conventional practices of politics but lacking in insight, imagination, and fertility of resource; consequently, he was quite at a loss where no precedents were apparent. There was none except Wilson's with respect to the President's dealing with the reorganized House and he could not use them. The fact that he cultivated close relations with Speaker Gillette shows how precedent-bound he was.[15] Far from being a czar, the Speaker had become almost a *roi fainéant*. Theodore Roosevelt would have been quick to recognize the new key man in the chairman of the Appropriations Committee and to cultivate a working understanding with him. President Harding, moreover, was confronted by another condition almost unprecedented among Republicans. The party solidarity McKinley had was gone and the President knew not how to mod-

14 *Op. cit.*, p. 241.
15 *Ibid.*, p. 245.

ify or adapt tactics, learned in the days of strict party discipline, to a loosely associated aggregation of individualists, at times definitely disrupted by the presence of the agricultural bloc.

In spite of his groping it is not to be assumed that President Harding had no successes. He discovered that he could sometimes play against the Senate the somewhat less intransigent House of Representatives, a method which might have proved more "unconstitutional than the leadership of the Roosevelt or Wilson kind." [16] For example, he had the emergency peace resolution held up in the House until he had his way against the Senate. He managed to enforce his will in the matter of the packer legislation and the Panama Canal tolls, which he wanted delayed until after the arms conference.[17] These were practically his only signal legislative victories. On the other side of the ledger was a long list of faltering, halfhearted, inept, or futile attempts at leadership. Once when Nicholas Murray Butler found Harding overwhelmed with paper work at his desk the President exclaimed, "I knew this job would be too much for me." So appalling was Harding's lack of judgment that he regarded his fellow senator Albert B. Fall "the ablest of international lawyers," and wanted to appoint him Secretary of State, but instead, as Fall desired, made him Secretary of the Interior where he bartered away, for a bribe, the Naval Oil reserved at Teapot Dome and was consequently sentenced to the federal penitentiary.

Even the Washington Naval Conference which was acclaimed in its day as a brilliant stroke of the foreign policy of the Harding Administration involved an element of historic irony. The request for the calling of

16 L. Rogers, "American Government and Politics," *Am. Pol. Sci. Rev.*, XVI, p. 47.
17 *Ibid.*, XVIII, pp. 91, 92.

the conference was forced upon the unwilling President through a Senate amendment, a rider attached to the Naval Appropriation Bill in the face of the President's efforts to prevent it. Thus the Senate had decisively taken the initiative in formulating foreign policy.[18] Nothing could be more indicative of the magnitude of the reaction against the Wilsonian type of Executive.

President Harding's extraordinary kindliness impaired his capacity to estimate character and select responsible administrators. His misplaced confidence in designing friends led to gigantic scandals that broke after his death in the summer of 1923, but his dawning awareness of the appalling consequences of his blunders in appointing corrupt subordinates is believed to have contributed to, if it did not cause, his physical breakdown and sudden death. He was succeeded by the impeccable Vice President Calvin Coolidge who was elected for another term a year later. So incapable was the Democratic party of exploiting the scandals of the Republican administration that their candidate John W. Davis polled only 28.7 per cent of the popular vote, the smallest share ever accorded a Democratic presidential candidate.

President Coolidge felt even less responsibility for leadership than his immediate predecessor. Of course he was not oblivious of the fact, as he put it, that "It is the business of the President as the party leader to do the best he can to see that the declared party platform purposes are translated into legislative and administrative action. . . ." But on the other hand he said, "I have never felt that it was my duty to attempt to coerce Senators or Representatives, or to make reprisals. The people sent them to Washington. I felt

[18] "American Government and Politics," *Am. Pol. Sci. Rev.,* XVIII, pp. 91, 92.

I had discharged my duty when I had done the best I could with them. In this way I avoided almost entirely a personal opposition, which I think was of more value to the country than to attempt to prevail through arousing personal fear." [19] It is the simple truth to say that following his overwhelming election in 1924, President Coolidge possessed enormous prestige, an indispensable asset of a strong President, but he chose to let it go to waste.

Coolidge's abdication of leadership is revealed in a statement made three years after leaving the presidency. In explaining why he had refused to take a stand on a pending issue he said, "I wouldn't take it. The situation had not developed. Theodore Roosevelt was always getting himself in hot water before he had to commit himself upon issues not well defined. It seems to me public administrators would get along better if they would restrain the impulse to butt in or be dragged into trouble. They should remain silent until an issue is reduced to its lowest terms, until it boils down to something like a moral issue." [20]

A somewhat more concrete revelation of Coolidge's philosophy appeared near the close of the first session of the Sixty-ninth Congress, when a news story giving the President's views was headed, "Coolidge stresses Congress' freedom—just before leaving for vacation he says it was free from dictation by him." The story contained the significant statement that ". . . it was mentioned, perhaps stressed, at the White House . . . that one of the reasons for the success of the session was that the Senate and House assumed their own responsibility and undertook to function as an inde-

[19] Calvin Coolidge, *The Autobiography of Calvin Coolidge*, pp. 231, 232.
[20] W. A. White, *Puritan in Babylon*, p. 433.

pendent branch of the government without too much subservience to the Executive." [21]

The key to an understanding of the presidential career of Calvin Coolidge is to be found in the fact that he had a distaste for legislation. He thought there were too many laws anyhow and the salvation of the country lay in administration, which was his major interest.[22] Of course he would not shirk his constitutional duty to inform Congress on the state of the Union and make recommendations concerning its problems. This, however, was done in a manner so formal and perfunctory that sometimes it was difficult or impossible for Congress to discover his views.[23] What, for example, did he desire with respect to agriculture, perhaps the outstanding domestic problem of his administration? Congress could not gather from his messages what he favored on this important issue even if his vetoes left no doubt as to what he disapproved. Apparently he wanted to attend to his constitutional function, recommend legislation, and then usually let the matter alone. He would not busy himself with congressmen, getting the measure passed. If Congress rejected his recommendation they could bear the odium while he reaped the credit for proposing them. Under President Coolidge the White House breakfast must have been little more than a social amenity. Congressmen were invited and attended but the President wrote concerning the breakfasts, "Although we did not undertake to discuss matters of public business at these breakfasts, they were productive of a spirit of good fellowship which was no doubt a help-

21 *New York Times,* July 7, 1926.

22 Gamaliel Bradford, "The Genius of the Average—Calvin Coolidge," *Atlantic Monthly,* CXLV, p. 8.

23 Arthur W. MacMahon, "American Government and Politics," *Am. Pol. Sci. Rev.,* XXII, pp. 665-67.

ful influence in the transaction of public business." [24] Coolidge admitted that he made appeals to the country through the press to influence Congress and was convinced that he got the Mississippi Flood Control Bill revised to a satisfactory form by that method. However, he believed that "a President cannot, with success, constantly appeal to the country. After a while he will get no response." [25]

The senators may have been a bit concerned lest they lose under Coolidge some of the advantage they had gained in the victory over Wilson and the elevation of Senator Harding to the presidency. At any rate Calvin Coolidge had been President by election no more than a few hours when for the first time since the Civil War the Senate rejected a President's nomination to a Cabinet position, that of Charles B. Warren to the office of Attorney General.[26] Warren had been an attorney of the Sugar Trust and to establish him in the office where he would be responsible for the enforcement of anti-trust legislation was rather too much for the Senate. This was no doubt due, in part at least, to a revival of vigilance on the part of the Senate because of the sorry experience with some of the members of the Harding Cabinet, whose nominations had been perfunctorily confirmed in accordance with long-established usage in respect to the President's immediate official family, and who had to resign when the scandals were publicized.

The Senate had no need to fear aggressiveness on the part of President Coolidge. For example, in the most critical stage of the struggle for ratification of the protocol of the World Court, which had been rec-

24 *Op. cit.*, p. 209.

25 *Ibid.*, p. 224.

26 L. Rogers, "American Government and Politics," *Am. Pol. Sci. Rev.*, XIX, p. 762n.

ommended by the President and made an administration measure if Coolidge ever had one, the senators received no word from the White House. When they went there to consult with him they were given no word of encouragement. While the administration senators were valiantly leading a losing fight the President was at the White House lunching with outstanding editors and authors who would return home and disseminate pleasant impressions about the President.[27] No one can say whether or not this was the President's deliberate method of enhancing the prestige of the President through favorable publicity and thus providing a check on Congress.

The aloofness of Calvin Coolidge led to the organization of the House of Representatives without any reference to the President's influence, that is to say, there was no disposition to place friends of the President in key positions in the committees. There was consequently no trace of that intimate relationship with congressional leaders that obtained during the leadership of McKinley and Theodore Roosevelt and to a lesser degree even Harding—no organic connection between the Executive and Congress. Nor was this aloofness necessary. The setup was now clearly at hand to effect the liaison, certainly by the beginning of Coolidge's elective term, when his great popular majority, too, enhanced his prestige. It required only a President with the slightest awareness of political realities to recognize the opportunity. "Leadership in the House was integrated and neatly effective in so far as it knew its mind; Speaker, floor leader, and steering committee merged almost undistinguishably with the chairman of the rules committee as an instrument." [28] One can easily imagine how prompt Theo-

---

27 T. R. B., "Washington Notes," *New Republic*, XLV, p. 326.
28 Arthur W. MacMahon, *op. cit.*, p. 608.

dore Roosevelt would have been to see in this situation an opportunity to translate public opinion into national policies. There is a penalty for such executive indifference. The time was to come when Speaker Longworth, leaving the chair and repairing to the floor, was to speak against the President's naval program, saying, "I agree with you as to the efficiency of the Bureau of the Budget and I believe in following them whenever I can. But, mind you, the Bureau of the Budget is not responsible to the people of the United States, and we are." [29]

President Coolidge usually failed to keep in touch with representatives waging the battles for the administration measures no less than in the case of the senators. Most Presidents in close contests would hold conferences with leaders, interview congressmen, and generally employ the prestige of the presidential office to carry measures. Even Harding, in spite of his pre-election pledge, did something of this kind. It was not, however, Coolidge's way—not often, at any rate.[30] His few attempts to influence senators by conference were usually unsuccessful.[31] When congressmen took the initiative and called at the White House the President was no more adroit. A group of congressmen went to the Executive Mansion in the winter of 1925 to ask an appointment for Governor Groesbeck of Michigan. The President met their request with a blunt and icy reminder that the resolution to override his veto of the postal salaries bill was then pending in the House. What did they intend to do about it? [32] Other Presidents had managed to make trades on occasions like

---

29 *Cong. Record*, 69th Cong., 2nd Session, p. 4703.

30 T. R. B., *op. cit.*, *New Republic*, Feb. 10, 1926, p. 326.

31 Mark Sullivan, "Coolidge versus the Senate," *World's Work*, Dec., 1925, p. 203.

32 William Allen White, *Calvin Coolidge*, pp. 140, 141.

this but not by dictatorial methods. Congress probably did just as well when he let it severely alone. Then there was the case of the influential Senator Reed of Pennsylvania, who repeatedly urged upon the President the appointment of a Pennsylvanian as ambassador to Spain only to discover later that the appointment of another had already been decided upon and the President had permitted him, nevertheless, to press his impossible request.[33] Under such circumstances cordial relations with Congress were simply out of the question.

The record of Coolidge's first year in the presidency speaks for itself. The President declared himself opposed to the soldier's bonus and Congress passed such a measure. He vetoed the measure and they passed it over his head. He opposed Japanese exclusion and they tacked it on an immigration bill. He urged adhesion to the World Court and the Senate refused it. He advocated the Mellon tax measure, reducing large surtaxes and they mutilated it beyond recognition and tacked on it the publicity requirement regarding income taxes in the face of his threatened veto which, however, he did not make good. Even after his election to the presidency by a decisive vote, when he bore a mandate from the electorate, his poor success with Congress is understandable only in the light of the methods he employed with them. In the short session after election Congress raised its own pay in the face of his disapproval. His recommendation with respect to agriculture was ignored. In spite of his plan for economy the postal salary bill was passed, vetoed, and escaped passage over his veto only by the vote of the floor leader of the upper house, Senator Curtis.[34] He

---

33 T. R. B., *op. cit.*, p. 240.
34 L. Rogers, "American Government and Politics," *Am. Pol. Sci. Rev.*, XIX, p. 762.

was not always so unsuccessful but this sample of his record is not far from typical of his experience.

Herbert Hoover came to the presidency in 1929 with the slightest genuine political experience of any President since General Ulysses S. Grant in 1869. He was, in fact, no less than "a novice in politics." [35] He had, of course, been Secretary of Commerce, almost, if not absolutely, the least political of the executive departments. It certainly did not in any sense provide an apprenticeship for the presidency. The President is, after all, a chief administrator. If the great function of an administrator is to mediate between the technician, the public, and the politician [Congress in this case] [36] then the presidency calls pre-eminently for special experiences and aptitudes and a man lacking them can never be happy in the office of President of the United States. The American people in 1868 called Grant to the presidency, thinking to put to shame the politician type of President. In 1928 they thought to do the same thing. They were disappointed in both cases and probably will be now and then again until they learn that no politically inexperienced man is ever equipped for that very political office.

The American people unquestionably expected Herbert Hoover to take charge of the government, assume a confident leadership in the shaping and execution of public policies, and to give energy and a sense of direction to the entire organization. Congress, it was hoped, would now need to flounder no longer. How did the President happen to get started off on the wrong foot? To answer this question in the case of any President it is necessary to inquire into his theory of

35 F. A. Ogg, and P. O. Ray, *Introduction to American Government* (1935), p. 286.

36 See Leonard W. White, *Introduction to the Study of Public Administration*, p. 16.

the relation of his office to the other branches of the government, especially to Congress. If we could know what Herbert Hoover's philosophy of the legislature was we might have a key whereby to interpret his presidential experience.

There is some evidence, amounting almost to a confession of faith, that he was a firm believer in the Republican dogma of the independence of the legislature. With him this idea was apparently a corollary of his doctrine of individual liberty. Perhaps it is unconsciously a manifestation of that tendency of business interests, apparent in the American Whigs and later in the Republicans, to look with suspicion on a strong Executive as a potential champion of the masses, and consequently to turn to Congress as a check upon the Executive. In the words of Herbert Hoover himself, "the militant safeguard to liberty . . . [is] . . . legislative independence. . . . More particularly does the weakening of the legislative arm lead to encroachments by the executive upon legislative and judicial functions, and inevitably that encroachment is upon individual liberty. If we examine the fate of wrecked republics over the world we shall find first a weakening of the legislative arm." [37] Then he proceeded with his illustrations, starting with the overthrow of the Roman Republic. This doctrine of legislative independence cannot be dismissed merely as an afterthought of President Hoover directed at the later aggressive leadership of Franklin D. Roosevelt. It corresponds too closely to the pattern of Hoover's dealings with Congress.

Less than a month after his inauguration he was being criticized for announcing that since tariff-making and farm relief were among the prerogatives of Congress, he could not furnish anything like a detailed

[37] *The Challenge to Liberty,* pp. 125, 126.

program of action.[38] A commentator, surveying the
first months of the administration near its end,
thought "it is hardly too much to say that a strange
paralysis seemed to rest upon Mr. Hoover during the
first year after Congress met," [39] in the special session,
of course. Congress had been in this session only a few
weeks when another commentator observed, "Frankly,
we like Mr. Hoover's attitude though we fear for him.
. . . He has maintained a dignified but hurt silence.
Yet we feel he would have better success in his clashes
with Congress if he moved actively to better relations
instead of bewailing them in the intimacy of the White
House study." [40] Evidently Herbert Hoover conceived
it to be the President's duty to leave to Congress alone
the initiation and formulation of legislation, reserving
to himself merely the specific constitutional duties of
recommending the fields in which legislation was
needed and exercising the veto power.

We can get an illuminating illustration of President
Hoover's method of dealing with Congress at the beginning of his term if we glance at the framing of the
tariff revision measure. Of course there is no semblance of the McKinley or Roosevelt method of handling the situation. Tariff revision was not the President's own idea in the first place but was urged upon
him by Senator Borah. In his message to Congress he
asked for a limited revision and Senator Borah introduced a resolution confining the revision to the
agriculture schedule. This lost by a single vote and
the way was opened for an old-fashioned logrolling
tariff revision with the ultimate result of one of the
most objectionable tariff measures ever enacted. It was

[38] Editorial, *New Republic*, LVIII, p. 184.

[39] Allan Nevins, "President Hoover's Record," *Current History*, July, 1932, p. 388.

[40] A. F. C., "Backstage in Washington," *Outlook and Independent*, May 29, 1929, p. 178.

currently believed that President Hoover might have used his influence to swing the one vote needed to carry the Senate resolution limiting revision as he desired but he did not lift his hand to that end.[41] If he failed to attempt what could have been done then it certainly was a major failure of his presidential career. When the measure left the House and came to the Senate, inquiries as to the President's desires concerning the bill brought forth no more illuminating information than Senator Smoot's statement, "I know that the President is in favor of protection." Late in the special session the President said in a press statement, "The President has declined to interfere or express an opinion on the details of rates or any compromise thereof, as it is obvious that, if for no other reason, he could not pretend to have the necessary information in respect to many thousands of commodities which such determination requires." [42] While this statement expressed an unquestioned truth, yet it carried an implication of presidential abdication of leadership such as the strong type of President would not have permitted.

Working in harmony with the President's avowed desire for moderate rates was a coalition of Democrats and Progressive Republicans, including the President's then-close friend, Senator Borah. Late in the special session the senator was able to say, "that those whom some are disposed to term the coalition are really now in charge of the making of the bill. The responsibility is upon us." [43] Senator Reed, of Pennsylvania, cried out in despair, "The coalition has made up its mind to knock out every increase in industrial rates,

41 Arthur W. MacMahon, *op. cit.*, p. 51; Allan Nevins, "President Hoover's Record," p. 388.

42 A. W. MacMahon, *op. cit.*, p. 56.

43 *Ibid.*, p. 52.

and we might just as well go ahead and have done with it." [44] Here was an opportunity for the President to promote his own desires, if not by lending aid to the group Borah was leading, by at least not interfering with them. Instead he lent aid and comfort to the general revisionists by accusing the coalition of being unwilling adequately to protect industry. Then the President maintained silence as the vicious logrolling went on apace,[45] the coalition losing control, and the measure finally passed the Senate with 1,253 amendments to the House bill.[46] The visible extent of the President's part meanwhile was two press statements urging a flexible provision permitting the President to raise or lower rates within limits and a White House breakfast, when the bill was in conference, at which the topic discussed was not how to get a reasonable adjustment but the tactics for getting the rather unsavory measure put through.[47] When the bill finally reached the President he signed it in the face of innumerable entreaties to veto it from all parts of the country, ranging from economic experts to prominent leaders of the President's party[48] and despite his reputed characterization of the measure to his friends as "vicious, extortionate and obnoxious." [49]

It will be noticed thus far that President Hoover's difficulties were not with the House of Representatives. The Senate, which had crippled Wilson, controlled Harding, and largely ignored Coolidge, were at first deeply concerned over the election of Hoover. Once more they feared they were to be confronted

[44] *Ibid.*, p. 53.
[45] Allan Nevins, "President Hoover's Record," p. 389.
[46] A. W. MacMahon, *op. cit.*, p. 923.
[47] *Ibid.*, p. 924.
[48] Allan Nevins, "President Hoover's Record," p. 389.
[49] Pearson, Drew and Allen, R. S., *Washington Merry-Go-Round*, p. 66.

with that greatest threat to their prestige, a President elected as a popular idol, intended as a strong leader of the Jackson-Lincoln-Roosevelt type. Unfortunately, President Hoover was from the very first decidedly persona non grata even to many of the leading Republican senators, who regarded him as only a recent convert to Republicanism and hence of doubtful party standing. There is food for reflection in the fact that even such an irregular as Senator George W. Norris had opposed Mr. Hoover's nomination in 1928, on the ground that he had no right to seek election to the presidency on the Republican ticket.[50] From the beginning there was no more than halfhearted support of his recommendations by Republican senators and on one occasion at least the Republican senators all sat silent while for a solid week the Democrats carried on a scathing attack on the President.[51] He had been President little more than a year when one of the Washington correspondents who had a very favorable opinion of the President in the early months of his administration felt compelled to report that "Mr. Hoover is most poisonously unpopular in Washington. Never have I seen the time when there was meaner talk about the occupant of the White House than there is today." [52]

President Hoover's leadership was impaired by his unhappy relations with the press. In a democracy where those who govern are necessarily very dependent upon public opinion in determining and executing public policies, officials are seriously crippled in the performance of their functions when such media of opinion as the newspapers become alienated. The members of the press covering the White House had

50 John Knox, *The Great Mistake,* p. 171.
51 T. R. B., *op. cit.,* Feb. 18, 1931, p. 18.
52 *Ibid.,* June 4, 1930, p. 72.

difficulty getting information they felt the public had the right to have. More than once they found that even the handouts they got were either false or misleading. Hence Hoover's statements were analyzed very critically. "No President needed a good press more than did Hoover; no President in modern times had worse relations with the fourth estate" observed Professor Warren.[53]

President Hoover had a very human sensitiveness to newspaper criticism which he once referred to as "wearing a hair shirt."[54] This was a handicap due to his political inexperience. Most Presidents have developed pretty thick protective hides on the road to that office. The attitude of the newspaper correspondents grew more and more hostile and by the middle of his term it was described as "rapidly degenerating into open warfare."[55] This unfortunate condition was not improved by the rumor, never denied, that the President was responsible for the removal of Robert S. Allen as Washington correspondent of the *Christian Science Monitor* because he was alleged to have been one of the authors of the *Washington Merry-Go-Round,* a book which dealt in no gentle manner with the President and his administration.[56]

As time passed President Hoover grew more active as a leader, and had his lot fallen in less critical times he might gradually have somewhat overcome his political inexperience. By the first session of the Seventy-

[53] Harris Gaylord Warren, *Herbert Hoover and the Great Depression,* 1959, p. 58.

[54] "The country got few impressions of Mr. Hoover as a human being. Almost the only self-revealing incident was the letter to President Thompson, of Ohio State University, suggesting that by way of reminder of sin and trouble Presidents were forced to wear 'hair shirts.'" L. Rogers, "The President and the People," *New York Times Magazine,* Apr. 9, 1933, p. 2.

[55] T. R. B., *op. cit.,* Oct. 14, 1931, p. 219.

[56] *Ibid.,* p. 219.

second Congress he was keeping that body informed on his views by frequent messages, sixty-three in that single session. He employed the veto and the threatened veto several times. In the cases of two measures "the tariff bill (H.R. 6662) and the relief bill (H.R. 12445), the President asserted himself as a director of national policy." [57] Yet his experience was far from happy. "When the President attempted to go beyond the sending of messages and signing of vetoes, his difficulties began. He was confronted with a dilemma; if he attempted aggressive leadership he was cried down as a dictator; if he made no specific suggestions, he was accused of shirking his burden of direction and guidance in a national emergency. The President's attitude was not entirely consistent; on some occasions he harshly called Congress to task for its dilatory tactics and on others he refrained from comment in the face of chaotic conditions in the legislature. For the most part, however, he held to a conciliatory viewpoint. He made frequent use of conferences at which legislators of both parties met with administrative officials. Yet in a situation demanding the closest cooperation between the administrative and legislative branches, friction developed." [58]

It was President Hoover's misfortune to have begun his administration with the belief that the system of free enterprise might soon extirpate poverty. Late in the very year of his inauguration, however, came the stock market crash that initiated the "Great Depression." This turn of events was especially embarrassing to a President representing the political party that had long proclaimed itself the guarantor of prosperity. "President Hoover's willingness to undertake

[57] E. Pendleton Herring, "American Government and Politics," *Am. Pol. Sci. Rev.*, XXVI, p. 855.
[58] *Ibid.*, p. 856.

the drastic measures needed for recovery was definitely limited by an apparently infrangible philosophy" observed Professor Warren.[59] Thus the budget had to be balanced in spite of its deflationary effect in an already galloping deflation; there must not even be federal "loans" for food for the drought-afflicted farmers of Arkansas because that would be a "dole." President Hoover even vetoed a bill to create an efficient Federal Employment Service. Such hard and fast ideology hampered presidential leadership of Congress enormously. "Former Secretary of Commerce," according to Richard Neustadt, "had a sense of purpose so precise as to be stultifying." [60]

Hoover had thrust upon him pressing social problems for the solution of which humanity is still groping. Under the circumstances his re-election was quite out of the question and his campaign for a second term could not have been much more than a gesture. In 1932 the American masses, out of the depths of almost universal economic distress, sought relief by rejecting the Republican candidate and choosing instead Governor Franklin D. Roosevelt of New York whom they doubtless hoped might prove to be another tribune of the people.

[59] *Op. cit.*, p. 143.
[60] *Presidential Power*, p. 182.

XIII

The Presidency of
Franklin D. Roosevelt

***

★

THE PHYSICAL misfortune that befell Franklin Roosevelt in his early forties was doubtless an important factor in his preparation for the presidency. It afforded him ample opportunity for wide, even if somewhat superficial, reading in the field of the social sciences at the same time that he was keeping alive and even expanding his acquaintance with key men in his party throughout the nation by means of a systematic and large-scale correspondence. Even in the interval between election and inauguration he continued his preparation. "I'm going ahead," he said at that time, "through a careful process of preparing myself for the job." [1] Franklin Roosevelt was the first Democratic President inaugurated after the Civil War

1 *Time*, Jan. 23, 1933, p. 11.

to whom the White House was already a familiar place.[2] After his marriage to Eleanor Roosevelt the two were occasionally White House guests of her uncle, Theodore Roosevelt, for whom Franklin had cast his first vote for President.[3] So Franklin Roosevelt was the first Democratic President-elect since James Buchanan to feel perfectly at home in official Washington.

In the sheer enjoyment of responsibility the two Roosevelts stood almost alone among the Presidents. The office that had proved a burden to Washington and to Lincoln seemed to stimulate and satisfy Franklin D. Roosevelt even as a generation earlier it had "delighted" his distant cousin Theodore. When asked in 1931 what authority he would want from Congress if he were elected President, Governor Franklin Roosevelt had instantly answered, "Plenty." He refused in office to be kept awake in bed by the perplexing problems of the presidency.[4] With never a hint of "hair shirts," he seemed positively to be doing just the sort of thing he liked to do.

Theodore and Franklin Roosevelt, in turn, had been compelled to overcome physical handicaps

[2] When as a boy of five his father had first taken him to the White House, the weary and worried President, Grover Cleveland, is reported to have taken the hand of the child and said, "I'm making a strange wish for you, little man, a wish no one else would be likely to make. . . . I hope you'll never be President of the United States. . . ." Sadyebeth and Anson Lowitz, *Franklin D. Roosevelt, Man of Action*, pp. 17, 20.

[3] *Ibid.*, p. 70. Anne O'Hare McCormick, "Roosevelt's View of the Big Job," *New York Times Magazine*, Sept. 11, 1932, p. 1. "One guesses that Theodore Roosevelt to whom he constantly refers and whose career his own parallels in so many particulars is the north star in Franklin Roosevelt's firmament." *Idem.*

[4] Anne O'Hare McCormick, "Preparing for the New Deal," *New York Times*, Jan. 15, 1932, Sec. 6, p. 1. Near the end of his third year as President his physician said, "The President's health is better today than it was when he came to the White House." *Cleveland Plaindealer*, Feb. 1, 1936. Col. 4.

through sheer force of will, and each emerged from the ordeal apparently triumphant over fear, self-confident and eager for difficult tasks. When the latter, in the midst of his first inaugural address, said "The only thing we have to fear is fear itself," he may have been speaking from the depth of a profound personal experience. Keen observers thought they noted in 1933 that something like a miraculous change had come over the Franklin Roosevelt of a dozen years before.[5]

By one of those inscrutable coincidences of history Franklin Roosevelt's pre-presidential experiences provided pragmatically almost exactly the preparation he needed to meet the issues that confronted him as President in 1933. Elected at the age of twenty-eight to an up-state New York senatorial district he was in time to consider his legislative experience an invaluable asset as Governor and as President. He was made Chairman of the Senate Committee on Forest, Fish, and Game, an appropriate apprenticeship for the future champion of conservation. Also as state Senator and as Assistant Secretary of the Navy his activity was to capture the enduring loyalty of labor. By frustrating his efforts as Governor to obtain cheap and abundant electric power in New York State the utility interests converted a President-to-be into a resolute and successful promoter of public power as the Tennessee Valley Authority attests to this day. So in 1933 there moved into the White House a president made to order "to fill the vacuum left by the confused leaders of business, industry, and his political opposition."

It is a curious but undoubted fact that the New Deal is rooted historically in the administration of Alfred E. Smith as Governor of New York. Thus

5 See Anne O'Hare McCormick, "Let's Try It, Says Roosevelt," *New York Times,* Mar. 26, 1933, Sec. 6, p. 19, Col. 3.

Governor Franklin Roosevelt inherited the maturing if not achieved legislative program of his immediate predecessor. In the fields of housing, education, budgeting, welfare, parks, and water power he was promoting state policies initiated by Governor Smith. It was the crisis consequent upon the Great Depression that gave Franklin Roosevelt the opportunity to exploit its challenge to his capacity for legislative leadership created by the obstinate obstructionist tactics of up-state Republican majorities in the legislature. One device Governor Roosevelt resorted to in order to overcome this opposition was the fireside chat at which he became an adept artist before he moved into the White House. So as President he was quite at home among many problems that confronted him as President and when he encountered a new one he tackled it with the method of the inveterate pragmatist.[6]

Perhaps when Governor Roosevelt was declaring so frankly that he would want plenty of authority as President he believed he was destined for leadership in the national crisis. Such a faith may be implicit in his words of the inaugural of March 4, 1933: "In every dark hour of our national life a leadership of frankness and vigor has met with that understanding and support of the people themselves which is essential to victory. I am convinced that you will again give that support to leadership in these critical days." [7]

The situation confronting the newly inaugurated President at noon of March 4, 1933, seemed made to order for one who professed such a striking doctrine of presidential leadership. The American people were then in the grip of a paralyzing financial panic that reached a dramatic climax on inauguration day. Not

[6] Bernard Bellush, *Franklin D. Roosevelt as Governor of New York*, p. 284.

[7] Franklin D. Roosevelt, *On Our Way*, pp. 255, 256.

the least alarmed were the business interests that had for a dozen years maintained implicit confidence in the Harding-Coolidge-Hoover type of government. There was something almost pathetic in the naïve faith with which millions looked for the promised political messiah. One ecstatic Hoover Republican presently pronounced Franklin Roosevelt "the greatest leader since Jesus Christ." [8] Nor did the faith then seem so misplaced, as the radio carried the inaugural address to a nation hanging almost breathless on every word. Out of the prevailing confusion came what sounded like confidence-commanding words, solemnly declaring: "It is to be hoped that the normal balance of executive and legislative authority may be wholly adequate to meet the unprecedented task before us. But it may be that an unprecedented demand and need for undelayed action may call for temporary departure from the normal balance of public procedure. I am prepared under my constitutional duty to recommend the measures that a stricken nation in the midst of a stricken world may require. These measures or such other measures as Congress may build out of its experience and wisdom, I shall seek within my constitutional authority to bring to speedy adoption.

"But in the event that the Congress shall fail to take

---

[8] Illustrative of the hysterical adulation of those strange days is the following episode. "In July, 1933," writes John T. Flynn, "riding into New York on the Long Island Railroad, I fell into conversation with a fellow commuter, a New York businessman whose name is not unknown to fame. . . . I ventured to criticize Mr. Roosevelt's course and to my surprise my companion—a businessman, a Republican businessman who had voted for Hoover—turned to me indignantly. He ended by saying that he had voted for Hoover but that he hoped God would forgive him and that he believed Franklin D. Roosevelt was the greatest leader since Jesus Christ." "Other People's Money," *New Republic,* Dec. 11, 1935.

these courses and in the event that the national emergency is still critical I shall not evade the clear course of duty that will then confront me. I shall ask the Congress for the one remaining instrument to meet the crisis—broad executive power to wage a war against the emergency as great as the power that would be given to me if we were in fact invaded by a foreign foe." [9]

With breath-taking promptness the new administration attacked the banking and monetary problems. Under a war-time statute the banks were closed for four days and an embargo was laid on the export of gold. A call was issued for a special session of Congress to convene only five days after the inauguration for the purpose of dealing with the banking crisis. Most congressmen having come to Washington for the inauguration ceremonies, the organization of both houses was determined in advance of their convening and no time was lost in preliminaries when they assembled at the appointed time.

Then followed a hundred days certainly without precedent in the history of the presidency. Congress was overwhelmingly Democratic in both branches. The inherently undisciplined nature of the Democratic party membership was now aggravated by the presence of 150 new and inexperienced congressmen. Democrats had never patiently submitted to any effective leadership by the Speaker or floor leader in the manner of the usually better-disciplined Republican party. Speaker Garner in opposing a steering committee had provoked the charge of a dictatorship, flung at him by his fellow partisans in the immediately preceding session. An admission of this charge was implicit in the remarks of newly elected Speaker Rainey when he said, concerning a new steering committee

[9] F. D. Roosevelt, *On Our Way*, pp. 260-61.

devised to mollify the Democratic congressmen: "It is a long step forward and it takes from the Speaker power he has arbitrarily exercised and gives it back to the House. Failures in the last Congress have been due to the fact that the determination of policies has come entirely from the Speaker's chair. We will put over Mr. Roosevelt's program." [10]

To satisfy the scruples of the turbulent majority a unique steering committee had been designed. The nation was divided into fifteen districts. The Democratic congressmen from each one of these elected one member of the committee and each of these was made an assistant whip. The chief whip effected the liaison with the Speaker. This headless organ seemed to be a satisfactory expression of the genius of a party that would brook no semblance of leadership of the Reed and Cannon type. Through this strange committee, acting as an intermediary between the party caucus and the leaders, the rank and file of the Democratic membership chose to consider themselves in charge of legislation. [11]

Regardless of apparatus devised to satisfy the Democratic congressmen, the real leader in legislation was President Roosevelt. The unprecedented public support behind him made most of his suggestions for the time being irresistible. In the face of it Republican opposition was futile and indeed practically abandoned. Instead of challenging the request of Floor Leader Byrns for unanimous consent to confine to only forty minutes the debate on the emergency banking bill, Republican Floor Leader Snell said, "The House is burning down, and the President of the United States says this is the way to put out the

10 Quoted by E. Pendleton Herring, "The First Session of the 73rd Congress," *Am. Pol. Sci. Rev.*, XXVIII, No. 1, p. 69.

11 *Ibid.*, pp. 69, 70.

fire," and he asked the Republicans to support the request.[12] Only the critical condition of the country can account for this complete disappearance of partisanship. Until nine o'clock of the night before the special session opened neither Senator Robinson, majority floor leader of the Senate, nor Speaker Rainey of the House had any idea of the legislative program of the President.[13] The bill had not yet been printed when the members voted on the emergency banking measure and they were compelled to depend solely on the reading of it by the clerk or to trust the President. Here is evidence that, as someone put it, the President commanded "a surplus of public confidence." [14] Passing the House without a record vote and the Senate a few hours later, the emergency bill was promulgated by the President the evening of the day of its passage.[15] President Wilson, the exponent and practitioner of the parliamentary theory of American government had never come so close as this to the realization of his ideas.

A crucial test of the President's leadership came on the following morning when he sent to Congress his message recommending severe reductions in the salaries of government officials and of the compensation of ex-servicemen. In the light of history such an attempt on the part of the President looked foolhardy indeed. In the absence of the regular congressional committees, not yet selected, there was created a special committee on the President's economy proposals. The rank and file of the Democratic congressmen insisted on opening the subject for debate in the caucus, where Speaker Rainey barely prevented the emasculation of the measure. On the floor of the House, how-

12 E. P. Herring, *op. cit.*, p. 70.
13 Anne O'Hare McCormick, "Let's Try It," p. 19.
14 *Ibid.*, p. 19.
15 E. P. Herring, *op. cit.*, p. 68.

ever, the attitude of the insurgents changed and they became docile. "Democrats who had viewed the bill unfavorably in secret caucus changed their viewpoint in the open debate, and the Democratic leaders found their hands strengthened by Republican support and by the public approbation of the administration's position. 'When the *Congressional Record* goes to President Roosevelt's desk in the morning' one of them asserted, 'he will look over the roll call we are about to take and I warn you new Democrats to be careful where your names are found.' Hisses and groans greeted this admonition, but the point struck home." [16]

The economy measure was not put through the House, however, without strenuous efforts on the part of the leaders. On one occasion only the Republicans who sided with the administration Democrats saved the bill.[17] A radio appeal to the nation by the President aided his cause. The opposition to the measure in the Senate was intense. The House was still torn by dissension over the pressure of the veterans' demands and a deadlock seemed imminent when President Roosevelt performed one of his feats of political magic. A seventy-two-word message from him electrified Congress with a proposal for the immediate modification of the Volstead Act. This response to the public demand for legalized beer instantly re-united the President's disintegrating following and two days later the Senate passed the economy bill.[18]

On passing from emergency enactments to subjects of presumably permanent reform the dizzy pace of legislation had to be somewhat slackened. Opposition of course arose, but the President dealt with it diplomatically through the friendly chat at the White House in which the director of the budget, the chair-

16 *Ibid.*, p. 71.
17 *Ibid.*, p. 72.
18 *Ibid.*, p. 73.

man of the Interstate Commerce   , the chairmen of congressional committees and even minority party leaders participated. The Republicans, however, played only a minor part and the President chose to work through his own party. No sooner was a presidential message read to the House than an administration congressman would rise, in accordance with a preconcerted plan, and present an appropriate bill to carry out the proposal of the message. That the tempo of congressional procedure was still rapid is revealed by the fact that an analysis of the time of passage of eleven of the President's outstanding measures through the House shows an average period of only three and two-thirds hours debate on each measure.[19]

President Lincoln had once almost infuriated Congress by sending them a proposed bill along with only a line or two of message recommending it to their consideration.[20] The storm he aroused was such as to discourage later Presidents until recently from a repetition of such a move. Even the fearless Theodore had once admitted that his messages to Congress were purposely made long and somewhat diffuse in order not to arouse the resentment of Congress at supposed executive encroachment.[21] Franklin Roosevelt's early messages were not only brief and to the point but he frequently sent along with a message a carefully prepared bill embodying the ideas of the message[22] and such was the character of the times that Congress readily accepted the practice. It has since become commonplace.

Throughout the special session the President's political stratagems proved infallible if not inexhausti-

[19] E. P. Herring, *op. cit.*, p. 75.
[20] Richardson, *op. cit.*, VI, p. 24.
[21] *Supra*, p. 259.
[22] E. F. Brown, "America Meets the Emergency," *Current History*, May, 1933, p. 210.

ble. The ex-servicemen who had hitherto proved to be an irresistible pressure group were checked for the time being by the President's frank and somewhat audacious laying of the case before the public in a radio address. When the inflationists were in a position to rush their program through Congress, the President canalized their flood of feeling to his own purposes by procuring from Congress permissive legislation for far-reaching monetary changes, lodging power to act or not to act in his own hands. Foreign observers assumed that these measures constituted merely a political gesture to satisfy the silver interests rather than a new economic policy.[23] In the face of an undisciplined party and an unstable public sentiment the President nevertheless maintained control of the situation. "By great good fortune," wrote Professor E. Pendleton Herring, "a skillful politician was in the White House who knew how to handle the public and how to negotiate with Congress. The President was able to outmaneuver his opponents and to compromise when a clear victory was impossible. His leadership supplied the unifying force." [24] Franklin Roosevelt, by the conduct of his office, according to one commentator, had "practically written a handbook on what every young President should know." [25]

It cannot be denied that the seerlike idealism of the inaugural address of March 4, 1933, was proclaimed by a stark realist in the realm of practical politics. Such a paradoxical combination will not astonish the

23 E. F. Brown, "The N.R.A. Runs Into Trouble," *Current History,* July, 1934, p. 466.

24 E. P. Herring, "The First Session of the 73rd Congress," p. 82. Professor Lindsay Rogers says of President Roosevelt that "he seems to be gifted with a greater knowledge of political psychology than any other statesman of whom I have seen any public record." *Crisis Government,* p. 124.

25 Radio round-table conference by Professors T. V. Smith, S. P. Weaver, and James Lynn of the University of Chicago, Sunday noon, Jan. 5, 1936.

informed, for it is not so rare in our history as might be supposed. One has only to recall how Abraham Lincoln, after laboriously distributing the post offices to importunate partisans according to wont and custom, proceeded to create captaincies, colonelcies, and brigadier-generalships galore to win and hold fast the political support necessary for the salvation of a democratic nation.[26]   Patronage likewise provided Franklin Roosevelt the cohesive power with which to cement, for the time being, the elements of an inherently discordant political following. Harding, too, had had such an opportunity to employ patronage when he succeeded Woodrow Wilson but he made no use of it as a device of presidential leadership and consequently dispensed it aimlessly in pleasing personal friends. Harding had left Coolidge no patronage and Coolidge in his turn had left none for Hoover, which did not matter much in the cases of Presidents loath to assume vigorous leadership. Into President Roosevelt's hands, however, the turn of the political wheel of fortune had brought the opportunity for a gigantic rotation in office.[27]   In addition to this the rapid creation of new offices in the expansion of the recovery agencies increased by tens and ultimately by hundreds of thousands the offices outside of the classified service or merit system.

[26] Civil War commanders unfamiliar with the exigencies of practical politics were disappointed with Lincoln's practice. Typical of their opinion is that of General William Tecumseh Sherman: "The greatest mistake made in our Civil War was in the mode of recruitment and promotion. When a regiment became reduced by the necessary wear and tear of service, instead of being filled up at the bottom, and the vacancies filled from the best noncommissioned officers and men, the habit was to raise new regiments, with new colonels, captains, and men, leaving the old and experienced battalions to dwindle away into mere skeleton organizations." *Memoirs*, pp. 387-88.

[27] See Earl Looker, *The American Way*, p. 67.

With the keen appetites of partisans who had fasted for a dozen long years the constituents of Democratic congressmen impatiently awaited the distribution of offices. The President was in no hurry and serenely bided his time, whispering to an inquiring congressman now and then, "We haven't got to patronage yet." [28] When at length the time came to relieve the pangs of hunger the President went at the task in a manner suggestive of Hamilton's conception of the "loaves and fishes" as an indispensable factor in executive control.[29] It may shock some to learn that such questions as "What was your preconvention position on the Roosevelt candidacy?" and "How did you vote on the economy bill?" confronted the congressmen seeking appointments for constituents. Yet throughout the special session, postponement was the policy so that, as someone put it, "his [the President's] relations to Congress were to the very end of the session tinged with a shade of expectancy which is the best part of young love." [30] When a congressman was asked to vote for a presidential measure in the face of local opposition his support was given the President on the frank basis of quid pro quo.

The emergency itself, the panic that had seized the nation, was the most important single factor in accounting for the President's having his way. Hitherto only the existence of an enemy in wartime had afforded a Chief Executive such well-nigh unanimous support as the American people gave Franklin Roosevelt in the first months of his administration. Editorial dissent disappeared for a season and partisan Republicans at first either held their tongues or joined in the chorus of acclaim. The question has been raised

28 *Ibid.*, p. 67.
29 Farrand, *op. cit.*, I, 376.
30 E. P. Herring, *op. cit.*, p. 82.

as to whether the American people, through their wholehearted support of President Roosevelt in March, 1933, did not vindicate representative government against the Fascist charge that democracies are timid and vacillating in a crisis.

President Roosevelt gained in prestige from the fact that he revealed in office rather greater capacity during the emergency than his previous career had led the public to expect. Fate was kind indeed to him in sparing him the misfortune of his immediate predecessor. Franklin Roosevelt had not been overadvertised. He was not handicapped with a public expectation of miracles. Walter Lippmann no doubt expressed the prevailing opinion of liberals in 1932 by disposing of Governor Roosevelt as "a pleasant man, who without any important qualifications for the office would very much like to be President." Fortunately no title corresponding to that of "The Great Engineer" had been created for him by some overzealous admirer. Indeed the first months of his administration seemed to show that, if anything, he had entered the office rather underrated. This proved to be a distinct advantage and served to increase his prestige when his handling of the emergency revealed unexpected capacities for leadership.

"For a hundred days," wrote Bernard Fay, "he kept Congress at work. And for a hundred days he collaborated with Congress. During these hundred days he avoided all conflicts and all quarrels with both houses. He had innumerable conferences with congressional leaders and, far from ever adopting a contemptuous attitude toward Congress he always treated it with the utmost courtesy. At no time did he proclaim the failure of parliamentary government. At no time did he make fun of parliamentary methods, and while newspapermen were comparing him with Signor

wisely declared a separation, but the impulse of a common purpose declares a union." [41]

Such was the doctrine. How was it to be implemented now that "crisis government" was no longer necessary? The answer appeared in the informal conference of leaders at the White House. The President was likely to start a typical day with a nine forty-five meeting of administration leaders, such as Secretaries Hull and Morgenthau, Budget Director Douglas, Senator Joseph Robinson and Speaker Rainey.[42] "In practice," wrote E. P. Herring, "he evolved a 'master ministry' of congressional leaders, cabinet officers, and executive officials working through the White House." [43] "He would spend hours at the telephone persuading, reasoning, mollifying and disciplining individual Senators and Congressmen." [44] The President had no formulas and he confessedly adopted the play-by-play tactics of the football team. A practical politician, he perceived that expediency is better than the inflexible rules of the doctrinaire. But, pliable as he might be on details, the Congressmen were to encounter Rooseveltian inflexibility on what the President chose to consider essentials. He had his "must" measures on which he demanded action.

Nor was it a rubber-stamp Congress after the presidential honeymoon had ended. It is significant that Federal Deposit Insurance, the National Labor Relations Act and Public Housing were statutes that originated in Congress. "In the early years Congress was as often to the left of Roosevelt as to the right." When persuasion played out, granting or withholding patronage from the Congressmen's districts were employed.[45]

41 F. D. Roosevelt, *On Our Way*, p. 204.

42 L. H. Robbins, "Serenely Roosevelt Carries On," *New York Times*, Mar. 4, 1934, Sec. 6, p. 1.

43 *Am. Pol. Sci. Rev.*, XVIII, p. 854.

44 A. M. Schlesinger, Jr., *The Coming of the New Deal*, p. 554.

45 A. M. Schlesinger, *op. cit.*, p. 555.

S
exec
outw
hou
vete
seek
adm
reso
Presi
most
any
eight
nectio
priati
end j
ernment nevertheless wondered how long Americans
would tolerate a system requiring such a questionable
and costly lubricant.

The mid-term congressional elections of 1934 were
looked forward to with intense interest. Republicans
confidently counted on a reduction of the overwhelming Democratic majority in the House of Representatives. Mark Sullivan had calculated that the gain of a
hundred seats by the Republicans would mean that
Franklin Roosevelt would be a one-term President.
Only once since the presidency of Martin Van Buren,
nearly a century earlier, had a President gained supporters in the lower house in the middle of a presidential term.[47]   The single exception had been in the
presidency of Theodore Roosevelt. But when the ballots were counted and reported in November, 1934, it
was apparent that the already overwhelming Democratic majority of 196 in the Seventy-third Congress
would be increased to one of 220 in the Seventy-fourth
Congress. No greater numerical majority had ever

[46] Oswald Garrison Villard in the *Nation*, June 27, 1934, p. 722.
[47] See table in the World Almanac, 1924, p. 881.

been received by any party in the history of Congress. It even exceeded the total membership of the House of Representatives at any time before the administration of Andrew Johnson. The election of 1934 had reduced the Republican representation to 102, or 23.4 per cent of the membership of the House of Representatives. It was the smallest fraction of the membership that the Republicans had ever provided. It was smaller even than the number of Republicans elected in 1854, the year of the birth of the party, when they sent to Washington 108 representatives, who constituted 56.5 per cent of the then total membership of the House.[48]

Startling as the tidal wave had been, it was impossible to determine what the election signified in terms of public policies ratified by the electorate. "If attention is directed from popular tumult to things that actually happened in Washington during the days preceding the election," wrote a discerning contemporary observer, "it is difficult to see just what the voters voted for. Speeches, news releases, Executive decrees and official announcements without end, activities and promises in administrative circles without number, indicated confusion triumphant." [49]

It was freely predicted that the new Congress would prove unmanageable.[50] "Never before," wrote Beard, "had such an aggregation of unknown quantities and inexperience appeared on Capitol Hill." [51] The House was not organized in a manner favorable to the President's program. The tide had turned within the Democratic party and the anti-Roosevelt forces were gathering strength. The Speakership went to J. W. Byrns, of Tennessee, a representative apparently not un-

48 *Ibid.*, p. 881.
49 C. A. Beard, "Confusion Rules in Washington," p. 333.
50 T. R. B., *op. cit.*, Jan. 9, 1935, p. 244.
51 "Our Foreign and Domestic Policies," *Current History*, Feb., 1935, p. 591.

friendly to the power interests with whom the President was engaged in open warfare, and other leaders unsympathetic with the New Deal occupied strategic posts. Nevertheless party loyalty impelled them generally to co-operate with the President. Concerned over the unruly character of the new recruits, veteran leaders of the House rushed through a new rule decidedly increasing the difficulty of getting a bill reported out of committee and on the floor for consideration. It raised from 145 to 218 the number of signatures required on a petition for such action. Since the Republicans could not have compelled action even under the easier conditions of the old rule, they were prompt to twit the Democratic leaders with the patent fact that they were afraid of their own following. It was frankly admitted that the purpose of the rule was to prevent pressure groups from forcing consideration of their measures to the obstruction of the President's program.[52] President Roosevelt fairly took the breath of the new Congress as well as the nation by asking for a blanket grant of $4,880,000,000 for the single matter of "recovery and relief." Not even the gentlemen of the press were able to extract from the President any idea as to the items in this sum, the largest single appropriation asked for in the history of congressional legislation. The President's reticence on this point was due to the fact that neither he nor anyone else had worked out the details in advance.[53] In the House of Representatives the unprecedented request evoked only perfunctory protests from Republicans and their floor leader, "the unimaginative Snell offered little more than grumbles." [54] In Republican districts no less than in Democratic, harassed local officers

[52] E. P. Herring, "First Session of the 74th Congress," *Am. Pol. Sci. Rev.*, XXIX, pp. 986-87.

[53] T. R. B., *op. cit.*, Feb. 6, 1935, p. 357.

[54] E. P. Herring, "First Session of the 74th Congress," *Am. Pol. Sci. Rev.*, XXIX, p. 985.

and taxpayers were clamoring for federal relief. Democratic congressmen hesitated only over the question of the distribution of the patronage to be created by the agencies for administering the dispensing of the gigantic appropriation. Satisfied presently on this point through a happy White House conference, they joined with Republicans in passing the appropriation as requested by an overwhelming vote of 329 to 18.[55]

The Senate, however, was not so easily satisfied. Here was to be witnessed the strange spectacle of Senator Carter Glass, chairman of the Appropriations Committee, an anti-administration Democrat, opposed in principle to federal aid, called upon to defend the bill and fight the amendment requiring the payment of the "prevailing wage" to relief workers.[56] Eventually the senators managed to get a qualified, lump-sum itemization which afforded them considerably more of the shadow than the substance of legislative control of expenditures. The President in the end had a free hand in expending the grand sum.[57]

As the winter of 1934-35 deepened it became increasingly apparent that Franklin Roosevelt was certainly no longer the confident captain of the ship of state who had taken the helm in 1933. The second anniversary of his inauguration found him in the midst of a scene of political confusion so striking as to afford unalloyed comfort to partisan Republicans. In marked contrast with the leadership displayed during "the hundred days" he was now unloading on Congress almost without comment the voluminous reports of the numerous commissions appointed to conduct studies and prepare plans for "the more abundant life." What

[55] See C. A. Beard, "The Month in America," *Current History*, Mar., 1935, p. 719.

[56] E. P. Herring, "First Session of the 74th Congress," *Am. Pol. Sci. Rev.*, XXXIX, p. 992.

[57] C. A. Beard, "The Month in America," p. 718; "Congress at Work," *Current History*, May, 1935, p. 183.

was his reason for failing to co-ordinate these useful surveys into a coherent program? Surely he knew how impossible the task is for Congress without executive leadership. Rumors of ill-health began to circulate to explain the change. When he confidently asked the Senate for the vote of adherence to the World Court, only to be refused the required majority, there could no longer be any question as to the decline of his prestige.[58] Viewing the political scene from the vantage point of the capital, Beard concluded "that the disintegration of President Roosevelt's political prestige proceeded with staggering rapidity during February and March. . . . President Roosevelt's spell of leadership has been definitely broken for the moment, if not for good." [59] Still there lurked a suspicion that the President might be quietly maturing a plan of strategy to win larger stakes.

Gradually the suspicion came to be confirmed by the grist of the legislative mill. As the session drew toward its close the President's repeated failures to secure the so-called death sentence for utility holding companies raised the hopes of his political opponents, until in the end it was discovered that he had, nevertheless, managed to secure a more drastic measure for dealing with holding companies than anyone would have believed possible a few months earlier. After Congress had adjourned, Beard, who certainly was not an apologist for the Roosevelt administration, concluded that "the victory of the President was complete all along the line. . . . After the democratic processes of debate and confusion were given free rein, leadership emerged in the end. When results were surveyed at the conclusion of the discussion and uproar, it could be truly said that seldom, if ever, in the long history

[58] T. R. B., *op. cit.*, Mar. 20, 1935, p. 158.
[59] "The President Loses Prestige," *Current History*, Apr., 1935, p. 64.

of Congress had so many striking and vital measures been spread upon law books in a single session." [60]

The second session of the Seventy-fourth Congress, which overlapped the earlier portion of the campaign of 1936, added nothing new to the pattern of the Roosevelt leadership. While the President's address on "the state of the Union" at the opening of the session was criticized as a political harangue, nevertheless it accurately forecast the character of the approaching campaign as a contest between the "masses" and "the interests." It was to be the old fight of Andrew Jackson against the money power over again, thought the Chief Executive. If the address was, as all but partisan Democrats felt, a breach of propriety the President evidently suffered no consequent loss of prestige among the rank and file of the citizens.

It was to have been a placid session of Congress confined to the performance of routine functions. A combination of circumstances, however, conspired to upset the program. The passage of the soldiers' bonus and the Supreme Court's opinion suddenly terminating the AAA farm-relief program and indicating that the processing taxes already collected might have to be returned forced upon the administration the staggering obligation of imposing heavy additional taxes on the eve of a presidential election. President Roosevelt attacked the problem with a unique proposal, among others, of a tax on the undistributed surpluses of corporations. Whether or not the resulting measure was "cockeyed," as Governor Landon characterized it during the ensuing campaign, the recommendation of the President surely came to the harassed Democratic congressmen as God's gift to the candidate for re-election—a new tax that seemed to fall on no one in particular.

In any case the average representative could not

60 "The Labors of Congress," *Current History*, Oct., 1935, p. 64.

make head or tail out of the maze of details in the bill drawn up to carry out the President's recommendations and so he contented himself, if a Democrat, with meekly obeying the whip's orders, while Republicans complained of having to vote on measures without printed committee reports and at other times even without copies of the bills being voted on. When the measure reached the Senate there came in due time from the Finance Committee a bill so different from that of the House as almost to challenge the constitutional provision that "all bills for raising revenue shall originate in the House of Representatives." On the floor of the Senate proposed amendments were passed on to the Conference Committee where, under President Roosevelt's influence, differences were composed. It was no mean achievement for the Chief Executive to have steered through Congress a measure for a substantial increase of revenue in an election year.[61]

Not since our presidential electors have been generally chosen by popular vote had there been anything comparable to Roosevelt's victory in 1936 over Governor Alfred M. Landon who carried only two small states. Half the states had elected no Republican Representatives in Congress and so weak was the party in the House that it was occasionally unable to muster even the one-fifth of the membership required by the Constitution to compel a roll call vote. So overwhelming was the Democratic majority that thirteen had to sit over on the other side of the aisle with the Republicans.

President Roosevelt who had declared during the campaign that he "had just begun to fight" inter-

---

[61] O. R. Altman, "American Government and Politics, Second Session of the Seventy-fourth Congress," *Am. Pol. Sci. Rev.*, XXX, No. 6 (Dec., 1936).

preted his overwhelming re-election as giving him an unequivocal mandate to speed up his program of social legislation. However, as he saw it, there were obstacles to be removed first. In nine notable decisions the Supreme Court had held outstanding New Deal legislation unconstitutional. No sooner had the new Congress convened than the President startled it by asking authority to appoint not more than six additional justices of the Supreme Court to aid those who had attained the age of 70 and who failed to retire in six months.

The President was to discover quite promptly that his overwhelming re-election conveyed no mandate for such drastic dealing with the sacrosanct Court. His recommendation stirred up an astonishing opposition. Showers of protesting letters and telegrams reached Congress and indignation meetings were held in New England towns. Editorial condemnation was overwhelming. The Republican opposition, stunned by its recent defeat, was galvanized into sudden life and even friends of New Deal legislation condemned the President's proposal. "Court packing" was one of the smear words overworked by the opposition which exploited to the limit the opportunity for an appeal to the emotions.

The sudden death of Majority Floor Leader Senator Robinson in the midst of the fight for the court reorganization measure demoralized support and led to compromise and an emasculated measure. One of the President's avowed purposes in asking for an increase of the membership of the Court was to relieve it of a backlog of cases. At this juncture Chief Justice Hughes who outmaneuvered the President at every stage reported that there was no backlog of cases.

The President's support was reduced by a widespread conviction that he had already won his objective by the astonishing reversal in the trend of court decisions. To the utter amazement of the bar associations the Supreme Court held constitutional the Wagner Labor Relations Act, minimum wages for women, and in fact every New Deal statute brought before it during the session. Thus the President emerged from the court reform defeat with his prestige scarcely impaired. Though he had lost a battle he seemed to be winning the war.

In less than six months after the 1936 election Democratic party unity was dissolving. Congress was examining critically the Roosevelt recommendations. Recurring economic distress had converted Congress into a forum of competing interests, blocs, pressure groups, and sections. These were particularly stubborn factors in the resistance to the President's request for authority to reorganize the administrative system. This request was based on the conclusions of the President's Committee on Administrative Management headed by Louis Brownlow. The bill's merit, long since demonstrated, was obscured by the falling into the lap of Congress just when its blood was up over the Court reform controversy.

Again passions were tattered in the battle to save the nation from "dictatorship." Hitler's invasion of Austria and the consequent proclaiming of the *Anschluss* was pointed to as a pertinent warning. Roosevelt's removal of A. E. Morgan as head of the Tennessee Valley Authority coincident with the Red Russian purges aggravated the preposterous phobia of presidential dictatorship. Newspapers persistently smeared the measure to reorganize the executive departments with the epithet, the "dictator bill." The insignificant but compact Republican minority in the House capitalized its nuisance value among the quarreling Democrats. Veterans, labor, farmers, and other interests in turn sought exemption of their own particular administrative agencies from the reorganization. Filibustering in both houses delayed passage until a denatured Act eventually emerged. It was universally regarded as a reverse for the President. Yet out of the authority granted the President by the reorganization legislation has emerged the Executive Office of the President including half a dozen agencies.

In time President Franklin Roosevelt developed virtually a routine procedure for important administration measures. The way was prepared for a particular proposal by the assembling of relevant data through preliminary studies made by nationally recognized specialists in the particular field of the proposed legislation. Meanwhile the President would be publicising the project with a view to creating a public demand and to bring to bear the influence of constituents on their Congressmen. When the bill reached the committee stage, answers were ready to the questions at the committee hearings. The President, through conference with congressional leaders, customarily took pains to see to it that an administration measure would not be referred to an inhospitable committee. Moreover proposed legislation was almost always accompanied by an appropriate draft of the proposed measure.[62]

62 "Congress Reasons for Delay in Passing the President's Bills." *United States News and World Report.* January 18, 1946.

$\star$ $\star$ $\star$ XIV $\star$ $\star$ $\star$

The Presidency
in World War II

$\star$

THE EQUANIMITY of the American people was scarcely
stirred at all by the ominous belligerency of the Axis
dictators and the Japanese invasion of China. Isolated
America was assumed to be secure enough. Conscious
of his responsibility for national security President
Roosevelt was determined to exert his leadership for
national defense and he accordingly "used the pulpit
of the White House to guide public opinion." In this
he was exceedingly hampered by the inflexible neutrality legislation public opinion had induced Congress
to enact in the mid-1930's under the assumption that
it would insure peace.

On October 3, 1937, the President, evidently meaning Japan, said: "When an epidemic of physical disease starts to spread, the community approves and
joins in a quarantine of patients in order to protect

the health of the community against the spread of disease." Here was a trial balloon that would not float, indicative of a public indifferent to the threat, and the President dropped the matter.[1]

As early as 1938, following the Munich crisis, he had expressed himself as favoring preparation for defense of the western hemisphere. Here was a Chief Executive convinced that the United States could not remain indifferent to or aloof from a general European war. Nor could he doubt the inevitability of such a war in the light of confidential information arriving from his diplomatic representatives. He accordingly assumed the extremely difficult responsibility of preparing the nation for war while the American people was yet psychologically unadjusted to the dread possibility or inevitability, as the President read the inauspicious omens. Meanwhile he was confronted with a partisan Republican opposition whose strength lay in the isolation-inclined interior regions of smaller cities, towns, villages, and countryside outside the South. The Republican congressmen from these districts quite naturally exploited the anti-war sentiment of their constituents by hampering the President in his preparedness program before we had become belligerents in World War II.

In April, 1939, the President let the chairman of the Senate Foreign Relations Committee know that he now favored repeal of the Neutrality Act. But on July 11 that Committee decided by a vote of 12 to 11 to consider no neutrality legislation that session. This vote shocked the British and French ministries. Roosevelt had been dealt a crushing blow. The Executive-Congressional impasse was to be broken only by the German invasion of Poland six weeks later. Then the President resumed leadership.

1 Walter Johnson, *1600 Pennsylvania Avenue*, p. 108.

When hostilities in Europe began with the German invasion of Poland, President Roosevelt issued a proclamation of neutrality and imposed the embargo upon exportation of arms, ammunition, and implements of war to the belligerents that was required by the Neutrality Act. Under statutory provisions with respect to an emergency he issued an executive order increasing the army, navy, and marine corps, in contrast with Lincoln's doing the same without authority either constitutional or statutory.[2] On September 7, 1939, under authority of the recent Reorganization Act, he issued Executive Order 8248 organizing the Executive Office and among other things he specified that it have "in event of national emergency or threat of a national emergency, such office for emergency management as the President shall determine." [3] A week later Roosevelt issued a call for a special session of Congress for the purpose of obtaining a radical revision of the Neutrality Act. When Congress convened, he urged the repeal of the embargo provisions of the Act as "the surest safeguard against involvement" of the United States in the European war.

President Roosevelt hoped that the course of the war in Europe would arouse the American people to an awareness of the threat it constituted to our own nation. He desired and needed a public opinion that would induce Congress so to revise the Neutrality Act as to enable the United States to aid substantially the nations fighting the Axis dictators. The conception of America as the "arsenal of democracy" was emerging from his pattern of thought and he hoped the public, too, would grasp it. He wanted to persuade Congress to adopt the "cash and carry" policy of the sale of war materials to the hard-pressed democracies. The exi-

[2] *Supra*, pp. 136-37.
[3] L. W. Koenig, *The Presidency and the Crisis*, p. 6℮.

gencies of party politics required that this formula be presented as a plan for ensuring peace. Already Roosevelt foresaw the almost inevitability of his candidacy for a third term. He wanted Congress to confine the special session to the revision of the Neutrality Act and he accordingly kept the administrative agencies from urging their favorite legislation and he himself made no nominations to fill vacancies. Giving his lieutenants in Congress a free hand in bargaining concessions he got the desired legislation and Congress adjourned.

With Germany's conquest of Poland consummated, the European war entered its "phony" stage and the American public grew complacent. Apparently there was nothing to concern us, since France was reputed to have "the finest army in the world" and that, together with the Maginot line, apparently baffled the Nazis. During the first half of 1940 economy-minded Congress busied itself mainly with the annual routine of appropriation bills, which it was systematically cutting below budget estimates. Then, in June, came the earth-rocking collapse of France and the President appeared before Congress to ask for fabulous appropriations in order to prepare the United States for defense against possible attack by the apparently irrepressible Nazis. Congressional economy promptly went out the window and the President's preparedness program, compulsory military training and the rest, was enacted without clearly drawn party lines and often with near unanimity. In contrast with the experience of Lincoln, who was bitterly denounced the only time he sent a prepared bill to Congress, Roosevelt's 1940 legislation was drafted or recommended by the administration.[4]

[4] F. M. Riddick, "The Third Session of the 76th Congress," *Am. Pol. Sci. Rev.*, Apr., 1941, pp. 284 ff.

As the President's preparedness program was being enacted the political campaign of 1940 got under way. In June the Republican National Convention nominated Wendell Willkie as its presidential candidate and at once the Gallup poll revealed his astonishing strength. Throughout most of the summer this poll steadily indicated that Willkie ought to carry states with enough electoral votes to assure his election. This trend suddenly ended with the bombing of London and the apparently imminent conquest of Britain which seemed to rally the electorate to Roosevelt. His percentage in the Gallup poll rose sharply to fifty-five per cent where it remained steadily until election day, when the President was returned for his third term.

Meanwhile President Roosevelt was making use of an extraordinary range of discretionary powers delegated to him in innumerable statutes scattered over more than half a century of congressional legislation. When Poland was invaded he declared, under such statutes, a "limited emergency" and used these powers rather sparingly in issuing executive orders. When France fell, however, he declared an "unlimited emergency" and thereby dipped freely into the vast reservoir of statutory delegations of power. Inasmuch as we were not then at war, these proclamations of emergency brought into relief the leadership of the President in a "peace time" crisis and his consequent responsibility for action.[5]

With the collapse of France the situation of Britain became desperate indeed. She had barely rescued her army at Dunkirk and her vast military equipment had been lost in France. Unless the "arsenal of democracy" came to the rescue the defense of the island might become hopeless. An immediate need of Britain was

[5] See L. W. Koenig, *The Presidency and the Crisis*, pp. 1-17.

destroyers and she desired some of our vessels of that type classed as over-age and some of our obsolete military material. It was a presidential campaign year and Roosevelt as a candidate for a third term had to be circumspect. He managed to accomplish his purpose through a "Yankee horse trade" by which he conveyed the destroyers to Britain in return for a 99-year use of naval and air bases on west Atlantic islands belonging to Britain. Here the President was skating on thin ice if he even had any authority at all for the transfer. His Attorney General's opinion on the President's power to make the transfer is quite unconvincing but Roosevelt was so elated over the acquisition of the bases that he proclaimed it "the most important action in the reinforcement of our national defense that has taken place since the Louisiana Purchase." [6]

In his annual message to Congress, as he was about to begin his third term, President Roosevelt had declared that the "future and safety of our country and of our democracy are overwhelmingly involved in events far beyond our border . . . the immediate need is a swift and driving increase in our armament production." Executive leadership became evident in the fact that the important measures of the session—even the appropriation bill—were sent to certain Senators or Representatives who then introduced them. When committee hearings were held, administration officials did most of the testifying. Nor did this practice escape the protests even of Democrats. Representative Monroney declared bitterly, "There is a criticism attaching to the Gore Bill, a blight that I am afraid may kill it, according to the popular conception on Capitol Hill, and that is that the Gore Bill originated in Congress." [7] Representative Randolph charged

[6] *Roosevelt Public Papers*, 1940, p. 5.
[7] *Cong. Record*, 77th Cong., 1st Sess., p. 9392.

that he could not get hearings on his bill providing for a separate air force because the President and the administration would not permit them to be held.[8]

It was through the magic device of the Lend-Lease statute which authorized the President to "sell, transfer title to, exchange, lease, lend, or otherwise dispose of any defense article" that President Roosevelt got the "arsenal of democracy" to supply the armed forces battling the Axis. The Lend-Lease Act, in its loose delegation of power to the President, is reminiscent of the National Recovery Act of the first weeks of Roosevelt's presidency and which the Supreme Court unanimously held unconstitutional and which Justice Cardozo denounced as "delegation run riot." Lend-Lease outdid the former act and, indeed, apparently left no American resource, either public or private, outside the scope of its sweeping terms.

Edward Borchard concluded that the Lend-Lease Act empowered the President to make military alliances "with any foreign nation for any purpose or on any terms that he sees fit" and to place at its disposal "any part of the military establishment in the United States." [9] The venerable John Bassett Moore, in a letter to Senator Hiram Johnson of California, criticised Congress for abdicating its power to "declare war," "grant letters of marque and reprisal," "make rules concerning captures on land and water," to "raise armies," to "provide and maintain a navy," and to "regulate land and naval forces." [10] Constitutional or not, President Roosevelt had available the powers

---

[8] F. M. Riddick, "First Session, 77th Congress," *Am. Pol. Sci. Rev.*, Apr., 1942, p. 300.

[9] Letter to Senate Committee on Foreign Relations, Jan. 25, 1941, *Hearings Before the Senate Committee on Foreign Relations on S 275, 77th Cong., 1st Sess.* (1941), pp. 652, 653.

[10] *Ibid.*, pp. 652, 653.

and freely used them. Thus, powers such as Lincoln cavalierly appropriated, Congress freely granted to Roosevelt.

Promptly following the attack on Pearl Harbor came the declarations of war and the end of the President's necessity of nursing isolationist opinion. Indeed opposition to the President almost disappeared. What all the artifices of the New Deal could not accomplish in stimulating full employment came in full force under the impetus of war production. By 1942 there was a shortage of labor. Never before had Americans attained such unanimity as the all-out war effort began. In contrast with the feeling prevailing in the First World War this unanimity was spontaneous and not induced by social pressures and a reign of judicial terror as in World War I. The appearance of unity in World War I had misled Woodrow Wilson, and Franklin Roosevelt narrowly escaped a similar deception. In his 1942 Labor Day address to Congress he coupled the demand for a repeal of the six-month old Emergency Price Control Act with the most ominous threat ever delivered by a President face to face with Congress. In part he said, "In event that the Congress should fail to act adequately, I shall accept the responsibility and I will act . . . I have given the most thoughtful consideration to meeting this issue without further reference to Congress. I have determined in this vital matter to consult with the Congress. . . . The American people can be sure that I will use my powers with a full sense of my responsibility to the Constitution and to my country. The American people can also be sure that I shall not hesitate to use every power vested in me to accomplish the defeat of our enemies in any part of the world where our own safety demands such defeat. When the war is won, the powers under which I act automatically revert to the people to whom they belong." [11]

What had become of the Franklin Roosevelt, familiar from early youth with the Federalist papers and other literature of the Founding Fathers and infallible, as Colonel Louis Howe had found him in 1933, "as to the meaning of a word a sentence or a passage in the Constitution." [12] Here Franklin Roosevelt went even beyond the constitutional theory of Cousin Theodore who had written that "the Executive power was limited only by specific restrictions and prohibitions appearing in the Constitution or imposed by Congress under its constitutional powers." Despite his constitutional obligation to see that the laws are faithfully executed, Franklin Roosevelt had told Congress in his Labor Day address that unless it repealed a statute he would, in effect, repeal it himself. Where did the President get this extraordinary power? From the people, he implied, for he said, "When the war is won, the powers under which I act automatically revert to the people to whom they belong." By what mystic means the sovereign conveyed these powers to the President is not revealed, for he could not, of course, cite article, section, and clause for powers that "revert automatically to the people."

"The crucial matter is, of course," wrote E. S. Corwin in a penetrating commentary on the Labor Day address, "the question of the right of the President to invade the field of Congress and to set aside Congressional legislation on his own finding that our war effort will be aided by doing so. That this question should have been raised is, however, by no means the fault of the President alone—Congress, too, is to blame. Moreover, until recently, it is the President rather

[11] *House Document* 834.
[12] *Supra,* p. 289.

than Congress that has enjoyed the support of dominant public opinion in this matter, a warning which Congress needs to take to heart. Unless Congress can, by improving its organization and reforming some of its procedures, render itself a more consistently useful public agency, it seems likely to be reduced to the level of a badly tarnished pageant and little more. And in this connection it should not escape attention that the operative Constitution of World War I has become since then, under the New Deal, the every day Constitution of the Country. There is always a tendency in democracies, for the emergency device to become the normal." [13]

Before one concludes that Franklin Roosevelt's theory of the scope of presidential power is unprecedented, it would be well to recall Lincoln's letter to Hodges in 1864 in which, among other things, he wrote, "My oath to preserve the Constitution imposed on me the duty of preserving by every indispensable means that government, that nation of which the Constitution was the organic law. . . . I felt that measures, otherwise unconstitutional might become lawful by becoming indispensable to the preservation of the Constitution through the preservation of the nation."

Early in the war the Truman Committee, set up to investigate waste in the production of war material, became almost a household term. It was due to the diligence and intelligent leadership of its chairman, Senator Harry S. Truman, that this congressional agency came to represent perhaps the highest development of the congressional investigating committee. So fearlessly and efficiently were its functions performed that no corporation, combination, or cartel, whatever its size, was exempt from the committee's

[13] "The War and the Constitution: President and Congress," *Am. Pol. Sci. Rev.*, Feb., 1943, pp. 24, 25.

scrutinizing investigation and frank appraisal. While most investigating committees discover mistakes too late to rectify them the Truman Committee was highly successful in locating waste and having it eliminated. In January, 1942, for example, Senator Truman called at the White House to inform the President that the Committee was about to recommend a one-man head of production and a day later Donald Nelson was announced as head of the Office of Production Management. The Committee's recommendation of a radical reorganization of this agency led to the prompt organization of the War Production Board.

It was the policy of the Truman Committee never to report its findings until the executive agency concerned had had an opportunity to read the report and point out inaccuracies. This is said to have been the only investigative committee that did this and this fair-play policy enhanced its prestige. Before Truman became Vice President more than thirty reports had been published.

"It was conceded by this time that the Truman Committee was the nearest thing to a domestic high command," wrote the Washington correspondent of the *St. Louis Post Dispatch*. "While it had no power to act or order, it got results by focusing public opinion on men who had the power, and by using Congress's prerogative to look critically and recommend. Cabinet members and business tycoons trooped into the committee hearings with a show of humility accorded few committees. Its outstanding work buttressed Congress's waning prestige." [14] Irving Brant was referring to this Committee when he expressed the opinion that, excepting only Roosevelt, Truman

[14] "Harry S. Truman," *Public Men, In and Out of Office*, pp. 14, 15.

contributed more to the winning of the war than any other civilian.[15]

In the ninth year of the presidency of Franklin Roosevelt there began to be apparent what would soon become a general assault on the President's program of social legislation. War supplies were, of course, freely voted. But Senators and Representatives were becoming deliberate in their opposition to the Administration's proposals on domestic issues, indicating a trend in their districts to be reflected soon in the mid-term congressional elections of 1942 which, for the first time in a dozen years, gave the Republicans almost an even representation with the Democrats in the House. As vacancies occurred and were filled by special elections, there came a time by the middle of 1943 when there were 216 Democratic, 212 Republican and 4 third-party Representatives, and the majority organization was compelled to consult Republican leadership before taking legislative action. If the President put forth sufficient effort he might still get what he sought, except on measures raising fundamental sectional interests which induced the coalition of Republicans with conservative Southern Democrats. In order to circumvent the President's veto power, which required a vote of slightly more than one-third of either house to sustain him, riders on appropriation bills were used by the coalition to terminate the National Youth Administration and the Home Owners Loan Corporation. The National Resources Planning Board was wound up through cutting down of its appropriation.

Despite the fact that the "rider" had long been condemned as a legislative practice and was assumed to be declining in use, the Seventy-eighth Congress carried its use to such an extreme in one act that the

15 "Harry Truman," *New Republic,* Apr., 1945.

Supreme Court felt constrained to set it aside as a violation of the Constitution's prohibition of bills of attainder. The House of Representatives had attached to an appropriation bill the provision: "No part of any appropriation . . . of this act . . . shall be used to pay any part of the salary or other compensation for the personal service of Goodwin B. Watson, William E. Dodd, Jr., and Robert Morss Lovett. . . ." The Senate at first voted this rider down unanimously but was compelled later to accept it by the stubborn refusal of the House to recede. Thus three officials were driven from office because one house chose, by indirection, to usurp the President's power of dismissal. By the time the Supreme Court had considered the matter the three were no longer in the public service.[16]

In February, 1944, the antagonism of President and Congress grew more tense, culminating in a sensational outburst of histrionics in the Senate. Against the urgent advice of Senator Barkley, Majority Floor Leader of the Senate, and Speaker Rayburn of the House, President Roosevelt decided to veto the Revenue Bill, the first instance in our history of a presidential rejection of that kind of measure. In words that remind one of Jackson's denunciation of the Bank Charter, Roosevelt said, "It is not a tax bill, but a tax relief bill providing relief not for the needy but for the greedy. . . . The nation will readily understand that it is not the fault of the Treasury Department that the income tax payers are flooded with forms to fill out which are so complex that even certified public accountants cannot interpret them. No, it is squarely the fault of Congress of the United States in using language in drafting the law which not even a

---

[16] See Frederick L. Schuman, "Bill of Attainder in the Seventy Eighth Congress," *Am. Pol. Sci. Rev.*, Oct., 1943, pp. 819 ff.

dictionary or a thesaurus can make clear. . . ." "Having asked Congress for a loaf of bread," he said, he might have been satisfied with "this small piece of crust" if it had not contained "so many extraneous and inedible materials."

The following day Senator Barkley, the President's chief liaison with the Senate majority, countered the veto with one of the most daring acts in Senate history. He denounced the veto message as "a calculated and deliberate assault upon the legislative integrity of every member of Congress. Other members of Congress may do as they please, but as for me I do not propose to take this unjustifiable assault lying down. . . . I dare say that, during the last seven years of tenure of majority leader I have carried the flag over rougher territory than ever traversed by any previous majority leader. Sometimes I have carried it with little help from the other end of Pennsylvania Avenue." Then, with respect to the President's criticism of the complexities of tax returns, the Senator continued, "Congress is to blame for these complexities to the extent and only to the extent, to which it has accepted the advice, the recommendations, and the language of the Treasury Department, through its so called experts who have sat in on the passage of every measure since I can remember." [17]

The following day, pursuant to his announced intention, Barkley presented his resignation as Senate Floor Leader to the Democratic caucus, which at once re-elected him by acclamation. This sensational break between the President and his party majority in the Senate was smoothed over as best it could be but a precedent had been established that encouraged party malcontent. Roosevelt's prestige was certainly not enhanced if such a Democratic party leader could re-

[17] *Cong. Record*, 78th Cong., 2nd Sess., pp. 1981-83.

pudiate the President, resign, and yet be unanimously
re-elected by a caucus of the President's own party.[18]
In the opinion of one commentator, "It seems abun-
dantly clear, in view of recent congressional action
that, after eleven years in the White House, Mr. Roosevelt (1) is a very poor dictator, (2) does not want to
be one, (3) has not found it possible to be one.
Whichever the case may be, this seems an appropriate
time to bury the accusation." [19]

The uproar created by the Barkley defiance of the
President led to speculation as to whether the spell
cast by Roosevelt over the electorate had not at last
been broken. Republicans had looked with unalloyed
glee upon the intra-party fracas of the Democrats.
Already the opposition had recovered the feel of
power from their effective alliance with Southern
Democrats, and the consequent bringing of the President's program of social legislation to a standstill. It
was presidential election year and conservative Southern Democrats, with the slogan of "White Supremacy," were laying plans to circumvent the possible
election of Roosevelt, even if the Republican candidate were defeated. They would nominate state tick-
ets of candidates for the Electoral College pledged not
to cast their ballots for Roosevelt if he were nominated.

As the end of Roosevelt's third term drew near it
could not be denied that the national government
had become, as even a decidedly pro-Roosevelt Washington correspondent denominated it, a "gerontoc-
racy"—a government by the aged. This journalist
supported his conclusion by producing a list of the

[18] F. M. Riddick, "The Second Session of the Seventy Eighth
Congress." *Am. Pol. Sci. Rev.*, Apr., 1945, pp. 317 ff.
[19] Karl Keyerleber, "Challenge to Roosevelt," *Current History*,
Apr., 1944, p. 314.

incumbents, with their ages, of fifteen key posts in the national government, including the most important cabinet members and chairmen of the principal congressional committees. Calculation readily revealed that the average age of these men was 74.5 years. So Governor Dewey, the Republican candidate for the presidency in 1944, touched a tender spot when he said in his acceptance speech that the Roosevelt administration "has grown old in office. It has become tired and quarrelsome."

Howevermuch Franklin Roosevelt, after the manner of his tribe, may have reveled in the powers of the presidency, he was evidently satiated with them in 1944. There is the ring of sincerity in the statement of his acceptance speech when he said, "All that is within me cries out to go back to my home on the Hudson River to avoid the publicity which in our democracy follows every step of the Chief Executive." But no matter how homesick he may have been for his Hudson home Franklin Roosevelt was caught in a clutch of circumstances planetary in scope. The mid-term congressional election had revealed a portentous Republican trend and, for the first time in a generation, that party now had nominated a vigorous and skillful campaigner. Roosevelt was apparently stronger than his party and the nomination of any Democratic candidate other than the President meant the probable election of a Republican President and a Congress ready to pare down the social gains of the Roosevelt regime.

Far above the preservation of his program of social legislation was Roosevelt's determination to win the war and rid the world of fascist dictatorship. Even this was merely preliminary to the establishing of a permanent world organization. He would dedicate his energy to seeing that this time the project would culminate in no Wilsonian debacle. In meetings of the "Big Three," where he had sat down and matched his wits dickering with Prime Minister Churchill and Marshal Stalin, Franklin Roosevelt had served his apprenticeship in global diplomacy and consequently possessed skills and precious understandings no other American could quite have. Quentin Reynolds, addressing the Democratic National Convention, merely gave picturesque expression to the party campaign strategy with his "never remove a pitcher when he is pitching a winning game." Evidently the electorate felt the same way, for they gave Roosevelt an emphatic endorsement at the polls in 1944.

Roosevelt started his fourth term with a good Democratic majority in the House of Representatives instead of the near balance of parties that the election of 1942 had produced. It was assumed that this would give the President a manageable Congress and break the power of the "unholy alliance" of Southern Democrats with the Republicans. But the session started with a portentous parliamentary coup. A motion was made to reinstate and make permanent the Dies Committee which had been generally assumed to be doomed to oblivion. This committee had been established to investigate un-American activities but instead had confined itself largely to the persecution of Roosevelt's strongest supporters in the public service. To the astonishment of the nation the motion carried by a vote of 207 to 186. The majority consisted of 70 Democrats, mostly from the South, and 137 Republicans.

By February, Congress was in open revolt. It was ignoring the President's recommendations for international economic agreements and showing no disposition to accept his proposals for post-war economic and social legislation. With rare exceptions presidential nominations for cabinet posts have been confirmed with little or no opposition. Roosevelt experienced one of these exceptions when he sent to the Senate the name of Henry A. Wallace as Secretary of Commerce. Wallace was the unblushing champion of the underdog—the urban masses, the little agrarians, and farm workers—and consequently his nomination aroused the fears of powerful industrial and financial interests. No nomination for a cabinet position had ever provoked such a furious conflict and Wallace's nomination was eventually confirmed only after the Commerce Department had been deprived of the Reconstruction Finance Corporation which controlled loans to larger businesses.

Persistent rumors of Roosevelt's ill health had circulated before the campaign of 1944 but they had been practically silenced by the President's campaigning in open cars through the autumnal rain and ice that tried the stamina of robust young journalists. In his fourth term he had abandoned the caution with which his physical handicaps had long been somewhat deliberately concealed and was instead delivering his addresses seated in his wheel chair. It had been presumed that this was done to conserve the strength of an extraordinarily hardworking war President. Despite reassuring reports by his physician as to his health, on April 12th the nation, and indeed the whole world, was stunned by the utterly unexpected sudden death of the President almost on the eve of the collapse of Germany.

The presidency can never lose the impress President Roosevelt made upon the great office and perhaps not more than two or three other Presidents influenced it as much as he. It was in the fifth year of his occupation of the White House that Beard wrote, "He has discussed in his messages and addresses more fundamental problems of American life and society than all the other Presidents combined. . . . Whatever else may happen, it seems safe to say that President Roosevelt has made a more profound impression upon the political, social, and economic life of America than any or all of his predecessors." [20] Nor is this the fervid eloquence of a convention orator nominating a favorite son, but the sober judgment of America's most eminent historian and political scientist of that generation who frequently saw fit to criticise caustically the very subject of this eulogistic judgment.

[20] "Roosevelt's Place in History," *Events,* February, 1938, pp. 85, 86.

★ ★ ★ XV ★ ★ ★

President Harry Truman

★

HARRY S. TRUMAN succeeded to the presidency at a moment in American history when that office would have taxed the sagacity of a Washington or a Lincoln. The United States was in the midst of a two-hemisphere war, the problem of a permanent world organization was pressing, and another "Big Three" meeting would soon have to be held. Already problems of reconversion were threatening to test to the limit our political institutions and way of life. Truman's only experience in public administration had been as a Missouri County Judge, that is, a member of a board that manages the county's business. The Truman Committee to investigate war contracts became virtually a household term and so successful was it that Truman was said to have done more to win the war than anyone except President Roosevelt.

Because Harry S. Truman had made a notable reputation as Chairman of the Senate Committee in-

vestigating war contracts he was a well-known
public man when he became Vice President.
To succeed the colorful Franklin Roosevelt was ordeal enough for this then very diffident man. Yet Truman was prompt to demonstrate that, by being his
own natural self, he, too, could play a presidential
role. When he coolly faced 348 alert newspaper correspondents at his first press conference as President
he answered their barrage of questions with such
promptness, simplicity, and confidence that these keen
men and women rushed from the conference to tell
the American people, as one ecstatic radio commentator expressed it over and over, "You have a President.
You have a President." Thus began a prolonged presidential honeymoon. In July the opinion polls indicated that Truman was more popular than Roosevelt had been at any time except in the "hundred
days" at the beginning of his first term. He benefited
particularly by not having been over-advertised.

Fortunately Harry S. Truman had read widely and
intelligently the history of the nation which fact
led Clinton Rossiter to observe: "Mr. Truman demonstrated a more clean-cut philosophy of presidential
power than any predecessor except Woodrow Wilson." [21] Truman was not, like Roosevelt, a political
evangelist. Yet those who predicted a distinct shift to
the right in the new President, particularly the conservative Republicans, were soon disillusioned by this
disciple of Franklin Roosevelt. His first message to
Congress contained an exceedingly significant sentence that proved to be the key to his domestic program. "Let me assure the forward looking people of
America," he said, "that there will be no relaxation
in our efforts to improve the lot of the common peo-

21 *The American Presidency* (1960), p. 155.

ple." Keen observers reported a pronounced cooling of conservative members at that sentence.[22]

It was freely predicted that Truman's relations with Congress would be in happy contrast with Roosevelt's. As a Senator he had won the cordial good will of his colleagues and was reputed not to have a personal enemy in Congress. Many assumed that this meant a renaissance of the relations with Congress by which McKinley had integrated the legislative and executive branches. By October the same coalition of Southern Democrats with Republicans that had plagued Roosevelt was prepared to block Truman's domestic program. Here is a congressional bloc not to be explained by any resort to the dogma of original sin. It is motivated as normally as any inter-sectional group at any time in American history. The assumption that Republican congressmen combine with anti-administration Democrats merely to embarrass the administration constitutes a misconception of the nature of our representative system. These coalition Congressmen, whether Democrats or Republicans, represent the dominant social forces, that is to say, the most influential interests in their predominantly rural districts reinforced by such sympathetic interests constitute the National Association of Manufacturers and Chamber of Commerce. By and large theirs is an anti-metropolitan ideology induced by a phobia of our American Babylons with their slums and laboring masses organized in unions that exert pressures at the polls through political action committees. By a strange paradox these conservative Congressmen are, in one striking respect, true sons of the Thomas Jefferson who, in 1784, wrote, "The mobs

[22] Irving Brant, "Harry S. Truman, II," *New Republic,* May 7, 1945.

of great cities add just so much to the support of pure government, as sores do to the strength of the human body."

These Republican Congressmen represent the regions that had chosen the Presidents during the 1920's. By combining with conservative Democrats, they act as a potent check upon Democratic Presidents who owed their election so largely to the urban masses. The thirteen largest American cities, according to the Gallup poll, were then 60 per cent Democratic. Here were the balances of voting power that could swing the most populous states in the Electoral College and thereby ensure the election of Democratic Presidents. Nor were the conservative Democrats to be dispersed by Truman's amiability any more than they were by Roosevelt's abortive "purges." Their existence is deep-rooted in our economic, political, and social structure and their behavior was thus a part of the normal functioning of our constitutional system. Despite friction between President and Congress considerable of Truman's legislative program of the 1945 session was enacted into law.

"Washington has begun to turn against him," wrote John Chamberlain in *Life* November 26, 1945. By December, 1945, practically the whole of Truman's post-war domestic program of legislation was deadlocked in Congress. For months the old Roosevelt following had been growing increasingly insistent that Truman assert his leadership in legislation. His response to this pressure came in the fireside chat of January 3, 1946, when the Congressmen were at home among their constituents. Aboard the presidential yacht *Williamsburg,* cruising in the winter fog and ice of the Potomac, with the aid of his secretaries and a group of trusted friends the appeal to the nation had been hammered into shape by the President. It was his first great effort to assume positive leadership of the Democratic party.[23] Among other things the President said, "This is our year of decision. . . . I can say with emphasis that the legislative branch of our Government has done its full share toward carrying out its responsibilities in foreign affairs. . . . When we return to our domestic problems we do not find a similar record of achievement and progress in the Congress." Then, after listing the measures he regarded as "must" legislation, he continued, "I urge you to tell your public servants your own views concerning the grave problems facing our country. In a free country the people must be heard." In order that he might not be misunderstood the President spoke of the people as the greatest "pressure group" in the country.

Why did this appeal to the people, and indeed Truman's leadership generally, fail to influence Congress? Strange to say, Truman was said not to be disposed to rely upon his own party organization in Congress. The Congressional "Big Four," Senate Majority Leader Barkley, president pro tem of the Senate McKellar, Speaker Rayburn, and the House Majority Leader McCormack saw the President weekly but he paid little attention to their advice. Their first inkling of the radio appeal came after the plans had been completed. Thus the leaders who knew Congress best were becoming discouraged with a President whom they wanted to work with. Truman ignored senatorial courtesy with respect to such old friends as Senators Hatch of New Mexico and Lucas of Illinois so that they had difficulty helping him get nominations confirmed.

Where President Roosevelt had been criticised for

23 See "Story of a Fireside Chat," *United States News*, Jan. 11, 1946, p. 32.

sending prepared bills to Congress, Truman dumped mere proposals in batches. Indeed, some Congressmen believed his fireside chat confused the public by the multitude of matters dealt with. Franklin Roosevelt knew how to drive for one thing at a time. He realized that legislation is a tedious process, that committee hearings must be held, giving the interests concerned an opportunity. The successful bill has to be drafted in accordance with the legislators' estimate of the strength and determination of the groups interested in it. Most of Roosevelt's social legislation represented the rewards of careful planning. Congressmen criticised Truman for not laying the ground work for his proposed legislation and not giving his own partisans an opportunity to co-operate. They blamed his advisers for the casual way in which difficult problems were tossed into the lap of Congress.[24]

It is doubtful whether superior tactics and strategy on his part would have solved Truman's problem, which, in fact, he had inherited from Roosevelt. Each was confronted with the stubborn fact that there were 248 non-industrial districts represented in Congress to 187 industrial districts. It was the former generally that provided the members of the Democratic-Republican coalition, so hostile to Truman's program of social legislation. The coalition smothered such measures in committees which it controlled through seniority, wiped out appropriations for agencies it disliked, and shaped measures generally to suit the desires of their agrarian constituents. By March, 1946, this bi-partisan bloc was caucusing as a unit, and had drafted its own housing plan for veterans in the face of the hardest fight against it by the President

[24] See "Congress's Reasons for Delay in Passing the President's Bills," *United States News*, Jan. 18, 1946, pp. 21 ff.

and Postmaster General Robert E. Hannegan, the Democratic National Chairman.[25]

In his Jackson Day speech President Truman argued that the Democratic Party had become powerful as a progressive party, pioneering in new fields to abolish abuses. He emphasized its responsibility as the majority party in Congress. Again he called for the enactment of health, education, social security, minimum wage, and more liberal housing legislation. It was in respect to the last of these that he revealed himself in the daring ad-libbed remark "My friends in Congress . . . have got to make up their minds whether they're for veterans' rights or whether they are going to bow to the real-estate lobby." [26] Whatever else might have been said of President Truman he was no quitter.

A President's popularity, according to Dr. George Gallup, tends to decline while Congress is in session and to rise again after it has adjourned. President Truman's popularity declined in one year from 87 per cent just after V-J Day, 1945, to 43 per cent as Congress was ready to adjourn early in August, 1946. A month earlier it looked as if the President might recover his lost popularity when he electrified the nation with his unexpected veto of a last-minute Congressional compromise renewing the Office of Price Administration. His strongly worded message had the effect of galvanizing into action a public alarmed by the trend toward inflation. Buyers' strikes were organized and Congressmen were flooded with demands for another price-control measure which they had no choice but to enact. For the moment the President had succeeded in arousing the usually dor-

25 "Barrier to Truman's Program, Bipartisan Coalition in Congress," *United States News,* Mar. 22, 1946, pp. 24, 25.
26 "Periscope," *Newsweek,* Apr. 8, 1946, p. 13.

mant consumer interests of the nation, rendering them articulate and pitting them against the producer interests, both industrial and agrarian, whose pressures bear continuously upon Congressmen.

The veto of the OPA Renewal Act was but an interlude in a year during which the President had lost control of his party in Congress. His party in turn had lost control of Congress to the combination of Southern Democrats with the Republicans, which, in the absence of a program of its own, was necessarily negative. Aside from the President's recommendations on foreign policy, all of which Congress enacted into law, his leadership was ignored or opposed by the lawmakers. "Of the 21 legislative recommendations he submitted to Congress at the beginning of the 1946 session, the President scored a total loss on 13, won about half of what he asked on two others—full employment and the retention of the United States Employment Services—and secured passage of six in the form he requested them. That is a batting average of .333—counted good in baseball but not good in government." [27]

It would be difficult to calculate the batting average of the Seventy-ninth Congress, and no poll of public opinion has measured its popularity. However, from the way in which outstanding members fared in the nominating primaries during the spring and summer of 1946, it could be assumed that public lack of confidence in the President was accompanied by no concurrent increase of confidence in Congress. The latter had been uneasily conscious of the public conviction that its national legislature was not living up to its possibilities. Despite deep-seated inertia and resistance to reorganization, Congress

[27] Roscoe Drummond, *Christian Science Monitor*, Aug. 3, 1946, p. 1.

fairly took the breath of the nation before adjournment in August, 1946, by passing the La Follette-Monroney bill providing for some radical reform in its organization.

The La Follette-Monroney Act dealt drastically with the long-recognized evil of too many congressional committees which sometimes led to one member's serving on as many as ten different committees. Under the new law, each Representative could serve on only one, and each Senator on two. The number of committees has been reduced from 33 to 15 in the Senate and from 48 to 19 in the House. Each committee will have for its jurisdiction a major activity of the federal government, such as Agriculture, Armed Services, Civil Service, Foreign Affairs, or Public Works. There is a standing committee that investigates each of the executive departments. To keep them informed, regular reports from the Comptroller General will show each committee how its particular government agency is spending the money Congress appropriates for it.

On the whole the reorganization proved disappointing. The drastic reduction of standing committees led to an astonishing multiplication of subcommittees until there were more than a hundred of them in the Eightieth Congress. The new standing committees found their burden greatly increased by the addition of functions of the discontinued standing committees. Members who had once been burdened by having to rush from one standing committee to another now found themselves hurrying from one sub-committee to another. Congress certainly experienced no such reform as the Revolution of 1890 when "Czar" Reed began counting present members who refused to answer roll call and refused to recognize members who intended to introduce dilatory motions.

The Eightieth Congress, elected in 1946, constituted a landmark in the history of the relations of the President to Congress. Its election reflected the reaction of an electorate to the frustrations incidental to civilian restrictions during World War II. The Republicans, jubilant over the first election of a Republican Congress in sixteen years, hailed the victory as an infallible harbinger of the election of a Republican President two years later. But the long years in acting the role of critic of the New Deal had handicapped Republican leadership in assuming responsibility for constructive legislation. By the end of the first session of the Eightieth Congress it had enacted only one of the President's proposals of his November 17th message and had ignored his ten recommendations designed to check inflation. On the other hand it had enacted several measures opposed by the President, notably the Taft-Hartley Act. This Act had been vetoed by Truman with a message so artful that it mobilized the American Federation of Labor and Congress of Industrial Organizations into militant supporters of Truman for President in 1948. Congress passed the Act over Truman's veto and one year later he was elected to another term after a campaign in which he stressed the Taft-Hartley Act as an issue.

President Truman's prestige declined to its lowest point during the Eightieth Congress. Democratic members of this Congress were frequently in outspoken opposition to the nomination of Truman for another term. But in spite of the efforts of leaders in the Democratic Convention of 1948 to find another candidate, Truman was nominated. At 2 A.M. of the last day of the Convention in the midst of his acceptance speech Truman perpetrated one of the most astounding coups in the history of political parties. He announced his determination to call the Eightieth Congress—the "do-nothing Congress" as he denominated it—into a special session to enact into law planks in the Republican platform—measures which he said he had been urging the Eightieth Congress to pass. Congress convened, with the Republicans in furious wrath, did "nothing" some more, adjourned and Truman, making the most of their inaction as he campaigned was elected along with a Democratic Congress.

President Truman interpreted his astonishing election as President in 1948 as a mandate to push through Congress the twenty-one points he had presented in a message in 1945 which had come to be known as the "Fair Deal." He had told both houses then that "every segment of our population and every individual has a right to expect from the government a fair deal." Yet Truman was only a little more successful in getting his recommendations enacted into statutes with the Eighty-first Congress than he had been with the Eightieth. Now that Southern Democrats occupied the committee chairmanships the President's Democratic support was sharply reduced. Because of a persisting liaison between the conservative Southern Democrats and the Republicans in Congress, Senator John Bricker of Ohio even proposed a new party alignment between these elements which voted down Truman's proposals.

In 1949 Truman's shrewdness in appointing ex-President Hoover head of a Commission of Organization of the Executive Branch of the Government paid off handsomely. The Commission's report comprised 277 recommendations. Congress authorized the President to carry out the plan and he began promptly to put the reorganization into effect. Senator Robert Taft even stood ready to aid Truman in revising the Taft-Hartley Law but the President insisted on its repeal, which proved to be impossible. Nevertheless it is astonishing how much of the Fair Deal program was enacted by a Congress in which hostility was present even in Truman's own party. So pleased was the President that he praised the achievement of the Eighty-first Congress at the end of its first session. Notable was the complete enactment by Congress of the cardinal items of Truman's foreign policies.

President Truman conceived the President to be, among other things, potentially the protector of the consumer interest against a Congress heavily weighted with representation of the producing interests. More than once he used his veto against legislation he deemed inimical to consumers, such, for example, as the transfer of off-shore oil rights of the federal government to the states and a later bill designed to repeal the Federal Power Commission's authority to control the price of gas at the well and transfer such control to the utility-regulating agencies of the oil-producing state which were under the pressures of the oil producers themselves and where the gas consumers of the great eastern cities could have no counter-influence whatsoever.

Another instance of President Truman's employment of the veto in the consumer's interest was his striking down the Basing-Point Bill which would have legalized certain price-fixing in the cement industry to the disadvantage of small business and the consumer interest generally. Had Truman signed this bill he would have risked alienating such element of his own political constituency as labor, farmers, and small business. Thus he would have repudiated his very own following and given aid and comfort to the Dixiecrats.[28]

The inclination of some scholars to rank Truman well up among the abler Presidents rests indubitably

[28] Earl Latham, *The Group Basis of Politics*, p. 220.

on his great decisions in foreign relations. It was he who made the momentous decision to drop the atom bomb. Once victory was attained the nation broke with tradition and plunged into world politics. With Britain's announced imminent withdrawal of armed forces from Greece and Turkey in 1946 leaving them open to communist absorption Senator Vandenberg urged Truman to make a personal appearance before Congress and scare hell out of the country. This was done at once with the consequence of a prompt appropriation of 400 million dollars for economic and military aid to the imperiled nations. Thus the Truman Doctrine of containment materialized, designed to check the inclusion of neighboring nations within the Russian sphere.

But Truman's masterpiece of management of a major problem in foreign affairs was his Economic Recovery Program better known as the Marshall Plan. Secretary of State Marshall's Harvard speech proposing economic aid to the European nations struggling out of their war-wrecked economic systems gave Britain's Foreign Minister the opportunity to seize upon Marshall's words and Truman promptly backed Marshall's proposal. Taking advantage of the opportunity Truman gave the emerging movement an impulse by a speech to the Canadians. He welcomed the support of Republican Senator Vandenberg who expected and got advance consultations step by step with Truman as the Senator established a functioning liaison between Congress and the administrative agencies concerned. Then Vandenberg asked for the appointment of a Republican, Paul Hoffman, as head of the European Recovery Authority, which request Truman complied with although he preferred another. Meanwhile the President kept reminding the nation of the required congressional action. As Richard Neustadt put it, "Truman got no help he did not pay for—and he paid the price required for their services." He had by resolute management overcome the handicap of his then low prestige and achieved a notable result. It is an example of Truman at his best in dealing with Congress.[29]

[29] *Presidential Power*, pp. 51-53.

$\star$ $\star$ $\star$ XVI $\star$ $\star$ $\star$

The Second Era of
Good Feeling

$\star$

THE INAUGURATION of Dwight D. Eisenhower as President in 1953 initiated the longest presidential honeymoon in American history. One scarcely exaggerates in saying that it lasted his entire eight years in the White House. As the victorious commander of the armies of the free peoples of the Western nations he had emerged as the symbol of the triumph of democracy over dictatorship. His cheerful ways and his infectious smile captivated the people wherever he appeared in any continent. He may have excelled Franklin Roosevelt in personal charm without inducing the intense animosity that Roosevelt's policies provoked in his frustrated political opponents. He appropriated the "fireside chat" enhanced as it was by its adaptation to television. No predecessor in the White House had ever enjoyed such immunity to carping criticism.

The bitter wrangling of the Truman and later Roosevelt years suddenly ceased. "He purged national life of rancor," as Walter Johnson aptly put it! [1]

Never before had an American party of the opposition been so impelled to caution for so long in playing its conventional role of critic of an administration. Eisenhower's convincing sincerity whenever he spoke, his high ethical standards, his ability to mediate between competing opinions and discover areas of agreement, no less than the prestige he brought to the great office, captivated the American people. President Truman had been so wrapped up in his duties that he almost forgot his role as Chief of State. Eisenhower reveled in it so that he was sometimes said to reign but not to rule. Moreover President Eisenhower restored the morale of the dispirited Republican party and made it the militant competitor that barely missed electing a Republican successor.

The history of West Pointers in the White House raises the question as to whether that institution stresses emphatically the tradition of the supremacy of civil authority over the military. We have seen that General Grant seemed never to have grasped the fact that when he doffed his uniform before his inauguration as President he had become a civilian. So his attitude toward Congress remained substantially what it had been when he was a general. To him Congress seemed to be pre-eminently the organ of the American people's will instead of a co-ordinate branch of the national government as was the presidency also.

Eisenhower seemed to start out as President with the same general conception and deference to Congress as the other West Point graduate in the White House, but it did not last long. No matter how deferential Eisenhower was to Secretary of the Treasury

[1] *1600 Pennsylvania Avenue*, p. 317.

Humphrey he occasionally took issue with him, as, for example, when he protested against Eisenhower's decision to ask Congress for credit controls in order to check inflation. Eisenhower then said he wanted to show that the administration is interested in the "little fellow".[2] Two years later at a conference of congressmen and cabinet members we find the President chaffing Humphrey for stating positively that a tax cut was possible then when no significant reduction of the budget seemed possible.[3] In another three months when Humphrey urged a tax cut to stimulate business the President countered with the statement that he had to see a surplus first.[4]

Early in 1954 Eisenhower, essaying the role of party leader, was proposing a legislative program of measures designed to provide an "umbrella" as he called it to fortify Republicans in the fall election. Thus he was proposing housing legislation in the face of conservative protests mindful again of the "little fellow." When, at one of these conferences, a conservative Republican Congressman protested that the President was pushing a conservative Congress too far it stung Eisenhower into retorting sharply that he had no pride in authorship of a program but was merely seeking every possible congressional advice. He wanted to do what was good for the country and if necessary "would carry it into the open."[5] Evidently Eisenhower was reading the newspapers more and making the transition from the catch phrases of "free enterprise," "creeping socialism" and "states' rights" to the realities of presidential politics.

Eisenhower had been President only a few months

2 Robert J. Donovan, *Eisenhower: the Inside Story*, pp. 34, 35.
3 *Ibid.*, p. 353-54.
4 *Ibid.*, p. 224.
5 *Ibid.*, p. 230.

when he expressed his exasperation at the opposition of the National Association of Manufacturers and the United States Chamber of Commerce to continuing the excess profits tax. He complained they did not understand that moderate Republicanism by its policy of making concession was the only way they could hope to share in the government. Lodge assured him that those two organizations could not do him much harm.[6] The President recognized that the New Deal was here to stay and every item of it was being incorporated in his Moderate Republican program.

President Eisenhower's promotion of his program was hampered, at first by his ineptitude as a political amateur and later by lack of continuous interest in his program. Before he had been President a year he was so exasperated at the failure even of Republican Congressmen to support his recommendations that he was talking about starting a new party unaware that no leader ever started a new American party that became a major party. Party leadership was foreign to his nature. "I am not one of the desk-pounding type that likes to stick out his jaw and look like he is bossing the show," said amiable Ike at a news conference. "I don't think it is the function of a President of the United States to punish anybody for voting as he likes," he said. Congressmen, as one Eisenhower associate said, "were scared of Roosevelt and Truman. They're not scared of Ike." When Eisenhower did use patronage among Republican congressmen it was not to "coerce, cajole, and seduce" them to support his program but he used it with such ineptitude that some Congressmen even turned it against the administration and Senator McCarthy even planted a personal partisan in the State Department where he created confusion and harrassed the administration.

[6] *Ibid.*, p. 61.

President Eisenhower in contrast with Truman and the two Roosevelts, got no pleasure out of the role of Chief Legislator. His support of his own legislative program was sporadic, and by failing to lift a hand at critical moments he would let down his own Moderate Republicans in Congress even on items of his own program. For example there was his own bill for federal aid for school construction. Of course, Secretary Humphrey had opposed it in a cabinet meeting where Vice President Nixon and Secretary of Health, Education, and Welfare Folsom saw the President privately and urged him to make a strong public statement for it before it came to a vote in the House. But Senate Minority Floor Leader Knowland, breakfasting with the President, berated the measure. Administration congressmen waited in vain for a word from the White House and it lost by three votes. When told at the next White House press conference that "Democrats were willing to go along with your bill, and their complaint is that you failed to go to bat for the legislation, so to speak," Eisenhower replied, "I never heard of that. . . . If that is true, why you are telling me something I never heard of." [7]

Presidents who have learned the art of politics from the precinct up move into the White House with few illusions as to the presidency. Early in his first term Eisenhower declared that he was getting damned tired of the pressures on him. The Hoover Commission had advised limiting the validity of appropriations to a year at a time, which provision was incorporated in H.R. 8002. Thus it was assumed Congress might recover some of its lost control of finance. Eisenhower came out for the bill and it passed the Senate unanimously. But when it reached the House Committee on Appropriations it encountered the vehement oppo-

[7] *Public Papers of the Presidents,* 1957, p. 576.

sition of the committee's two veteran watch dogs, Representatives Cannon and Taber. Secretary of Defense Wilson, under questioning before the Committee, admitted that this provision "might endanger national security"—a cabinet member thus criticising an administration bill. Thereupon Ex-President Hoover called at the White House and persuaded the President to have prepared for his signature a letter to the House supporting the bill. But before it was signed Taber got a White House appointment and argued vigorously that the bill would waste money, which, the President admitted, was an entirely new point of view. At this juncture Representative Clarence Brown, a sponsor of the bill, indignantly called up Herbert Hoover, then in New York, who telephoned the White House, whereupon a news release announced that the President was all out for the bill. Not to be outwitted Cannon and Taber then released the closed-session criticism of the bill by Defense Secretary Wilson, who felt impelled to deny the plain meaning of his statement. The bill was now dead. Only veteran politicians like Truman and the Roosevelts can preserve their equanimity under such confusing pressures.

Some Presidents are veritable artists in so conducting themselves in the great office as to cultivate and magnify their prestige and influence. All the great Presidents have been adept at this. Andrew Johnson possessed the same presidential authority as Abraham Lincoln but circumstances and the course of events together with Johnson's ineptitude reduced his power as President to the point where he barely escaped removal from office. President Eisenhower entered upon his duties with a prestige surpassed by few of his predecessors. Only belatedly did he learn the art of utilizing that prestige in dealing with Congress.[8]

[8] Stewart Alsop, *Toledo Blade* (editorial page), August 7, 1957.

President Eisenhower submitted his budget for the fiscal year 1958 on January 16, 1957. It called for relatively generous expenditures for the development of resources, welfare, school construction, defense, foreign aid—virtually a Moderate Republican program —totaling $72 billion. But that very day Secretary of the Treasury Humphrey declared at a news conference that if the government cannot reduce the terrific tax burden of the country, "I will predict that you will have a depression that will curl your hair." The almost incredible fact is that Eisenhower knew that Humphrey's statement was to be made but did not protest. To some Presidents, Humphrey's statement would have been an act of insubordination to be penalized by removal. But three days after his second inaugural President Eisenhower, alluding to Humphrey's demand for reduction of the budget, said, "If they can, I think if Congress can, its committees, it is their duty to do it. . . . So with the thought behind the Secretary's statement I am in complete agreement. . . ." Moderate Republican congressmen were dismayed and felt deserted. The public demand for tax relief swelled into an organized torrent. March 1 the House with mingled anger and prankishness passed a resolution asking the President just where to cut his own budget. By April Eisenhower was confronted with deep and indiscriminate Congressional cutting even of national defense and foreign aid. Something like utter confusion as to the budget was developing. Eisenhower shifted back and forth from defense of his budget to praise of budget cutting. By May he was compelled to defend the budget and got around to assuming the necessary legislative leadership on this matter.

The effect of President Eisenhower's indecision as to the budget had a startling after-effect. "Early in

1958," wrote Richard Neustadt, "a technician from the Bureau of the Budget testified before a subcommittee of the House on the provision of a pending bill within his field of expertise. As he concluded, he remarked for emphasis, that what he recommended was essential 'to the program of the President' whereupon everybody laughed. The hilarity was general and leaped party lines; to a man committee members found the reference very funny." [9] The episode reflected the then prevailing low opinion of the President's prestige. It had struck bottom as a consequence of the debacle of his handling of his budget. He had demonstrated how not to protect presidential prestige.

The recovery of the President's prestige was a phenomenon only somewhat less remarkable than its decline had been. In 1959 the President himself took charge of his office and the New Eisenhower emerged. "Moderate Republicans were gratified," wrote Neustadt. "Democrats began to reassess. 'Old Guard' Republicans prepared to give some ground. So far as I know nobody laughed." He had recovered his prestige and with it his power to rule. No longer did he just reign.

One reason for Eisenhower's tardiness in learning the art of presidential politics was the extraordinary protection provided him by the White House Office— the staff dominated by Administrative Assistant to the President Sherman Adams. Eisenhower seems not to have realized the potential use of the veto power to protect the consumers against the producing interests over-represented in Congress by the gerrymandering of congressional districts to the disadvantage of urban constituencies. Truman and Roosevelt had used the veto as a counterbalance in favor of consumers. Thus

[9] *Presidential Power: the Politics of Leadership,* pp. 64, 65. *Ibid.,* p. 74.

Truman vetoed the bill that would have transferred from the Federal Power Commission's control the price of gas at the well to state utility commissions under the complete domination of the producers of gas. A similar bill was pending in the Eisenhower Administration when a delegation of mayors of Eastern cities representing the concern of their constituent consumers of gas appeared at the White House to urge Eisenhower to veto the bill. The President was so astonished at this point of view that he is said to have exclaimed, "Why didn't someone tell me about this?" Significantly the emergence of the "New Eisenhower" coincided with the departure of Sherman Adams from the White House Office.

In May, 1954, after having endured for many months the inquisition of a sub-committee of the Senate Committee on Government Operations dominated by Senator McCarthy, the Administration caught it asking for information where the precedents since the Administration of Washington were uniformly against the request. In a controversy between the sub-committee and the War Department the sub-committee asked for information on the conversations by which a certain administrative decision had been arrived at. At this point President Eisenhower directed the Secretary of Defense not to divulge such information because it would constitute an invasion by Congress of the power of the Executive. The President stated, "Because it is essential to efficient and effective administration that employees of the Executive Branch be in a position to be completely candid in advising with each other in official matter and because it is not in the public interest that any of these conversations or communications or any documents or reproductions concerning such advice be disclosed you will instruct employees of your department that in all their appearances before the sub-committees of the Senate Committee on Government Operations regarding the inquiry now before it they may not testify to any such conversations or communications or to produce any such documents or reproductions." [10]

The President accompanied his directive to the Secretary of Defense with a long memorandum from Attorney General Brownell supporting the directive with precedents beginning with the first President. Among other things Brownell said, "The messages of the presidents reveal that almost every one of them found it necessary to inform Congress of his constitutional duty to execute the office of president, and, in furtherance of that duty, to withhold information and papers for the public good." [11] Somehow Brownell's memorandum omitted the most vigorous defense of the point which was contained in President Jackson's statement of his refusal to comply with a Senate resolution demanding that he give information as to what happened in a Cabinet meeting.

During his campaign for the presidency in 1952 Eisenhower had at times been critical of Truman's involvement in the war in Korea and this came to have a peculiar effect on his own relations with Congress during his presidency. In the third year of his first term President Eisenhower felt impelled to ask Congress for a resolution approving in advance the use he might make of armed forces in the defense of Formosa. He admitted that he had the authority as Commander-in-Chief to act without such resolution, but he hoped to get insurance against any action he might take being dubbed an Eisenhower War as some

[10] *Public Papers of the President,* 1954, pp. 483, 484.
[11] *Ibid.,* p. 484. Incidentally Brownell's memorandum relied heavily on an earlier edition of *President and Congress* to which he gave appropriate credit.

had denounced the Korean intervention as Truman's War. Congress gave the President the resolution he desired but, as Richard Rovere pointed out, "any future president who neglects to ask Congress' leave in a matter of this sort will be accused of ignoring the admirable precedent set by Mr. Eisenhower in 1955." [12] In effect this would amount in practice to a reduction of the constitutional power of the Commander-in-Chief in sharp contrast with Lincoln's serene expansion of that power, as, for example, in basing the Emancipation Proclamation on it.

But President Eisenhower did not find Congress quite so complaisant when in January, 1957, in the midst of the Middle East crisis he again asked it for a blank check authorizing possible intervention with armed forces there. This time complaints were heard in Congress that Eisenhower was "trying to pass the buck to Congress." Congress did appropriate 200 million dollars for economic and military aid and then passed a curiously phrased resolution that "if the President determines the necessity thereof, the United States is prepared to use armed force to assist any nation or group of nations requesting assistance against armed aggression from any country controlled by international communism." [13] This put the responsibility of the Commander-in-Chief right back where the Constitution had put it.

Only once since the Civil War had the Senate rejected a nomination to a Cabinet post when in June, 1958, it rejected Eisenhower's nomination of Lewis Strauss as Secretary of Commerce, which office he already held on a recess appointment. The rejection came in spite of perhaps the greatest White House

12 "Letter from Washington," *New Yorker*, February 26, 1955.
13 See Thomas A. Bailey, *A Diplomatic History of the American People* (1958), pp. 444, 445.

behind-the-scenes effort ever made to induce the Senate to confirm. No doubt the President was unaware of some of the pressures exerted by his partisans, such, for example, as the inducement held out to some Southern Senators with powerful textile constituents that Strauss would restrict importation of competing Japanese textile imports. Two West Virginia Senators were promised restriction of Caribbean petroleum residue imports which competed with coal and the United Mine Workers added their pressures for confirmation of Strauss on these two Senators but in vain. Some Northern members of the Judiciary Committee were reported to be ready to join Southern members in holding up in committee a civil rights bill in return for support of Strauss. A Wyoming businessman, induced by a message from Washington, telephoned his Senator to "lay off Strauss," saying the Jewish people were charging him with anti-Semitism. The pro-Strauss forces were even boasting, "We've got Herman Talmadge in the bag," presumably under the pressure of the Georgia Coca-Cola interests, which expectation proved to be erroneous. Majority Floor Leader Lyndon Johnson was to epitomize the outcome of the pressure campaign with his remark to Minority Floor Leader Everett Dirksen that the heat was so great that it helped to burn Strauss in the end.[14]

[14] Joseph Alsop, "Pressure to Win Strauss Confirmation Self-Defeating," *Toledo Blade*, June 22, 1960.

$\star$ $\star$ $\star$ XVII $\star$ $\star$ $\star$

Summary and Conclusions

$\star$

THE AMERICAN presidency is an office rooted deep in colonial experience. Its prototype is the colonial governor who, as the representative of the Crown and agent of the dominant economic interests of Britain, was constantly confronted with the counterforces of emerging American democracy represented in the elective assembly in each of the colonies. Here was a conflict that ended only with the flight of the royal governors when the patriots seized power at the opening of the Revolutionary War and set up their own state governments. They made their state legislatures "omnipotent," while they reduced the state governors to mere agents of the legislatures except in New York and Massachusetts where the governors were popularly elected. The shadowy government of the Continental Congress and the Articles of Confederation proved satisfactory enough to the democratic forces of the post-Revolutionary period, since it left them quite securely intrenched in power in the omnipotent state legislatures. However, as the years of the 1780's slipped by, this governmental set-up grew increasingly obnoxious to the very strong commercial, financial, and greater planter interests of the coastal communities.

The framing and ratification of the Constitution were largely the work of this group of coastal interests and it represented remarkably well the consummation of their desires. The debates of the Philadelphia Convention reveal a powerful and concerted drive against "democracy" which the delegates identified with the state legislatures, unrestrained by any central government. The specific evidence that they achieved the satisfaction of their desires is found in such provisions of the Constitution as the federal power to regulate commerce and thereby end the chaos of state regulations, the treaty-making power by which commercial agreements might be made with foreign nations, the prohibition of the states' power to emit bills of credit or make anything but gold or silver a tender in the payment of debts, or enact laws impairing the obligation of contracts.

Furthermore, the Constitution authorized the enactment of federal statutes and the establishment of enforcement agencies acting directly on the individual. Thus for the first time in American history a powerful set of distinctly American executive agencies was created, potentially, if not actually, popular in its nature. It apparently made necessary a Chief Executive. The proponents of the Constitution, the Federalists, thus became champions of the idea of a vigorous national executive and the anti-Federalists were closely identified and more or less satisfied with the powerful unchecked legislatures of the states and the feeble Congress of the Confederation.

When the time came to establish the government under the Constitution it was extremely fortunate for the Federalists that they had within their group the leader to whom all turned as the one man for the presidency. George Washington was a national hero endeared to the masses as the father of his country. He was fitted by character, aptitude, and appropriate experience for the office of Chief Executive. He had served a magnificent apprenticeship in administration on a large scale by his exceptionally shrewd management of his vast plantation and by his performance of duties as Commander in Chief of the Continental army. His dealing with the Continental Congress had afforded him an invaluable experience with politicians and given him a foretaste of the difficulties inseparable from the office of President. Ever mindful of the proper subordination of the military to the civil authority, he had yet learned the bitter lesson of governmental impotence as manifested by the Congress during and after the Revolutionary War. Moreover, the character of the executive office devised by the constitutional framers would certainly have been less imposing if it had not been created in the full understanding that its first incumbent would be General Washington himself. Thus the personality of this remarkable man contributed to the strengthening of the Executive.[1]

After ample opportunity to survey the evidence in the case, the late Albert J. Beveridge came to the conclusion that the lifelong determination of John Marshall to obtain a strong national government de-

[1] See letter of P. Butler, May 5, 1788, in Farrand, *op. cit.*, III, p. 301.

rived from the profound impression made on him by the incompetence of the civil administration under the Continental Congress during the Revolution.[2] He had served as a soldier under Washington, as had also young Alexander Hamilton, who came in contact with the same executive futility under the Congress. These three key men of the Federalist party, Washington, Marshall, and Hamilton, no doubt saw eye to eye when their thoughts turned to legislatures. They were also affiliated with the economic and social groups that had charge of the government during the first decade under the Constitution.

Circumstances of various sorts, then—the previous experience of these outstanding Federalists in the Continental army, the interests of several powerful economic and social groups, the unrestrained conduct of some of the state legislatures dominated by the debtor element—these and other factors combined to induce the Federalists to assign to the Executive the function of leadership in the new government. The Federalist scheme of government was apparent from the very beginning. Congress, of course, created the departments and prescribed their functions and President Washington nominated the heads. The Treasury Department was the most important. Hamilton was placed at its head and in accordance with instructions from Congress made his famous Reports and followed them up with appropriate measures supported through his active influence on Congressmen. The product was the remarkable financial program ever since associated with Hamilton's name. This was the Federalists' idea of executive leadership and their correspondence of the period revealed that they believed it to be the ultimate solution of the problem of the proper relationship to be maintained between the political

2 *The Life of John Marshall,* I, pp. 146, 147.

branches of the government.[3] The executive heads of the departments under the President's titular leadership constituted a ministry which was to function freely and frankly in the full light of publicity. Congress was to have in this ministry a legislative reference bureau plus an active political leadership unencumbered by congressional committees.

In this matter, however, the agrarians had been taken off their guard. So far from suspecting peril to their interests in the Federalist pattern of government, they had even played into the hands of their opponents by consenting to the referring of matters to the executive heads instead of organizing the House internally for handling such matters by establishing a system of standing committees.[4] The landed gentry of Virginia had found themselves able to get along at home in the House of Delegates, working through the Committee of the Whole and as the largest delegation in the federal House of Representatives they had succeeded in imposing this procedure on Congress.[5] There was, however, a vital difference between the situations in Virginia and in the federal government. In the former the agrarians encountered no significant commercial interests in opposition. In Congress they faced the vigilant, intelligent, and powerfully motivated commercial interests and, moreover, the administration was in the latter's hands. The agrarians were as yet inadequately organized and led, their future chief, Thomas Jefferson, being in a sense a captive of the Federalists as Washington's Secretary of State, even victimized, so he thought later, by Hamilton's political trade of the location of the capital on the Potomac in return for Jefferson's delivery of the

3 See *supra*, p. 40.
4 *Supra*, p. 42.
5 *Supra*, p. 41.

votes of some Southern congressmen for the assumption of state debts.

Exasperated by the manner in which they had unwittingly contributed to the success of Hamilton's program, the agrarians soon awakened to the disadvantage under which they were placed by the Federalist method of executive leadership. Under the astute but secret generalship of Jefferson their strategy began to take shape. Not the least significant feature of it was, as might have been expected, a drive against the Executive, not as a person—Washington's prestige made that too perilous—but as a branch of the government, particularly as represented in the Treasury Department. From that vantage point Hamilton had exercised almost a mastery of the government, easily putting through Congress the measures that the agrarians believed rendered them tributary to the financial interests. On that stronghold of Federalism, the agrarians large and small concentrated the attack that did not slacken until Hamilton had been driven back to private life. Jefferson sought to discredit the Federalists by denominating them "monocrats" while he led the "Republicans." This latter term was meant to imply the advocates of a type of government in which the main organ was the legislature. The agrarians thus claimed to be the champions of legislative authority. As they conceived it, Congress, composed of representatives of the numerous communities of the country, was decentralizing in its tendency while the Executive had already proved to be a tremendous factor in nationalizing the government in the interest of the commercial and financial classes.

It is almost certain that the Federalists were blind to the spirit of the times and overplayed their hand. They defeated their purposes by the vigor with which they exercised the power of the executive office as well as by the inordinate claims they publicly made for that branch of the government. The landed gentry of the South and the agrarians generally were exasperated by Hamilton's claims for the Executive as set forth in his letters signed "Pacificus." Perhaps, plausible as the reasoning seemed, it was imprudent for him to point out that while the powers of Congress are specifically enumerated, the President is not thus limited but is under oath to "execute the office of President," thus implying a vast uncharted field of executive prerogative.[6] It has long been customary to regard the display of force, fifteen thousand militiamen, against the "whisky rebels" as a prudent demonstration of the authority of the national government but the Federalists paid a heavy price for it in the loss of party prestige—it seemed to confirm the direst predictions of the agrarians as to the designs of the military monocrats against the people. It was Jefferson's testimony concerning the Whiskey Rebellion that: "The information of our militia returned from the westward is uniform, that though the people there let them pass quietly they were the objects of their laughter not their fear."[7] It almost certainly marks the turning point of Federalist power. Henceforth the party was on the defensive. The final piece of folly was the Alien and Sedition Acts, the latter of which conferred dictatorial power on the President with respect to deporting resident aliens. Unquestionably the personality of John Adams was not adequate in the presidential office, as the successor of Washington, to maintain the great prestige of the presidency. He failed to retain the support of his Cabinet and

6 *Supra*, p. 52.
7 Jefferson to Madison, Thomas Jefferson, *Writings* (1903), IX, pp. 293-97.

left the office with the Executive decidedly on the decline.

In 1801 Thomas Jefferson was elected to the presidency by the agrarians of both large and small holdings. He entered office determined to put the ship of state "on the Republican tack." No single element in the Republican party had been more influential than the Virginia gentry. Their delegation in Congress had been most persistent in checking the executive "usurpations" of Secretary of the Treasury Hamilton. They would not have permitted Jefferson to pursue a policy of bold leadership even if he had desired. He chose instead a role admirably suited to his temperament and managed Congress through secret influence somewhat after the manner of a political boss, although without any implication of corruption. Congress, however, was getting out of hand by the end of his administration, and under his successor, Madison, leadership in the government passed quite definitely to Congress. The House was thoroughly organized for action independent of the Executive and took the initiative in determining public policies. The trans-Allegheny West came into control and under the Speakership of Henry Clay the coastal gentry saw the reins of Congress pass permanently from their hands. So completely did the Republicans now succeed in the application of their doctrine of congressional "sovereignty" that for a quarter of a century the President was by election or nomination the choice of Congress. While not actually an agency of Congress, the presidency had nevertheless come to have a distinctly subordinate place in the government.

The subordination of the presidency was destined, however, to pass. The agrarians had reduced it and now they restored it and gave it a pre-eminent place in the federal government. The pioneer farmers of the

West had enjoyed universal white manhood suffrage for years and in the hope of checking migration the older states also had been compelled reluctantly to grant it. This created a situation suitable for the election to the presidency of a popular hero, a champion of the masses consisting of the urban working classes and the little agrarians everywhere, in short, the "underdogs." The landed gentry did not welcome such an innovation, but they were helpless when Andrew Jackson was a candidate in 1828. His election marked the beginning of the idea that the President is a "tribune of the people," privileged to exercise a vigorous veto in the people's behalf. The party of the agrarians had made a direct about-face on the doctrine of congressional sovereignty.

The now-defunct Federalist party finally got a successor in the Whigs, particularly the Northern wing of that party. Here reappeared as a political party an economic group combination that had once championed the Executive and profited so much by Hamilton's initiative and leadership in that branch of the government. This was the combination that had suffered so much from legislative excesses during the "critical period" of the Confederacy. One might expect them now to manifest once again their historic distrust of the legislature. But something had happened to induce an about-face in this group also. The threat of populism, once so imminent in legislatures, had now passed to the presidency. The commercial and industrial interests felt impelled to transfer their allegiance from the federal executive to the federal legislature. The eloquence of Clay and Webster, both figuratively and literally agents of these interests, was directed against the Executive as a governmental agency dangerous to the liberties of the "people." Something far deeper than the exigencies of politics and economics in that day is necessary to account for this historic reversal in the attitude of business toward the presidency. Ever since the days of Andrew Jackson the business interests of the United States have always been uncomfortable when a popular, aggressive leader has reached or even threatened to reach the office of President. Every "tribune of the people" from Jackson to Franklin D. Roosevelt has looked like a potential if not an actual "rabble rouser" to the capitalistic interests. Such an Executive, fearless both in initiative and in the use of the veto power, puts the control of the government quite definitely beyond their power.

The Whigs and, of course, the business interests generally, sought in vain to subordinate the Executive once more to the control of Congress and were finally reduced to the necessity of depending on capturing the presidency through a resort to rabble rousing on their own part. Accordingly in 1840 they offered as their candidate a military hero, General William Henry Harrison, and after the most boisterous campaign in our history elected him. In his inaugural address he promised to be the kind of a President the Whigs prescribed, duly subservient to Congress, but he did not live long enough to show how that would be done. The four-year term was completed by the Vice President, John Tyler, a strong-willed, Virginia, states-rights Democrat affiliated with the Whigs but who used the veto with deadly effect on the Whig program.

Throughout the first generation of the industrial revolution in the United States the political party of commerce, finance, and the industrial interests was pretty completely frustrated in its efforts to secure the legislation it desired from the federal government. It was able frequently to control Congress but the new type of Executive, ready with a veto message when he felt impelled to use it, either checked or prevented measures for internal improvements, a new Bank of the United States, and high protective tariffs. The second Whig President, General Zachary Taylor, was ready to use the veto himself on the Compromise Bill of 1850, designed by Clay and supported by Webster, and was only prevented from doing so by his untimely death. Almost all the experience the Whigs ever had with the presidency inclined them to look on that office with extreme distrust.

By the forties the southern slavocracy managed to wrest control of the Democratic party from the masses that had shouted for Jackson. The preservation of the institution of slavery became their paramount political passion. Numerically a minority, they could not hope to control Congress, which, in any case, would have been insufficient for their purpose. They must obtain and maintain control of the presidency since the Jacksonian type of Executive had come to stay. Their master stratagem for this purpose was the fastening of the two-thirds rule for presidential nominations on the Democratic National Nomination Convention. The result was that even when they could not nominate a slaveholder they could, at any rate, prevent the nomination of a candidate inhospitable to slavery. In time the typical Democratic candidate became the "doughface," a Northern man with Southern principles. No matter what party controlled Congress, the veto power in the hands of a Pierce or a Buchanan made the slavocracy secure against legislation disadvantageous to their interests. Moreover, the most capable statesmen of the South, even if denied the presidency, found positions of commanding influence in the Cabinets of the "doughface" Presidents. Outnumbered in both House and Senate, the slave power had come to depend for the protection of their institution on the control of the presidency and thereby maintain the rule of a minority. The failure to retain this control in 1860 threw them into the panic that precipitated the secession movement.

The platform on which Lincoln was elected appealed strongly to the masses of free laborers and little farmers, because of its proposal to keep the territories free from the odium of slavery and to open them to settlers through homestead legislation of the type which Buchanan, under the influence of the slave power, had recently vetoed.[8] Industrial interests were attracted to the party by the promise of protective tariffs and railroad promoters by the promise of a Pacific railroad. The campaign was waged along the lines of the one by which Harrison had been elected twenty years before. Lincoln was presented as pre-eminently a man of the people. He readily accepted the idea and as President conducted himself as a tribune of the people. This doctrine was the beginning of his difficulty with the directorate of the Republican party. It was a democratic dogma repulsive to the former Whigs, from whose ranks many of the leaders of the Republican party had come. A list of the Republicans in Congress who at one time or another used against Lincoln's conduct as President the dogma of congressional superiority to the Executive included such names as those of Senators B. F. Wade, Charles Sumner, Zachary Chandler, James W. Grimes, and William Pitt Fessenden, and such members of the House of Representatives as Thaddeus Stevens and Henry Winter Davis. Not one of these former Whigs had divested himself of the fundamental Whig doctrine that the President is more or less responsible to Congress, which alone was assumed to be representative of the people. Most of them were lawyers whose

8 Richardson, *op. cit.*, V, pp. 608-14.

clients were often the business interests. Taken by and large, they represented ideas that had always been basic policies of the Northern Whigs. These politicians welcomed no popular leader of the type Lincoln was assuming to be in the presidential office. The real Lincoln could never be a satisfactory type of President to the great industrial and financial leaders that came in time to constitute such an influential element in the Republican party. Only a mythical Lincoln could make that group happy at any time before or since his death. While never actually a rabble rouser, he could not play the role of a tribune of the people without seeming to be a potential one. The danger may have seemed implicit in the well-known passage in his first annual message to Congress: "Labor is prior to and independent of capital. Capital is only the fruit of labor, and could never have existed if labor had not first existed. Labor is the superior of capital, and deserves much the higher consideration." [9]

The haunting specter of populism has induced the business interests since the Civil War to seek constantly to put "safe and sane" men in the White House. Grant was quite satisfactory. He was almost infatuated with men of wealth and usually let Congress have its way, happily, however, checking the inflationists with a veto of the greenback "heresy." Cleveland was the independent type, dangerous at first because of his unorthodox views on protective tariffs manifested in his shocking tariff message of December, 1887, but he redeemed himself in his second term with his anti-inflation policy and his vigorous employment of federal authority in labor disturbances[10] and

---

9 Richardson, *op. cit.*, VI, p. 57.
10 In addition to keeping mails moving by use of federal troops at the Chicago R.R. strike of 1894, an army officer boasted of the

he consequently occupies today a secure place in their hall of fame. McKinley was "safe"; he worked with Congress. He saved the country from what the business interests regarded as the most dangerous arouser of the masses in our history. In 1896 William Jennings Bryan threw the business interests of the United States into a panic almost incomprehensible today.[11] Some were planning to leave the country if Bryan were elected. It was felt that such a candidate had to be defeated for the presidency to save society from dissolution.

Theodore Roosevelt had a similar capacity for arousing popular enthusiasm and with his "big stick," his "square deal," his program of social reform, and his remarkably successful leadership in legislation. He was the least typical of the Republican Presidents. By 1912 he looked to the Old Guard like another Bryan and, despite the strong demand of the rank-and-file Republicans, they, nevertheless, defeated his nomination in the convention. The business interests were then willing to see the Republican party reduced temporarily to the rank of a third party in the hope of permanently eliminating such a "dangerous" man from party leadership. Woodrow Wilson's capacity to get the public ear, focus attention on the disorders

---

purpose to "break the strike." C. A. Beard, "Emerging Issues in America," *Current History,* Nov., 1934, p. 203.

[11] The reader may judge for himself the hysteria of the commercial East by an editorial from the New York *Tribune* written just after Bryan's defeat for the presidency in 1896: "He was only a puppet in the blood imbued hands of Altgeld, the anarchist, and Debs, the revolutionist, and other desperadoes of that type. . . . He goes down with the cause and must abide with it in the history of infamy. He had less provocation than Benedict Arnold, less intellectual force than Aaron Burr, less manliness than Jefferson Davis. He was the rival of them all in deliberate wickedness and treason to the republic." Quoted, H. F. Pringle, *Theodore Roosevelt,* p. 162.

and abuses of business, and compel prompt enactment of such measures as the Underwood Tariff, the Clayton Act, the Federal Trade Act, and the Federal Reserve Banking Act in the face of the powerful opposition of the business interests made him worthy to be placed in the great succession of Democratic Presidents following Jefferson and Jackson and to be considered just as obnoxious to the "interests" as his predecessors. Franklin Delano Roosevelt, hailed first as a savior of all, took his place with the other outstanding Democratic Presidents. Elevated to the presidency by a combination of farmers, laborers, and the disappointed middle class, he was bound sooner or later to arouse the resentment of powerful business interests. The determined but futile insistence on the "death sentence" for utility holding companies would make a marked man of any President. The whispering campaign against "that man" that followed was perhaps as inevitable as in the case of Woodrow Wilson or even Jackson and Jefferson, except that in those early days they shouted instead of whispered.

The cult of isolationism in America virtually ended with the 1930's and this profoundly affected the presidency. Not only did the burden of the office increase enormously during the presidencies of Truman and Eisenhower but its very nature underwent a profound change. War, both hot and cold, shifted the center of gravity of the presidential office from domestic issues into the very midst of world problems with the eyes of the human race centered on the President. To him fell decisions as to whether to contribute aid to save the post-war European economy from collapse and chaos, whether to repel communist aggression in Korea, to act promptly to save Greece and Turkey from inclusion within the Russian sphere, to land American forces in the Near East or suddenly to decide whether the moment of all-out attack had arrived that called for letting loose the American nuclear arsenal against the assumed attack. Meanwhile he may be perplexed by domestic issues that persist in having planet-wide implications, whether it be slums, labor strife, or desegregation riots.

The gigantic change within the lifetime of millions of Americans living today can be measured by the fact that President Cleveland managed the presidential office with a single secretary, when he had any at all, while in 1960 the Executive Office of the President contained half a dozen agencies with a total personnel of 2814 while the White House Office, his immediate staff, the counterpart of Cleveland's single secretary, had a personnel of over 400. And with it all the President is overburdened.

A President who considers himself a tribune of the people, when possessed with flair for publicity and a fearless personality will inevitably start powerful interests demanding that Congress resume its "proper" function of legislation and cease being a "rubber stamp." The "dictator" has been violently condemned in the case of every President of the type under consideration. The words of Henry Clay, uttered a century ago, sound like an extract from a campaign philippic against Franklin Roosevelt: "We are in the midst of a Revolution, hitherto bloodless, but rapidly tending toward a total change of the pure republican character of the government, and to the concentration of all power in the hands of one man. The powers of Congress are paralyzed, except when exerted in conformity with his will. . . ."[12] Every President who has exercised any degree of leadership has inevitably provoked an outburst of "constitu-

[12] *Supra*, p. 96.

tionalism." Democrats in the first decade of the twentieth century condemned Theodore Roosevelt as intemperately as Republicans attacked his cousin in the 1940's.

The experience under the Constitution certainly reveals that the problem of integrating the executive and legislative branches has not yet been solved. There are those who confidently propose resort to the magic formula of a parliamentary system in which the executive can dissolve the legislature and "appeal to the country" in a general election. There was an epidemic of such proposals when Roosevelt and Truman in turn were deadlocked with Congress by the alliance of Southern Democratic with Republican congressmen which prevented extension of the presidential program of social legislation.

The theory of the English parliamentary system is fascinating to amateurs who know neither its historical evolution nor its prosaic practical operation. Of course it was by no means a product of planning but is instead a natural outgrowth of the experience of Britain's peculiar society groping through the centuries for adjustments, expedients, and makeshifts that would solve immediate governmental problems. Out of such innumerable trials do constitutions emerge and evolve. Whenever transplanted elsewhere the original parliamentary system may behave as an exotic plant. It could not do otherwise in America. This does not signify that it would be impossible here but that its performance would be unpredictable.

The American constitutional system is just as much the product of our own society and environment as the parliamentary is of another. Certainly our federal government today is no artificial creature. It, too, is rather the result of innumerable fortuitous day-to-day adjustments over three and a half centuries of governmental experience in the American environment. Such is the complexity of American society, with its conflicts of interests and of sections, that a resort to prompt settlement of its major issues by the simple majorities implicit in a parliamentary system might prove positively explosive. Conflicts inherent in our society are not to be resolved by a simple shift in the mechanics of government. These very conflicts, indeed, determined the nature of our constitution, and this constitution cannot be held responsible for such clashes.

A practicable national policy, translated into a federal statute, represents rather the net results of the concurrences and balances of the dominant interests of the sections, states, and congressional districts. Congress functions at its best when its statutes are most successful in striking an approximate equilibrium of these interests. It was a shrewd observation of the late Frederick Jackson Turner that our federal statutes resemble the international adjustments of general European treaties. So continental in its character is the United States that Turner further concluded, "The more the nation is organized on the principle of direct majority rule and consolidation the more sectional resistance is likely to manifest itself."

It may then be that the very opportunity our system gives for such a phenomenon as the "unholy alliance" of Southern Democrats with Northern Republicans provides the safety valve for what would otherwise be irreconcilable minorities in a parliamentary system. Doubtless the bloc represents ideologies already becoming obsolete. Local pressures may yet produce the "concurrent majorities" which, in contrast with simple national majorities, provide the only sound basis of national legislation in the United States.

In any case, whatever its merits, a parliamentary system is out of the question in the United States in the foreseeable future. There are, however, feasible reforms called for clearly within the framework of our traditional constitutional system. Rural population is over-represented in both Houses of Congress. In the Senate, on the other hand, the cities make themselves felt through the balances of urban voting strength that the Senators in many states disregard only at their peril. In the House the effect of poll taxes is to give to a handful of voters in certain agrarian states gross over-representation. Moreover, the rural population in many states is given an advantage in congressional representation through the failure of state legislatures during the last generation to redistrict the state in accordance with the enormous growth of city populations.

The function of the President in our system is to discover and somehow or other to promote the public welfare amid the mosaic of conflicting interests represented in Congress. No one has expressed it better than President Coolidge in his statement, "It is because in their hours of timidity the Congress becomes subservient to the importunities of organized minorities that the President comes more and more to stand as the champion of the rights of the whole country." [13] We need Presidents expert in the kind of leadership that make this championship effective. Let us see what our experience has been.

Since the Civil War the training school for successful Presidents has been the gubernatorial office in the

[13] Calvin Coolidge, "The President Lives Under a Multitude of Eyes," *The American Magazine* 108, Aug., 1929, p. 146.

states, where they seem to serve an incomparable executive apprenticeship. The list of governors elevated to the presidency since 1865 is indeed impressive: Hayes, Cleveland, McKinley, Theodore Roosevelt, Wilson, Coolidge, and Franklin Roosevelt. While they varied in quality, not one failed, and several belong among the great Presidents. Elected to fill intervals between these abler Chief Executives were Grant, Garfield, Benjamin Harrison, Taft, Harding, and Hoover.[14] So striking is the contrast of the latter list to the former that it might be mistaken for a deliberate attempt to catalogue the less happy choices of the American electorate for the presidency. It is, however, merely a list of the Chief Executives who lacked experience as governors of their states. With rare exceptions, in the half century following the Civil War the American people alternated the two types of President.

Commencing with Harding, the alternation ceased. Three Presidents, each conforming closely to the Republican type and "safe" from the point of view of business, not at all disposed to rouse the populace, came in succession to the presidency. There has perhaps never been a decade in our history when business was more contented with the conduct of government than during the "prosperous" twenties. Government in its operation conformed to the Whig-Republican model. Congress legislated with no pronounced leadership on the part of any of the three Presidents. Harding, Coolidge, and Hoover were "constitutional" Presidents so far as any disposition to lead Congress was concerned. The decade of the twenties was one of relative economic calm, sometimes spoken of as the era of "Coolidge prosperity."

14 Since only "elected" Presidents are considered, Arthur and Truman are omitted.

Business got the protective tariffs it wanted and the Presidents vetoed "dangerous heresies" such as "uneconomic" farm relief or "heretical" ventures in government ownership. The era was singularly barren of regulative legislation. Not a single one of the great statutes of the kind that stand forth as landmarks in the legislation of the twentieth century was enacted in this decade of the 1920's.

There are those today who are disposed to put the cart before the horse and assume that this type of government brought economic calm, instead of economic calm determining the character of the government. They are forgetful of the fact that it was under this very regime that the great depression began and the kind of government then existing did not demonstrate its capacity to deal with the economic catastrophe it encountered. It may be, after all, but a fair-weather type of government. Surely it will not suffice as "crisis government." It is perhaps a truism that crises call for leaders in the presidential office capable of commanding confidence, and since the old myth that every great crisis brings forth a great leader was long ago exploded, the American people are rather reduced to the necessity of hoping for the good luck of getting a competent leader along with a major crisis. And Presidents with capacity for leadership ought not to be unwelcome even in "normal" times.

BIBLIOGRAPHY

ADAMS, GEORGE BURTON, *An Outline Sketch of English Constitutional History*. New Haven, 1918.

ADAMS, HENRY, *History of the United States*. 9 vols. New York, 1889-91.

———: *The Education of Henry Adams*. (The Modern Library) New York, 1931.

———: *The Life of Albert Gallatin*. New York, 1880.

———: "The Session," *North American Review*, CXI, CXIX.

ADAMS, JOHN QUINCY, *Memoirs of John Quincy Adams*, edited by Charles Francis Adams. 12 vols. Philadelphia, 1874-77.

A. F. C., "Backstage in Washington," *Outlook and Independent*, May 29, 1929, p. 178.

ALTMAN, O. R., "American Government and Politics," *American Political Science Review*, XXX, Number 6.

AMES, FISHER, *Works of Fisher Ames*. 2 vols. Boston, 1854.

ANDERSON, D. R., "The Insurgents of 1811," *American Historical Association Reports*, 1911, I.

Annals of the Congress of the United States. 42 vols. Washington, 1834-56.

Annual Cyclopedia and Register of Important Events. New York, 1885.

Anonymous, "Our New President," *Atlantic Monthly*, Mar., 1869.

Anonymous, "The Intellectual Character of General Grant," *Atlantic Monthly*, May, 1869.

Atlantic Monthly.

BADEAU, ADAM, *Grant in Peace: a Personal Memoir*. Hartford, 1885.

BAGEHOT, WALTER, *The Works and Life of Walter Bagehot*. 10 vols. London, 1915.

BAILEY, THOMAS A., *A Diplomatic History of the American People*. New York, 1955.

BEALE, HOWARD K., *The Critical Year: a Study of Andrew Johnson and Reconstruction*. New York, 1930.

BEARD, CHARLES A., "Confusion Rules in Washington," *Current History*, Dec., 1934, p. 333.

———: "Congress at Work," *Current History*, May, 1935, p. 183.

———: *Economic Origins of Jeffersonian Democracy*. New York, 1915.

———: "Emerging Issues in America," *Current History*, Nov., 1934, p. 203.

———: "Our Foreign and Domestic Policies," *Current History*, Feb., 1934, p. 591.

———: "The Labors of Congress," *Current History*, Oct., 1935, p. 64.

———: "The Month in America," *Current History*, Mar., 1935, p. 719.

———: "The President Loses Prestige," *Current History*, Apr., 1935, p. 64.

———: "Roosevelt's Place in History," *Events*, Feb., 1938, p. 80.

BEARD, CHARLES A., and BEARD, MARY R., *The Rise of American Civilization*. 2 vols. New York, 1927.

BEER, THOMAS, *The Mauve Decade* (Overseas Edition).

BELLUSH, BERNARD, *Franklin D. Roosevelt as Governor of New York*. New York, 1955.

BENTON, THOMAS H., *Thirty Years View*. 2 vols. New York, 1854-56.

BEVERIDGE, ALBERT J., *Abraham Lincoln*. 2 vols. Boston and New York, 1928.

———: *The Life of John Marshall*. 4 vols. Boston, 1916.

BIGELOW, JOHN, *Public Writings and Speeches of Samuel J. Tilden*, New York, 1885.

BINKLEY, WILFRED E., *American Political Parties: Their Natural History*. New York, 1943.

BISHOP, J. B., *Theodore Roosevelt and His Times*. 2 vols. New York, 1920.

BLACK, H. C., *The Relation of the Executive Power to Legislation*. Princeton, 1919.

BLAINE, JAMES G., *Twenty Years in Congress*. 2 vols. Norwich, 1884.

BLAUVELT, MARY TAYLOR, *The Development of Cabinet Government in England*. London, 1902.

BOUTWELL, GEORGE S., *Reminiscences of Sixty Years in Public Affairs*. 2 vols. New York, 1902.

BOWERS, CLAUDE G., *Jefferson and Hamilton: the Struggle for Democracy in America*. Boston and New York, 1925.

———: *The Tragic Era: the Revolution after Lincoln*. New York, 1929.

BRADFORD, GAMALIEL, "The Genius of the Average—Calvin Coolidge," *Atlantic Monthly*, CXLV, p. 8.

BRANT, IRVING, "Harry S. Truman," *New Republic*, Apr. 30, 1945.

———: "Harry S. Truman II," *New Republic*, May 7, 1945.

BROOKS, NOAH, *Henry Knox, a Soldier of the Revolution*. New York, 1900.

BROWN, E. FRANCIS, "America Meets the Emergency," *Current History*, May, 1933, p. 210.

————: "The N.R.A. Runs into Trouble," *Current History*, July, 1934, p. 466.

BROWN, GEORGE ROTHWELL, *The Leadership of Congress*. Indianapolis, 1922.

BROWNING, O. H., *Diary of Orville Hickman Browning*. 2 vols. Springfield, 1925, 1933.

BRYCE, JAMES, *American Commonwealth*. 2 vols. (Commonwealth ed.) New York, 1908.

BURGESS, JOHN W., *Reconstruction and the Constitution*. New York, 1902.

————: *The Administration of President Hayes*. New York, 1916.

————: *The Civil War and the Constitution*. 2 vols. New York, 1901.

————: *The Middle Period, 1817-58*. New York, 1901.

BUSBEY, L. WHITE, *Uncle Joe Cannon*. New York, 1927.

CARPENTER, WILLIAM SEAL, *Democracy and Representation*, Princeton, 1925.

————: "The Separation of Powers in the Eighteenth Century," *Am. Pol. Sci. Rev.*, XXII, p. 37.

CLARK, DELBERT, *New York Times Magazine*, September 1, 1935, p. 3.

CLAY, HENRY, *The Life and Speeches of Henry Clay*. 2 vols. Philadelphia, 1854.

————: *The Life and Speeches of Honorable Henry Clay* (Daniel Mallory, editor). 2 vols. New York, 1843.

CLEVELAND, GROVER, *Presidential Problems*. New York, 1904.

Cleveland Plaindealer.

Congressional Debates. 29 vols. Washington, 1825-37.

Congressional Globe, Containing the Debates and Proceedings. 108 vols. Washington, 1834-73.

Congressional Record, 1865-. Washington, 1865.

COOLIDGE, CALVIN, *The Autobiography of Calvin Coolidge*. New York, 1929.

————: "The President Lives Under a Multitude of Eyes," *The American Magazine* 108, Aug. 1, 1929, p. 146.

CORWIN, EDWARD S., *The President: Office and Powers*. New York, 1941.

————: "The Progress of Constitutional Theory, 1776-87," *American Historical Review*, XXX.

————: "The War and the Constitution: President and Congress," *Am. Pol. Sci. Rev.*, XXXVII, Feb., 1943.

COX, J. D., "The Administration of President Hayes," *Atlantic Monthly*, LXXI, p. 831.

CROLY, HERBERT DAVID, *Marcus A. Hanna, His Life and Work*. New York, 1912.

CULLOM, SHELBY M., *Fifty Years of Public Service*. New York, 1911.

CURTIS, GEORGE TICKNOR, *Life of Daniel Webster*. 2 vols. 1870.

DENNETT, TYLER, *John Hay* (American Political Leaders). New York, 1933.

DeWITT, DAVID MILLER, *The Impeachment and Trial of Andrew Johnson*. New York, 1903.

DIMOCK, M. E., *Congressional Investigating Committees*, Baltimore, 1929.

Documents Illustrative of the Formation of the Union of the American States. 69th Congress, 1st Session, House Document, No. 398.

DODD, W. E., *Woodrow Wilson and His Work*. New York, 1922.

DONOVAN, ROBERT J., *Eisenhower: the Inside Story*. New York, 1956.

DUNNING, WILLIAM A., *Essays on the Civil War and Reconstruction*. New York, 1931.

———: *Reconstruction, Political and Economic*. New York, 1907.

———: "The Constitution of the United States in Civil War," *Political Science Quarterly*, I, 188.

ECKENRODE, H. J., *Rutherford B. Hayes, Statesman of Reunion*. New York, 1930.

Editorial, "The Movement for General Grant," *Harper's Weekly*, Jan. 11, 1868.

ELLIOTT, JOHNATHAN, *Debates, Resolutions and Other Proceedings in Convention on the Adoption of the Federal Constitution*. 6 vols. Washington, 1827-45.

FARRAND, MAX, "The Compromises of the Constitution," *American Historical Review*, IX, p. 479 ff.

———: *The Records of the Federal Convention*. 3 vols. New Haven, 1911.

FAY, BERNARD, *Roosevelt and His America*. New York, 1933.

FLYNN, JOHN T., "Other People's Money," *New Republic*, Dec. 11, 1935.

FOLLETT, M. P., *The Speaker of the House of Representatives*. New York, 1896.

FORD, HENRY JONES, *The Cleveland Era*. New Haven, 1921.

———: *The Rise and Growth of American Politics*. New York, 1898.

———: *Woodrow Wilson, the Man and His Work*. New York, 1916.

FORD, PAUL LEICESTER, *Pamphlets on the Constitution of the United States*. Brooklyn, 1885.

——— (editor): *The Federalist: a Commentary on the Constitu-

tion of the United States by Alexander Hamilton, James Madison, and John Jay. New York, 1898.

GALLATIN, ALBERT, *The Writings of Albert Gallatin* (Henry Adams, editor). 3 vols. Philadelphia.

GALLOWAY, GEORGE B., "The Investigative Function of Congress," *Am. Pol. Sci. Rev.*, XXI, p. 47.

GARNER, J. W., "Executive Participation in Legislation as a Means of Increasing Legislative Efficiency," *Proceedings of the American Political Science Association*, X, p. 180.

GETTELL, RAYMOND G., *History of American Political Thought*. New York, 1928.

GIBBS, GEORGE, *Memoirs of the Administrations of George Washington and John Adams*. 2 vols. New York, 1846.

GLASS, CARTER, *An Adventure in Constructive Finance*. New York, Garden City, 1927.

GODWIN, PARKE, *Life of William Cullen Bryant*. 2 vols. New York, 1883.

GRANT, ULYSSES S., *Personal Memoirs*. New York, 1885.

GREEN, E. B., *The Provincial Governor* (Harvard Historical Studies), VIII. New York, 1898.

HACKER, L. M., *The Triumph of American Capitalism*. New York, 1940.

HAMILTON, ALEXANDER, *The Works of Alexander Hamilton* (Henry Cabot Lodge, editor). 9 vols. New York, 1885.

HARLOW, RICHARD VOLNEY, *The History of Legislative Methods in the Period before 1825*. New Haven, 1917.

Harper's Weekly.

HART, ALBERT BUSHNELL, *American History Told by Contemporaries*. 5 vols. New York, 1929.

HART, JAMES, *The American Presidency in Action, 1789*. New York, 1948.

Hearings before the Committee on Foreign Relations on S 275, 77th Cong., 1st Sess. (1941).

HENDERSON, JOHN B., "Emancipation and Impeachment," *Century Magazine*, LXXXV, No. 2.

HERRING, E. PENDLETON, "American Government and Politics," *Am. Pol. Sci. Rev.*, XXVI, p. 855.

———: "The First Session of the Seventy-third Congress," *Am. Pol. Sci. Rev.*, XXVIII, p. 69.

———: *Presidential Leadership*. New York, 1940.

HERTZ, E., *The Hidden Lincoln*. New York, 1940.

HOAR, GEORGE F., *Autobiography*. 2 vols. New York, 1903.

HOLLISTER, OVADNO J., *Life of Schuyler Colfax*. New York, 1886.

HOLST, HERMANN EDWARD VON, *The Constitutional and Political History of the United States*. 8 vols. Chicago, 1881-92.

HOOVER, HERBERT, *The Challenge to Liberty*. New York, 1934.

HOUSTON, DAVID F., *Eight Years with the Wilson Cabinet*. Garden City, N. Y., 1926.

HOWARD, BENJAMIN C., *Report of Cases argued and determined in the Supreme Court*. 24 vols. Philadelphia, 1843-1861.

HURD, CHARLES W. B., "The President's Job," *Current History*, Dec., 1935, p. 233.

HYMAN, HAROLD M., "Johnson, Stanton and Grant: A Reconsideration of the Army's Role in the Events Leading to Impeachment." *The American Historical Review*, Vol. LXX, No. 1. (October, 1960), pp. 85-100.

JAMESON, J. F., "Origin of the Standing Committee System," *Political Science Quarterly*, 1894.

JEFFERSON, THOMAS, *Notes on the State of Virginia*, 1784.

——: *The Writings of Thomas Jefferson*. 9 vols. Washington, D. C., 1853.

——: *The Writings of Thomas Jefferson* (Paul Leicester Ford, editor). 10 vols. New York and London, 1892-99.

——: *The Writings of Thomas Jefferson*. 20 vols. Washington, D. C., 1903.

JENKS, EDWARD, *Parliamentary England*. New York, 1903.

JOHNSON, ALEXANDER, *History of American Politics*. New York, 1882.

——: "What the Federal Constitution Owes to the Constitutions of the Several States," *New Princeton Review*, Sept., 1887.

JOHNSON, ALLEN, *Dictionary of American Biography*, 20 vols. New York, 1925-36.

——: *Readings in American Constitutional History, 1776-1878*. Boston, 1912.

JOHNSON, WALTER, *1600 Pennsylvania Avenue*, Boston, 1960.

Joint Committee on the Conduct of the War, Report of. Washington, 1865.

Journal of the Senate of the United States. Annual volumes since 1789. Philadelphia and New York.

JULIAN, GEORGE W., *Political Recollections, 1840-1872*. Chicago, 1884.

KENNEDY, J. P., *Memoirs of William Wirt*. 2 vols. Philadelphia, 1849.

KEYERLEBER, KARL, "Challenge to Roosevelt," *Current History*, Apr., 1944.

KNOX, JOHN, *The Great Mistake*. Washington, D. C., 1930.

KOCH, ADRIENNE AND PEDEN, WILLIAM; *The Selected Writings of John and Quincy Adams*. New York, 1946.

KOENIG, WILLIAM K., *The Presidency and the Crisis*. New York, 1944.

LaFOLLETTE, ROBERT M., *LaFollette's Autobiography*. Madison, 1960.

LATHAM, EARL, *The Group Basis of Politics*. Ithaca, New York, 1952.

LATHROP, THORNTON KIRTLAND, *William Henry Seward*. Boston and New York, 1896.

LAWRENCE, DAVID, *The True Story of Woodrow Wilson*. New York, 1924.

LEARNED, H. B., *The President's Cabinet*. New Haven, 1912.

LEECH, MARGARET, *In the Days of McKinley*. New York, 1959.

LEWIS, W. D., *The Life of Theodore Roosevelt*.

LINCOLN, ABRAHAM, *Writings*. 10 vols. New York, 1905.

LODGE, HENRY CABOT, *Alexander Hamilton*. Boston and New York, 1898.

LOOKER, EARL, *The American Way*, New York, 1933.

LOWELL, A. LAWRENCE, *The Government of England*. 2 vols. New York, 1912.

LOWITZ, SADYEBETH and ANSON, *Franklin D. Roosevelt, Man of Action*. Garden City, 1933.

McCALL, SAMUEL W., *The Life of Thomas B. Reed*. Boston, 1914.

McCONACHIE, LANROS G., *Congressional Committees*. New York, 1898.

McCORMAC, EUGENE IRVING, *James K. Polk, a Political Biography*. Berkeley, Cal., 1922.

McCORMICK, ANNE O'HARE, "Let's Try It," *New York Times*, Mar. 26, 1933, Sec. 6, p. 19, Col. 3.

———: "Preparing for the New Deal," *New York Times*, Jan. 15, Sec. 6, p. 2.

———: "Roosevelt's View of the Big Job," *New York Times Magazine*, Sept. 11, 1932, p. 1.

———: "Vast Tides that Stir the Capitol," *New York Times Magazine*, May 7, 1933, p. 2.

McCULLOCH, HUGH A., *Men and Measures of Half a Century*. New York, 1888.

McELROY, ROBERT M., *Grover Cleveland, the Man and the Statesman*. 2 vols. New York, 1923.

McLAUGHLIN, ANDREW C., *A Constitutional History of the United States*. New York, 1935.

MACLAY, WILLIAM, *Journal of William Maclay*. E. S. Maclay, editor. New York, 1890.

McMAHON, ARTHUR W., "American Government and Politics," *Am. Pol. Sci. Rev.*, XXII, pp. 665-67.

MAITLAND, F. W., *The Constitutional History of England*. Cambridge, 1908.

MALLON, PAUL, "Roosevelt's Ear to the Ground," *New York Times Magazine*, Jan. 14, 1934, p. 1.

————: "Roosevelt Gets His Story Over," *New York Times Magazine,* Nov. 19, 1933, p. 2.

MANN, MRS. MARY (editor), *Life and Works of Horace Mann.* 5 vols. Boston, 1865-68.

MERRIAM, CHARLES E., *American Political Ideas.* New York, 1920.

MILL, JOHN STUART, *Autobiography.* New York, 1873.

MONROE, JAMES, *The Writings of James Monroe* (S. M. Hamilton, editor). 7 vols. New York, 1898.

MORISON, SAMUEL E., *The Oxford History of the United States.* 2 vols. London, 1927.

MUZZEY, DAVID SAVILLE, *The United States of America.* 2 vols. Boston, 1922.

MYERS, WILLIAM STARR, *The Republican Party, a History.* New York, 1928.

NEUSTADT, RICHARD, *Presidential Power: the Politics of Leadership.* New York, 1960.

NEVINS, ALLAN, "President Hoover's Record," *Current History,* XXXVI, p. 88.

————: *The War for the Union.* 2 vols. New York, 1959.

————: "Warren G. Harding," *Dictionary of American Biography,* VIII, p. 252.

New Republic.

New York Herald.

New York Nation.

New York Times.

New York Tribune.

Newsweek.

NICHOLS, ROY F., *Franklin Pierce.* Philadelphia, 1931.

NICOLAY, JOHN G. and HAY, JOHN, *Abraham Lincoln: a History.* 10 vols. New York, 1890.

————: *Works of Abraham Lincoln.* 10 vols. New York, 1894.

Niles Weekly Register. 75 vols. Baltimore, 1811-49.

OBERHOLTZER, E. P., *History of the United States since the Civil War.* New York, 1917.

OGG, F. A. and RAY, P. O. *Introduction to American Government.* New York, 1935.

OLCOTT, *William McKinley.* 2 vols. Boston, 1916.

PATTEE, FRED LEWIS, "Chester Alan Arthur," *Dictionary of American Biography,* I, p. 373.

PATTERSON, CALEB PERRY, *American Government.* Boston, 1929.

PAXSON, F. L., "Theodore Roosevelt," *Dictionary of American Biography,* XVI, New York, 1928.

————: "William McKinley," *Dictionary of American Biography,* XII, p. 107.

PEARSON, DREW and ALLEN, R. S., *Washington Merry-Go-Round*. New York, 1932.

PECK, HARRY THURSTON, *Twenty Years of the Republic, 1885-1905*. New York, 1913.

Philadelphia Inquirer.

PLUMER, WILLIAM, *The Missouri Compromises and Presidential Politics, 1820-1825*. Letters of William Plumer, Jr., edited by E. S. Brown. St. Louis, 1926.

POORE, BENJAMIN PERLEY, *Perley's Reminiscences of Sixty Years in the National Metropolis*. 2 vols. 1886.

PRINGLE, H. F., *Theodore Roosevelt, a Biography*. New York, 1931.

RANDALL, HENRY STEPHENS, *The Life of Thomas Jefferson*. 3 vols. New York, 1858.

RANDALL, J. G., *Constitutional Problems Under Lincoln*. New York, 1926.

RAY, P. O., *The Repeal of the Missouri Compromise*. Cleveland, O., 1908.

Republican Campaign Textbook, 1920.

Review of Reviews.

RHODES, JAMES FORD, *Historical Essays*. New York, 1909.

———: *History of the United States from Hayes to McKinley, 1877-1896*. New York, 1919.

———: *History of the United States from the Compromise of 1850*. New York, 1893-1906.

———: "The Presidential Office," *Scribner's Magazine*, Feb., 1903.

RICHARDSON, JAMES D., *Messages and Papers of the Presidents, 1789-1897*. 10 vols. Washington, 1897.

RIDDICK, F. M., "The Third Session of the 76th Cong., *Am. Pol. Sci. Rev.*, XXXV, Apr., 1941.

———: "The First Session of the 77th Cong.," *Am. Pol. Sci. Rev.*, XXXVI, Apr., 1942.

ROBBINS, L. H., "Roosevelt Seeks Guidance in History," *New York Times*, Jan. 28, 1934, Sec. 6, p. 3.

———: "Serenely Roosevelt Carries On," *New York Times*, Mar. 4, 1934, Sec. 6, p. 1.

ROGERS, LINDSAY, "American Government and Politics," *Am. Pol. Sci. Rev.*, XIX, p. 762.

———: *Crisis Government*. New York, 1934.

———: "Presidential Dictatorship," *Quarterly Review*, CCXXXI, p. 141.

———: "The President and the People," *New York Times Magazine*, Apr. 9, 1933, p. 2.

ROOSEVELT, FRANKLIN D., *On Our Way*. New York, 1934.

Roosevelt Public Papers.

ROOSEVELT, THEODORE, *An Autobiography*. New York, 1913.

———: "The Duties of American Citizenship," *Works of Theodore Roosevelt*. 20 vols. New York, 1925.

SALTER, J. T. (editor), *Public Men: In and Out of Office.* Chapel Hill, 1946.

SARGENT, NATHAN, *Public Men and Events from the Commencement of Monroe's Administration.* 2 vols. Philadelphia, 1874.

SCHLESINGER, JR., A. M., *The Coming of the New Deal.* Boston, 1959.

SCHOULER, JAMES, *History of the United States under the Constitution.* 6 vols. New York, 1880-1913.

SCHURZ, CARL, *Life of Henry Clay.* 2 vols. Boston and New York, 1887.

————: *Reminiscences.* 3 vols. New York, 1908.

SEWARD, WILLIAM H., *Works of William H. Seward* (George E. Baker, editor). 5 vols. Boston, 1853.

SHERMAN, JOHN, *Recollections of Forty Years in the House, Senate and Cabinet.* 2 vols. Chicago, 1895.

SHERMAN, WILLIAM T., *Memoirs of W. T. Sherman.* New York, 1890.

SHORES, VENILA LOVINA, *The Hayes-Tilden Controversy, 1877-1879.* Smith College Studies in History, IV, No. 4.

SLOSSON, P. W., "Warren G. Harding, a Revised Estimate," *Current History,* XXXIII, pp. 174-79.

SMITH, THEODORE CLARKE, *Life and Letters of James A. Garfield.* 2 vols. New Haven, 1925.

Statutes at Large of the United States of America. Boston and Washington, 1850-.

STEPHENS, ALEXANDER H., *Speech before Georgia Legislature, Nov. 14, 1860.* Pamphlet No. 36 of Loyal Publication Society. New York, 1865.

STEPHENSON, N. W., *Lincoln.* Indianapolis, 1922.

SULLIVAN, MARK, "Coolidge versus the Senate," *World's Work,* Dec., 1925.

SWISHER, CARL, *American Constitutional Development.* Boston, 1954.

TAFT, WILLIAM H., *"Our Chief Magistrate and His Powers.* New York, 1916.

————: *The McKinley Birthplace Memorial.* 1918.

THACH, CHARLES C., JR., *The Creation of the Presidency,* Johns Hopkins Studies in History and Political Science, Series XL, No. 4.

THAYER, WILLIAM ROSCOE, *Life and Letters of John Hay.* Boston and New York, 1915.

THOMAS, H. C., *The Return of the Democratic Party to Power in 1884.* Columbia University Studies in History, Economics, and Public Law, LXXXIX, 1919.

Time.

T. R. B., "Washington Notes," *New Republic,* XLV.

TUMULTY, J. P., *Woodrow Wilson as I Knew Him.* New York, 1921.

TYLER, LYON G., *Letters and Times of the Tylers.* 3 vols. Richmond, 1884, 1885, 1896.

UNDERWOOD, OSCAR W., *Drifting Sands of Party Politics.* New York, 1928.

United States News.

United States News, "Barriers to Truman's Program," Mar. 22, 1946.

———: "Congress's Reasons for Delay in Passing the President's Bills," Jan. 18, 1946.

———: "Story of a Fireside Chat," Jan. 11, 1946, p. 32.

UPSHUR, ABLE P., *A Brief Enquiry into the True Nature and Character of Our Federal Government.* Petersburg, 1840.

VAN BUREN, MARTIN, *Inquiry into the Origin and Course of Political Parties in the United States.* New York, 1867.

VILLARD, OSWALD GARRISON, *Nation,* June 27, 1934, p. 722.

WALSH, C. M., *The Political Science of John Adams.* New York and London, 1915.

WARREN, HARRIS GAYLORD, *Herbert Hoover and the Great Depression.* New York, 1959.

WASHBURN, C. G., *Theodore Roosevelt, the Logic of His Career.* Boston and New York, 1916.

Washington Federalist.

WEBSTER, DANIEL, *Writings, and Speeches.* 18 vols. Boston, 1903.

WEED, THURLOW, *Life of Thurlow Weed, Including His Autobiographical Memoir.* 2 vols. Boston and New York, 1883-84.

WELLES, GIDEON, *Diary of Gideon Welles.* 3 vols. Boston and New York, 1911.

WELLEVER, JUDSON C., "President Harding," in A. B. Hart, *American History told by Contemporaries,* V, p. 831.

WEST, WILLIS M., *American History and Government.* Boston, 1913.

WHEATON, HENRY, *Reports of Cases Argued and Adjudged in the Supreme Court.* 12 vols. Philadelphia, 1816-27.

WHITE, HORACE, *Money and Banking.* Boston and New York, 1908.

WHITE, LEONARD D., *Introduction to the Study of Public Administration.* New York, 1926.

WHITE, WILLIAM ALLEN, *A Puritan in Babylon: The Story of Calvin Coolidge.* New York, 1938.

———: *Calvin Coolidge.* New York, 1925.

———: *Masks in a Pageant.* New York, 1928.

WILLIAMS, CHARLES SMITH, *Diary and Letters of Rutherford B. Hayes.* 5 vols. Columbus, 1922.

————: *The Life of Rutherford B. Hayes.* 2 vols. Boston, 1914.

WILLOUGHBY, W. F., *The Government of Modern States.* New York, 1919.

WILSON, JAMES, *The Works of James Wilson.* Chicago, 1896.

WILSON, JAMES GRANT (editor), *The Presidents of the United States.* 4 vols. New York, 1914.

WILSON, WOODROW, "Cabinet Government in the United States," *International Review*, August, 1879, VI, pp. 46-163.

————: *College and State Papers* (R. S. Baker and W. E. Dodd, editors). 2 vols. New York and London, 1925-27.

————: *Congressional Government.* Boston, 1885.

————: *Constitutional Government in the United States.* New York, 1907.

————: "The Presidency in 1879," *International Review*, VI.

————: *The State: Elements of Historical and Practical Politics.* Boston, 1898.

WINSTON, ROBERT W., *Andrew Johnson: Plebeian and Patriot.* New York, 1928.

WISE, HENRY A., *Seven Decades of the Union.* Philadelphia, 1871.

WOODBURY, LEVI, *Writings, Political, Judicial and Literary.* 3 vols. Boston, 1852.

World Almanac, 1924.

Index

WILFRED E. BINKLEY was born in Lafayette, Ohio, in 1883. Graduated in 1908 from Ohio Northern University, where he has taught since 1921 as Professor of Political Science, he received in 1910 a bachelor's degree from Antioch College; in 1926 he received his master's degree and in 1936 his doctorate, both from Ohio State University. Dr. Binkley was awarded the first Fulbright Lectureship to England in 1949-50 and taught at Oxford University. He has also taught at Columbia University, Ohio State University, and Bowling Green State University; by special appointment of the War Department, he taught political science to soldiers awaiting redeployment at the American University in Biarritz, France, in 1945-6. Dr. Binkley was twice appointed by President Eisenhower to the National Historical Publications Commission. He has been President of the Ohio Academy of History and the Mid West Political Science Association, as well as Vice President of the American Political Science Association. In 1960, at a convocation honoring his forty years teaching at Ohio Northern University, he was awarded by the University the degree of Doctor of Laws.

Dr. Binkley's books include *American Political Parties: Their Natural History* (for which he was awarded an Alfred A. Knopf Fellowship in History), *A Grammar of American Politics* (with Malcolm Moos), and *The Man in the White House*.

THE TEXT of this book was set on the Linotype in *Baskerville*, a facsimile of the type designed by John Baskerville, Birmingham, England, in 1754. The Linotype copy was cut under the supervision of George W. Jones of London. Composed, printed and bound by H. WOLFF BOOK MANUFACTURING COMPANY, New York.

V-198	Bardolph, Richard	THE NEGRO VANGUARD
V-42	Beard, Charles A.	THE ECONOMIC BASIS OF POLITICS and Related Writings
V-60	Becker, Carl L.	DECLARATION OF INDEPENDENCE
V-17	Becker, Carl L.	FREEDOM AND RESPONSIBILITY in the AMERICAN WAY OF LIFE
V-191	Beer, Thomas	THE MAUVE DECADE: American Life at the End of the 19th Century
V-199	Berman, H. J. (ed.)	TALKS ON AMERICAN LAW
V-211	Binkley, Wilfred E.	PRESIDENT AND CONGRESS
V-44	Brinton, Crane	THE ANATOMY OF REVOLUTION
V-37	Brogan, D. W.	THE AMERICAN CHARACTER
V-72	Buck, Paul H.	THE ROAD TO REUNION, 1865-1900
V-98	Cash, W. J.	THE MIND OF THE SOUTH
V-190	Donald, David	LINCOLN RECONSIDERED
V-264	Fulbright, J. William	MYTHS AND REALITIES IN AMERICAN FOREIGN POLICY AND DOMESTIC AFFAIRS
V-31	Goldman, Eric F.	RENDEZVOUS WITH DESTINY
V-183	Goldman, Eric F.	THE CRUCIAL DECADE—AND AFTER: America, 1945-1960
V-95	Hofstadter, Richard	THE AGE OF REFORM
V-9	Hofstadter, Richard	AMERICAN POLITICAL TRADITION
V-120	Hofstadter, Richard	GREAT ISSUES IN AMERICAN HISTORY, Volume I (1765-1865)
V-121	Hofstadter, Richard	GREAT ISSUES IN AMERICAN HISTORY, Volume II (1864-1957)
V-242	James, C. L. R.	THE BLACK JACOBINS
V-102	Meyers, Marvin	THE JACKSONIAN PERSUASION
V-189	Miers, Earl Schenck	ROBERT E. LEE
V-84	Parkes, Henry B.	THE AMERICAN EXPERIENCE
V-212	Rossiter, Clinton	CONSERVATISM IN AMERICA
V-52	Smith, Henry Nash	VIRGIN LAND
V-253	Stampp, Kenneth	THE PECULIAR INSTITUTION
V-179	Stebbins, Richard P.	U. S. IN WORLD AFFAIRS, 1959
V-204	Stebbins, Richard P.	U. S. IN WORLD AFFAIRS, 1960
V-222	Stebbins, Richard P.	U. S. IN WORLD AFFAIRS, 1961
V-244	Stebbins, Richard P.	U. S. IN WORLD AFFAIRS, 1962
V-110 V-111	Tocqueville, Alexis de	DEMOCRACY IN AMERICA, Volumes I and II
V-103	Trollope, Mrs. Frances	DOMESTIC MANNERS OF THE AMERICANS
V-265	Warren, Robert Penn	LEGACY OF THE CIVIL WAR
V-208	Woodward, C. Vann	BURDEN OF SOUTHERN HISTORY

VINTAGE BIOGRAPHY AND AUTOBIOGRAPHY

A free catalogue of VINTAGE BOOKS will be sent at your request. Write to Vintage Books, 457 Madison Avenue, New York, New York 10022.